# Entering the Conversation

## A Guide to the World of Great Books

Samuel Joeckel
AND Tom St. Antoine, Editors

Printed in the United States of America

First printing, 2019
ISBN 978-0-578-54901-9

Tressler Press
Caliskynovel@gmail.com

# CONTENTS

*Dedicated to the students—past, present, and future—in the Supper Honors Program at Palm Beach Atlantic University*

# ACKNOWLEDGMENTS

We express gratitude for the editorial assistance of Lauren Sumner, who exemplifies the intellectual rigor of Palm Beach Atlantic University's Supper Honors Program. We also thank Palm Beach Atlantic University for awarding us a grant to complete this book.

# INTRODUCTION

## Tom St. Antoine and Samuel Joeckel

*"The person who doesn't read lives only one life. The reader lives 5,000. Reading is immortality backwards."*

—Umberto Eco

Sometime during their final semester at Palm Beach Atlantic University, students in the Supper Honors Program take their oral exams. Every honors course taken and every honors text read over the course of four years are fair game as students face questions that they are expected to answer intelligently. Usually, at some point in the exam, honors faculty ask this question: how has the honors program changed you?

It is not unusual for students to begin to cry while answering this question. They are not emotional because they are unable to offer insights on their learning or because they are asked questions to which they have no reply. Rather, they are moved by this climactic moment when they reflect on their journey. When they were freshmen, the honors reading list had seemed like a mountain to be climbed. It was so high. The peak had appeared to be insurmountable. The climb had seemed treacherous. Yet now they find themselves on the mountaintop, and the view is breathtaking.

Students speculate on what they would have been like had they not made the climb. They consider the ways that the wisdom of these great books, now a part of who they are and how they think, transformed their lives, thus moving them to tears.

The obvious assumption in this standard oral-exam question is that the honors program *does* in fact change students. But for those familiar with the program, especially for those who have experienced it firsthand, the assumption is hardly unwarranted. Year in and year out, the PBAU Honors Program does change students. It changes the way they think as well as what they think about. It shapes worldviews, sometimes in significant and surprising ways.

How? By introducing students to some of the greatest minds in recorded history. On the first day of the honors First-Year Experience course (FYE), students are greeted with a syllabus headed with an epigraph from Proverbs 13:20: "He who walks with the wise grows wise." For the next four years, honors students keep company with these wise people, from Plato and Aristotle to Shakespeare and Milton: people who have written what are often referred to as the Great Books of the Western World.

Why should university students in the twenty-first century care about these books? Because they ask long-enduring questions and explore issues that have been foundational to the human condition. Today we are inundated with information. With just a touch of our phones, we can potentially access more knowledge in seconds than the best scholar living a hundred years ago could research in a lifetime. Although this ability is in many ways a great innovation, it brings with it distinct red flags: all of this knowledge contends for our attention, which is necessarily limited, and much of this knowledge is not even worth our attention. Yuval Noah Harari puts it well:

> In the past, censorship worked by blocking the flow of information. In the twenty-first century censorship works by flooding people with irrelevant information. We just

> don't know what to pay attention to, and often spend our time investigating and debating side issues. In ancient times having power meant having access to data. Today having power means knowing what to ignore. So considering everything that is happening in our chaotic world, what should we focus on?[1]

We contend that university students should focus on the Great Books. The Great Books are not something that university students, or anyone for that matter, should ignore; they are at the center of what has been called the Great Conversation.[2]

This metaphorical Great Conversation stretches through history. It occurs when, say, a philosopher builds upon the work of another philosopher, as is the case with Aristotle reshaping Plato's ideas. It happens when, for instance, a thinker completely rejects another thinker, as transpired when Francis Bacon critiqued Aquinas and the legacy of Thomistic thought. Or it occurs when a poet shapes the work of another poet, as when Homer influenced Milton. As students in the honors program progress, as they advance from one class to the next, the conversation they hear becomes increasingly multi-vocal and audible; they make connections between the ideas of great minds; they pick up on themes and repeated questions; they see lines of influence as they receive a

1 Yuval Noah Harari, Homo Deus (New York: Penguin, 2016), 462.

2 We are not unaware of the significant ways that the Great Books Tradition has been challenged over the past few decades. We recognize that the great-books canon—the list of books that we read in the honors program—was established by white, European males and that it almost entirely excludes non-whites, non-Europeans, and females. We find the subsequent critique of the Great Books Tradition, which is much too complex to reproduce here, to be formidable and thus at the very least worth acknowledging. Our position is that the Great Books Tradition provides our students with a foundation to build upon. We encourage students to build upon this foundation by studying non-white, non-European, and female literatures, historical accounts, and theoretical approaches. We also welcome multicultural, postcolonial, and feminist approaches to the Great Book Tradition, whether in class discussion, writing assignments for class, or even during the honors oral exam.

fuller picture of how everything fits together. To switch metaphors, the PBAU Honors Program enables its students to "stand on the shoulders of giants."

According to Alasdair MacIntyre, standing on these shoulders is a foundational component in fulfilling a primary aim of education: cultivating virtue. According to MacIntyre, the so-called cardinal virtues—charity, hope, faith, wisdom, justice, courage, and temperance—are "...required to sustain the kind of households and the kind of political communities in which men and women can seek for the good together."[3] Drawing from these virtues, wise minds through history have asked the sorts of questions that allow us to interrogate our own character. They help us to order our lives and our loves.

The PBAU Honors Program fosters this process. If you are reading this Introduction for the first time, chances are you are an incoming honors student about to undergo this process. Honors professors might very well ask you how you fared in four years when you take your oral exam. For now, we will introduce you to seven virtues you need to know *before* you embark on your journey through the honors program: the seven virtues of a good reader. Thus far, we have mentioned virtue as a consequence of learning. However, there are certain virtues that also serve as a precursor to learning. Those who are in possession of these virtues are better able to grow in wisdom and to have their minds and lives ordered by the truth.

## *How to Read like an Honors Student*

### *1. Read with Curiosity*

Human beings have a natural desire to know things. We are born with a love of learning, and we find deep satisfaction in what Socrates calls the examined life. Curiosity is the fuel that propels students forward in their reading; curiosity has also fueled human learning

3 Alasdair MacIntyre, *After Virtue* (Notre Dame: University of Notre Dame Press, 2007), 219.

and advancement. One could even argue that the examined life is an important part of our Christian walk. Arthur Holmes calls the life of the mind "a continuous doxology of praise to God."[4] Indulging one's intellectual curiosity can be a way of worshipping God, who created the very objects of our curiosity.

In college, curiosity manifests itself in a number of ways. Curious students, for example, often struggle to settle on just one major because they are curious about a great many things. Those students hate to focus on just one subject to the exclusion of all others. That is okay. While university education requires students to declare a major, students should also indulge this curiosity: the biology major should feel encouraged to take a course in creative writing; the theater-arts major should feel free to learn more about marine life.

Because higher education is often viewed through radically utilitarian lenses, wide-ranging curiosity can make us appear to be unfit for the world. We look impractical, as if we are not thinking about our future; we feel anxious if we are not focusing exclusively on a career. This anxiety increases when the labor market tightens and the value of a degree is measured in terms of return on investment. College is justified as a hedge against unemployment or underemployment.[5] A college degree, from this point of view, is pursued specifically to prepare students for careers, to enter the workforce, and to climb the ladder of success. Many people today still believe that university education centers on this preparation: higher education as a means to an end.

Anything we pursue in life as a means to an end, however, should be put in its proper context; metaphorical stepping stones are merely instrumental. After relishing an exquisite meal at a

4 Arthur Holmes. *Building The Christian Academy* (Grand Rapids: Eerdmans, 2001), 5.

5 See, for example, Nick Roll, "College A Buffer Against Great Recession." *Inside Higher Ed.* June 30, 2017. The author presents evidence that millennials with a college education fared better in the great recession than their counterparts without a degree.

world-class, five-star restaurant, we do not proclaim, "What fantastic silverware!" The meal is the final end of the dining experience; the fork just gets the meal into our mouths. Millennia ago, Aristotle identified the *summum bonuum*, the highest good, as the final end we pursue in our lives. The means are inferior, for they are only ways to get to the ends. This is why Aristotle deemed theoretical, abstract knowledge to be more valuable than practical, concrete knowledge. One pursues the latter as a means to an end, whereas one seeks the former for its own sake. The examined life is valuable in and of itself; it is an intrinsic good.

Similarly, higher education, by which we mean your opportunity to experience the examined life, is not merely instrumental either. While the liberal arts do possess *some* instrumental value (for instance, they cultivate critical-thinking skills), the liberal arts are so much more than that. When we think with curiosity, we seek knowledge for the sake of knowledge itself. To conceive of higher education as a means to an end is to run the risk of redefining what it means to be a human being. Do we value knowledge because of its instrumental value or because it opens our eyes to the wonder of being alive in a world that God has created?

The great books are thus more than preparation for something. They are a break from something, a break from the prevailing utilitarian wisdom of the world. They give us time to pursue the transcendent. On the subject of the busy life, the Roman Stoic Seneca laments, "Are you always on the go, allowing yourself no time to turn from things human to things divine?"[6] Honors students read and discuss these books with curiosity, proudly defying the educational instrumentalists who find this activity to be folly.

Christianity has a rich history of receiving and then owning the accusation of "folly." Recall that the apostle Paul was accused of folly…and was proud of it! He boldly proclaimed the "folly of

6 Seneca, *On the Private Life*. In J.M. Cooper & J.F. Procope, eds, *Seneca: Moral and Political Essays* (New York: Cambridge University Press, 1995), 177.

the cross" (1 Cor. 1:18-31). Much later, in his book *The Praise of Folly* (1511), Erasmus reminded his readers that true Christian wisdom often appears absurd in this world. He observed that in scripture, those who are destined for eternal life are called sheep, the most foolish of creatures. Erasmus observed that God "is most pleased with those who are farthest removed from the slyness of the fox."[7] The wisdom of the world tells us to be mighty like a lion and shrewd like a fox. The wisdom of Christ encourages us to become sheep, to follow a shepherd. This is not a call to ignorance or anti-intellectualism; it is the opposite. Linking the examined life to the experience of a Christian, we can see the mission of the honors program as a call to see everything through a Christian lens whereby, "transformed by the renewing of the mind," we come to possess a wisdom that the world calls foolishness (Romans 12:2).

### 2. *Read with Creativity*

An imaginative reader examines assumptions and challenges accepted definitions, able to envision worlds that do not yet exist. The imaginative reader seeks to know more than "what this book is about." Imagination allows the reader to take books that seem to come from a remote time and place and make them personal, contemporary, and relevant. Consider the way Seneca (4 BCE-65 CE) approaches Homer's *The Odyssey*, a text that might seem ancient and foreign. Seneca makes it personal and contemporary: "Show me rather, by the example of Ulysses, how I am to love my country, my wife, my father, and how, even after suffering shipwreck, I am to sail toward these ends, honourable as they are."[8]

Making personal connections like this creates multi-directional lines of influence between text, reader, and the world in which the

---

7 Erasmus, *The Praise of Folly,* 2nd Edition, trans. Clarence H. Miller (New Haven: Yale University Press, 2003), 176.

8 Seneca, "On Liberal and Vocational Studies" in *Seneca In Ten Volumes* vol. 5, trans. R.M. Gummere (Cambridge: Harvard University Press, 1970), 353, 355.

reader lives. The convergence of these influences nourishes creativity. Let's consider each one of these lines of influence. First, personal connections encourage readers to bring their own perspectives to bear on the great books. Your unique perspective affords you a unique lens through which to view and analyze the projected world of a text; you are thereby positioned to offer a creative interpretation. Second, when we make ourselves vulnerable to texts, their ideas can help us creatively re-engage our own. With works of fiction, the imagined world of the text collides with our own worldview; if the collision is powerful enough, we can creatively integrate some of that imagined world into our own perspective. Finally, a text can supply us with the tools to creatively interact with our everyday world. Works of fiction, for instance, often cultivate in us empathy for literary characters; this empathy does not simply vanish when we close the book and enter the world.

When we read creatively, we come to understand concepts from many angles. Let's take a look at the concept of "greatness" and our ability to imagine what it is and how it applies to us. While most students strive for greatness, it is more important to conceive of a range of answers to the question, "What is greatness?" Imagining alternative definitions of greatness is at least as important as knowing how to become great. In Greek culture, greatness shared a conceptual kinship with *Arete*, which means "excellence in all things." *Arete* was achieved through well-rounded greatness of mind, body, and spirit. Neil Postman points out that the Athenians' greatness did not come from economic or military might but from a love of knowledge, contemplation, and reason.[9] The dystopian novel *Canticle for Liebowitz* warns of the dangers of using the wrong metrics to determine greatness. In the novel, the character Marcus Apollo is asked, "How can a great and wise civilization have destroyed itself so completely?" He answers, "Perhaps

9 Neil Postman, "My Graduation Speech," in *Conscientious Objections: Stirring Up Trouble about Language, Technology, and Education* (New York: Vintage Books, 1992).

by being materially great and materially wise, and nothing else."[10] It is instructive to consider these expressions of excellence in contradistinction to the proclamations of more modern voices urging material greatness and power. Through the centuries, great books teach us that there are many alternative ideas about true excellence. Reading creatively expands possibilities of meaning.

Likewise, there has been much talk about greatness in higher education. Students and their families are drawn to the prestige and status of a college's brand or ranking and to the success associated with acceptance to a prestigious institution. In *Where You Go Is Not Who You'll Be,* Frank Bruni counters this materialist logic: "College is a singular opportunity to rummage through and luxuriate in ideas, to give your brain a vigorous workout and your soul a thorough investigation, to realize how very large the world is and to complete your desired place in it."[11] Your education should lead to more than status; it should lead to *Arête.* As we have seen in this section, reading any text with imagination will lead you to unexpected and original insights and help you to relate those ideas to your life and assist in your efforts to achieve *Arête.*

### *3. Read with Purpose*

Historically, the great books have been the basis of the liberal arts, or those studies which liberate us or make us free. Free from what? From unconsidered, limited, provincial views. The notion of the liberal arts descends from Greek and Roman Stoic conceptions of education. Drawing from these conceptions, Martha Nussbaum explains that education is "'liberal' in that it liberates the mind from the bondage of habit and custom, producing people who can func-

10 Walter M. Miller, Jr., *A Canticle For Leibowitz* (New York: EOS Harper Collins, 2006), 127.

11 Frank Bruni, *Where You Go Is Not Who You'll Be* (New York: Grand Central Publishing, 2015), 10.

tion with sensitivity and alertness as citizens of the whole world."[12] Reading with purpose thus means preparing for world citizenship.

Christian higher education builds upon this project by establishing faith as a guide. That is, Christian truths and the Christian imagination serve as compasses as we examine all ideas from a distinctly Christian perspective. We thus liberate our minds from the bondage of secular habits and customs as we employ faith as an interpretive lens; at the same time, we continually reassess our own understanding of the faith. A Christian approach to the liberal arts thereby engages the whole person, mind and soul, preparing us for world citizenship as Christians.

The goal of a great-books education is to make one whole. It is to equip students for a life well-lived. It makes one free from all the unreflective thinking that can enslave the mind. Adam Smith says that human beings who do not use their intellectual faculties are "mutilated" and "deformed." They have not realized their full human potential.[13] Shelley's *Frankenstein* gives us an interesting perspective on the dangers of this sort of mutilation and deformation. The novel encourages us to think about what it means to be a whole human being. The character of Victor Frankenstein becomes enslaved by his obsession with creating life, losing sight of the moral and spiritual implications of his reckless science experiment. We are led to wonder if the creature is not more human than Victor who, by the book's end, seems himself to be mutilated and deformed, a wretched being chasing the creature to the ends of the earth.[14] A truly humane education liberates us to become fully human, nourishing our minds and souls.

In his book *The Liberal Arts: A Student's Guide*, Gene Fant proposes this syllogism:

---

12 Martha Nussbaum, *Cultivating Humanity: A Classical Defense of Reform in Liberal Education* (Cambridge: Harvard UP, 1997), 8.

13 Adam Smith. *The Wealth of Nations* (New York: Random House, 1994).

14 Mary Shelley, *Frankenstein, 1818 Text* (New York: Oxford University Press, 1993).

Major Premise – Education is the pursuit of truth.

Minor Premise – The truth will make you free.

Conclusion – Education will make you free. [15]

The author goes on to explain that "freedom is not found in this world but is effected by the divine rescue of persons from their selfish fallen natures [...]. Genuine freedom that transcends the created order may be found solely within the context of Christ-centered education rather than self-centered training."[16] A great-books education will set students on a path to freedom from the consumer desires, the technological demands, the irrational assumptions, and the vapid rhetoric of this world. They are freed from the cubicles of bureaucracy, from the empty promises of advertising, and from the common herd of popular culture. Students are set free from these drives not only so that they might be better *than* others but also so that they might become better *for* others.

The contemplative life is a vehicle for our liberation. It leads us out of the darkness of Plato's cave and into the light. The book *The Art of Freedom: Teaching Humanities to the Poor* is a memoir about Earl Shorris's work with the underprivileged. Shorris recognizes that, in order to break the cycle of poverty and to transcend the forces which surround and subjugate the poor, they must progress "from a life of reaction to one of reflection."[17] He says, "The humanities are a foundation for getting along in the world, for thinking, for learning to reflect on the world instead of just reacting to whatever force is turned against you."[18] Progress from reaction to reflection frees all of us who are poor in spirit. And we who

15 Gene C. Fant, Jr., *The Liberal Arts: A Student's Guide* (Wheaton: Crossway, 2012).

16 Ibid, 18.

17 Earl Shorris, *The Art Of Freedom: Teaching Humanities To The Poor* (New York: Norton, 2013), 146.

18 Ibid, 23.

have had the privilege of a liberal-arts education are bound by the purpose to help free others.

### *4. Read with Confidence*

Every student in the honors program belongs and has something to offer. Some students worry that they will add nothing to a discussion of the great books because they are not smart enough. Others worry that one must be an expert in the humanities to really get something out of these texts. Still others fear that they will not be interested in the great books because they do not come from the right background. On the contrary, the great books will be of interest to all students because the great books chronicle the history of ideas. All who are passionate about ideas will find something to love in the great books. They speak to *all* of us. They address questions that have remained universal for generations, and they have benefitted all sorts of people at all sorts of times in all sorts of places.

Reading with confidence emboldens students to wrestle with these questions. With each honors class they take, students see how ideas shape the world and their lives. Ideas have consequences. In the world today, people suffer the consequences of bad ideas while good ideas suffer the consequences of neglect. Honors students are among the few who continue to read the books that ask the great questions. Because of that, they will be leaders in making the world a more humane place by taking up the cause of good ideas.

Our reading suggests that the world would be different if everybody read the great books. Our political system would function differently. The Church would be more effective in its work. Business would be practiced more humanely. And people would have a better sense of the good life. The Honors Program aims to produce students who show the world why everyone ought to read the great books.

These texts are useful not only to liberal arts majors. Business majors, biology majors, exercise-science majors—all majors—can read with confidence. The great books do not belong to any one discipline. They belong to all. Most of these texts were written in an age when there were no academic departments protecting their turf. An author like Aristotle has something to say to historians, economists, rhetoricians, philosophers, scientists, political scientists, and others. Oftentimes, students read a primary text in preparation for class and feel like they do not understand it. Then they confidently bring the scraps of understanding to class with them and begin a discussion. It is nothing short of miraculous that fifteen or twenty partial understandings or even misunderstandings can come together to assemble a truly solid, insightful understanding of the text. Confidence inspires each student to recognize that his or her perspective is valid and contributes to a larger understanding. It allows us to think out loud without fear of being proven wrong. And, in the end, it gives each student the joy that comes with conquering a difficult text and achieving a new understanding, thereby gaining even more confidence.

### *5. Read with Courage*

Students read the great books with the courage that comes from the knowledge that learning can be traumatic. The trauma often occurs when the ideas of a text challenge the worldview of a student. The experience is a dizzying sensation in which dearly held assumptions are compellingly called into question, seemingly turning the world upside down. But this trauma, when confronted with courage, need not eventuate in the erosion or eradication of belief. On the other side of educational trauma, most students reencounter their beliefs with newfound wisdom and make them their own, though often in revised forms. All that is required is a commitment to truth and an understanding that sometimes truth will lead to uncomfortable places.

Students who lack courage evade the challenges that the great books often present. One evasive maneuver that is common among readers is what our colleague David Horkott calls the inoculation analysis. The inoculation analysis occurs when a student begins the reading of a book with a foregone conclusion that the ideas presented in the book are wrong. As a flu shot inoculates you from the flu, the inoculation analysis inoculates a student from the perceived threat of a book with which the student disagrees from the outset. The inoculation analysis comes in various forms, all of which involve triumphalism and intellectual fraud: the student who begins to read the Koran already convinced that everything in it is wrong, or the student who goes into Charles Darwin's *On the Origin of Species* with his or her mind already settled that the theory of evolution is incompatible with Christianity.

Another evasive maneuver is the assumption of certainty. If you are certain that you are correct, then *any* idea that contrasts with your own is necessarily wrong. If you are certain that you are right, then the study of other ideas becomes defensive, protective, and thus superficial; the mind operates primarily or even solely in critique mode (the mode of the inoculation analysis). Reading with confidence, in contrast, necessitates an attitude of intellectual humility and curiosity: to study, for instance, the existentialism of Soren Kierkegaard and the postmodern ideas of Richard Rorty with genuine interest—and not with an initial, settled conviction that they are evil and just plain wrong, an approach that will always confirm what it assumes from the beginning.

It takes courage to find truth where we least expect to find it. But truth is no less true when it goes unrecognized and unappreciated. We do not possess the truth. When rightly understood, truth cannot be possessed. Instead, we are possessed by it. The goal for students is not to know truth but to become obedient to the truth, to submit to the truth, wherever it may appear. We submit to truth with courage and reverence, and, in so doing, we allow ourselves to be formed by it.

The great books include a variety of ideas which will challenge every reader. At times, this challenge will produce trauma. Courageous readers can handle this trauma and thus be willing to interrogate their own presuppositions, knowing that the result will be a refined set of commitments and a renewed commitment to truth.

### 6. *Read with Humility*

As fallen, finite beings, we seek a truth that transcends us. Knowing this is a necessary precursor to all other knowledge. According to the Christian worldview, those who believe that all things can be grasped by human understanding begin their quest for knowledge with a flawed presupposition. On the other hand, those who acknowledge not only the fallenness of the will but the fallenness of the intellect embrace the epistemological humility that is necessary for all learning. Put simply, we must acknowledge both that we are wrong about some things and that there are some things we will never know. Intellectual history has revealed that each generation has been certain about some things that turned out not to be true. We too can be certain that our descendants will correct a good many of our certainties.

Pride endangers our learning. This is another reason why the assumption of certainty is dangerous. Students who come to college believing that they already know everything are deceiving themselves. In fact, their decision to go to college was a mistake, for, when they are certain that they are right, there is nothing that they can be taught. In the Classical Tradition, Socrates shows that learning reveals how much we don't yet know. Our humility allows us to put ourselves not at the center of all things but to be open-minded toward the books we read and charitable toward those who are reading with us. Only then do we open ourselves up to new, previously unimagined possibilities. C.S. Lewis famously said, "A proud man is always looking down on things and people; and, of course, as long as you are looking down, you cannot see something that is above you."[19]

The history of ideas is also filled with warnings for the "overreacher." We have in us the tendency to lose a sense of propriety and to ignore our own limits. Literary characters like Icarus, Faust, Frankenstein, and Milton's Satan all show us what can happen when we ignore our own fallenness and attempt to transcend our own place in God's creation. These overly ambitious characters think they can know all things and can do all things. They reveal a fundamental human disobedience in which we wish to put ourselves in the place of God. In their effort to become more than human, they fail spectacularly, and their ignorance is to be pitied.

Students of the great books are also humbled by the responsibility that comes with their education. The mind is like a vessel to be filled by education. As with any vessel, if nothing is poured in, nothing can be poured out. If you are constantly pouring out, the vessel is emptied, and there is nothing to be shared. Those who seek to serve others and who have allowed themselves to be filled by reading, thinking, and discussing the history of ideas have more to share with others. Humility reminds us that we are to be a vessel that needs to be filled.

### *7. Read with Gratitude*

The great books are filled with wisdom that has been discovered and shared graciously by thinkers through the ages. A grateful reader does not take for granted this wisdom but reads with a sense of awe. Readers of the great books recognize the privilege that we have to spend time reading, discussing, and writing about the most profound ideas. The liberal arts were first called liberal because they were pursued by free citizens. The luxury to contemplate ideas like truth, beauty, and justice—to lead the examined life—assumes that

19 C.S. Lewis, *Mere Christianity* (New York: Harper Collins, 1980), 124.

we have the time and resources and freedom to give to our study. If we think of all of the people who have lived in all of the times and places throughout history, we quickly recognize that today's college students have a great privilege.

Our gratitude should include a thankfulness for the books and authors that we have inherited, but it should also be extended to the people with whom we share this experience. In college, we establish friendships that will last a lifetime. For Cicero, a healthy friendship should have its basis in a shared love for virtue.[20] What better place to cultivate friendships than within a community of scholars dedicated to the pursuit of virtue! Mark Schwehn writes that "academies at their best can and should become communities where the pleasures of friendship and the rigors of work are united."[21]

Our gratitude also extends to a thankfulness for the rigors and hard work of study. To many in the modern world, the good life is characterized by the absence of work. Seemingly, a life of leisure without work is today's dream. The contemporary world seems to have dedicated itself to creating technologies that eliminate work from our lives. To the reader of the great books, however, work is a blessing. To have meaningful work enriches our lives. That we can live well and not have work is illusory. The contemplative life does not replace work. Instead, it makes our work more fulfilling.

Education is an act of gratefully receiving and graciously giving. Those thinkers who came before us, in an act of generosity, recorded the wisdom that was revealed to them. And, as readers of their books, we are to receive that wisdom with gratitude. Our education is best understood as an inheritance. It is our good fortune that the wisdom of great thinkers has been passed down to us. This privilege is also burdensome. Like so many who have come before us, we

20 Cicero "Laelius On Friendship" *Cicero On the Good Life* Trans. Michael Grant (New York: Penguin, 1971).

21 Mark Schwehn, *Exiles From Eden: Religion and The Academic Vocation In America* (New York: Oxford University Press, 1993), 61.

have the responsibility of good stewardship. This inheritance is not ours to consume. We must care for it, adding to it when we can, and sharing it with others. And we are grateful that those who came before us took this burden seriously for our sake.

### *Final Words of Encouragement*

The chapters that follow are organized into two parts. The first part consists of historical background that will help contextualize the readings for the courses; the second part provides brief glosses (paraphrases and explanations) of required texts in those courses. Hopefully, you will find this book useful in your study of the great books. In these texts are hidden the treasures of intellectual history. They have transformed minds and shaped lives for centuries. Yet they remain relevant and contemporary in our own age. To any reader, they offer much. But, to the careful, introspective reader, they hold even greater promise. These texts have the potential to challenge you, to shape your character, to bring true joy into your life, and to ignite a love of learning. And only those who read the great books know what they would have missed had they not been introduced to these thinkers and their ideas.

The faculty and alumni of the Frederick M. Supper Honors Program have contributed the following chapters with the hope of introducing these authors to you in their own historical context. The chapters are not intended as a substitute for the books themselves, but as primers that will inspire you to go further and to frame the reading, making it less intimidating and more interesting. We hope that you will enjoy these historical backgrounds and textual glosses, and that they will enhance your time in the honors program.

# CHAPTER ONE

# THE WORLD OF POLIS AND COVENANT

**DAVID HORKOTT AND NATHAN MAXWELL**[1]

*What has Athens to do with Jerusalem?*[2]

Our modern culture is like the Mississippi River. It is a wide current fed by many tributaries. The major tributaries of the Mississippi are the Arkansas, Illinois, Missouri, Ohio, and Red Rivers. Similarly, the wide stream of our Western European culture can be traced to its major sources. The World of Polis and Covenant does just that by focusing on two of the major sources of our way of life: the ancient cultures of the Greeks and Hebrews. These ancient cultures make for a muddy but fertile mixture. The title of this course (like some other Supper Honors courses) indicates a juxtaposition or incongruity—for the world of the ancient Greeks was

1 The historical overview and glosses on Greek texts were written by David Horkott. The introduction to the Old Testament and Old Testament glosses were written by Nathan Maxwell.

2 Tertullian put it this way, "What has Jerusalem to do with Athens, the Church with the Academy, the Christian with the heretic? [...] After Jesus we have no need of speculation, after the Gospel no need of research." http://www.newadvent.org/fathers/.

a world apart from that of the ancient Hebrews. This course is an immersion in the contrary relation between Athens and Jerusalem. The Greeks were obsessed with excellence and sought beauty and perfection in and through the humanities. The ancient Hebrews focused their energy on following the righteous instructions of a holy God. And here you are at a Christian university where you are required to study the humanities, which share the greatest affinity with Greek thought. According to Louise Cowan, there will always be a tension when Christians study the liberal arts:

> For the liberal arts are indisputably Greek in their orientation: and yet those bright gods on Mt. Olympus, who mingled with men (and women!), jealously coveted sacrifices, and accepted official commemoration in marble temples and olive groves, have little to do with the hidden presence who spoke from a burning bush and forbade David to build him a temple. And the center of our faith—that lonely one who hung on the cross at Golgotha and redefined the purposes of life—took as his earthly ancestry the Hebrew tradition, with its pervasive tendency to regard as idolatry any representation such as we in the West have called art.[3]

Cowan not only observes that Greek and Hebrew cultures influence us in contrary ways, but she makes two bolder claims. First, that the Western intellectual tradition contains a Hebraic strain even more surely than it does a Greek one.[4] Second, that, far from being a schizoid culture, our culture benefits from a doubleness of vision that provides us with unique creative genius. Cowan's bolder claims are supported by an earlier cultural diagnostician: the nineteenth-century philosopher Friedrich Nietzsche. Nietzsche argued

---

3 Louise Cowan, "Jerusalem's Claim on Us" in *The InterCollegiate Review* Fall/Spring 2000-01, 14.

4 Ibid., 14.

that the single greatest event in all of human history has been a protracted war between the value system of Jews (and Christians) and that of the Greeks (and Romans). Even though Nietzsche was convinced that our culture is still a battleground, he believed that Jewish/Christian values had won the decisive battles over Greek and Roman values. In The World of Polis and Covenant you will explore the origins and meanings of both value systems.

The Greek mode of thought is speculative, scientific, and creative. Edith Hall describes the ten qualities shared by most ancient Greeks most of the time: "seagoing, suspicious of authority, individualistic, inquiring, open to new ideas, witty, competitive, admir[ing of] excellence in talented people, wildly articulate, and addicted to pleasure."[5]

The ancient Greek-speaking world has left us an amazing legacy. In this course you will read Herodotus, who has become known as our first historian. His account of the speech of Pericles will show you just how proud Athenians were of their democracy. The Greeks gave the world theater, and you will gain a sense for the Greek love for drama as you read and discuss their tragedies. The Olympic Games—the oldest and best sporting competition—were Greek contributions, and they show the Greek predilection for ranking in order of most flawless (gold, silver, and bronze medals). Finally, our fullest understanding of happiness (*eudaimonia*) comes from the ancient wisdom of Aristotle, the Stagirite.

The ancient Hebrew culture left us with another amazing legacy. According to the Jewish philosopher Martin Buber, the real contribution of the Hebrews was to work with a recalcitrant material: human hearts.[6] The Hebrews do not give us monuments but rather a community.[7] Nietzsche would agree with Buber. In his estimation, the Hebrews were humanity's greatest geniuses in terms

5 Edith Hall, *The Ancient Greeks: Ten Ways They Shaped the Modern World* (New York: Vintage, 2016), 21.

6 Hall, 21.

7 Ibid.

of value-creation. In fact, no other culture on the planet has come close to their moral genius.[8] Most all cultures (including ancient Greek culture) had a priestly caste, but in addition to its priests the Hebrews were on the whole a priestly people. The priestly psychology that permeated Hebrew culture reflected its interest in having a special relationship to God.

If we credit the Greeks with the idea that humans are worth regarding, we can credit the Hebrews with the notion that humans are the pinnacle of creation because we were made in the image of God. Humans alone are able to mirror God's qualities such as justice, wisdom, righteousness, and love. In the second account of creation, man is made from earth but inspirited with God's own breath, and woman is taken from his side. Our greatest gift from the Hebrews is this: we learn that God loves humankind and has made a covenant with those who hear his voice.[9] After completing The World of Polis and Covenant, you will become familiar with the Greek quest for perfection and obsession with beauty as well as the Hebraic sense of moral community and their experience of God's awe-inspiring mystery (*mysterium tremendum).*

This course will be one of the first you take in the Frederick M. Supper Honors Program, and right away you will discover that the conception of what makes an excellent human in these ancient cultures will be startlingly divergent. You will find strikingly different responses to the question, "What is it that gives humans their humanity?" If a great conversation consists in great minds discussing a great topic, then The World of Polis and Covenant is an absolutely better-than-fantastic introduction to what is called the Great Conversation. In The World of Polis and Covenant, you will participate in a conversation that centers on the most significant topics humans can discuss. Bear in mind that whenever you refer-

8 Nietzsche, *GM* I section 16.

9 Jews wear phylacteries (small leather boxes containing biblical verses related to the covenant with God) to remind them of the privilege of being given divine commands.

ence or refine the thinking of writers that have preceded you, then you too will be contributing to the Great Conversation. This course will awaken you to the task of becoming more deeply human.

## *Prolegomena to the Greek and Hebrew Glosses*

Greek civilization has lasted a long time. It has had numerous iterations. Please refer to the timeline below for a short historical sketch:

I. The Archaic Age (800-475 BCE)

A. Epic Poetry

. Homer 750-650

B. Pre-Socratics

. Thales 620-540

. Anaximander 610-546

. Pythagoras 569-475

. Xenophanes 570-475

. Heraclitus 535-475

II. The Hellenic Age (475-320 BCE)

A. Greek Tragedy

. Aeschylus 523-456

. Sophocles 496-406

B. Greek History

. Herodotus 485-425

. Thucydides 472-400

. Peloponnesian War 430-404

C. Sophists: Protagoras 490-420

D. The Academics

| | | |
|---|---|---|
| . | Socrates | 470-399 |
| . | Plato | 428-347 |
| . | Aristotle | 384-322 |

E. Cynicism

| | | |
|---|---|---|
| . | Diogenes of Sinope | 412-320 |

III. The Hellenistic Age (323-31 BCE)

| | | |
|---|---|---|
| A. | Skepticism: Pyrrho | 360-270 |
| B. | Epicureanism: Epicurus | 341-270 |
| C. | Stoicism: Zeno of Citium | 334-262 |

IV. The Rise of Rome: Polybius 200-118

The rest of this chapter conforms to the timeline introduced (above) with two variations. In the first part of the remainder of this chapter, ages and authors will be treated generally. The second part of the chapter (the "glosses" section) will examine select works and authors with a view toward helping students gain an initial orientation to them.

## I. *The Archaic Age (800-475 BCE)*

In about 800 BCE the Greeks emerged from a period of stagnation known as the "Dark Ages." An increasing awareness of Greek identity formed around a common mythical parent, Hellen. Hellen was a male who fathered three major Greek tribes: the Ionians, the Aeolians, and the Dorians. They called their land Hellas and started to organize small city-states (*poleis*).

### A. *Epic Poetry*

The first phase of ancient Greece is known as the Archaic Age. One of the first figures discussed in The World of Polis and Covenant is Homer.[10] According to critics, the first praise of genius should go to the creators of epic poems because epic poetry combines all of the artistic powers found individually in other art forms.[11] And the greatest of epic poets was Homer.

B. *Pre-Socratics*

The Pre-Socratic era is when those early Greek philosophers who had not been influenced by Socrates did their thinking. Thales, Anaximander, Anaxagoras, Pythagoras, Xenophanes, and Heraclitus are sometimes called Pre-Socratics, but that is not chronologically accurate in all cases. These thinkers, by and large, looked to explain events in the natural world in terms of natural causes. Pre-Socratics did not rely on magic or myth to explain natural events. They were associated with impiety and even atheism because of their naturalism. Very little of their writing has survived. If more of these archaic works had survived, then we might be giving them more attention than the works of Plato and Aristotle.

These archaic philosophers did not limit their thinking to what appears to humans in ordinary experience. The story of philosophy begins with metaphysical wonder.[12] The archaic Greeks wondered about the underlying nature of things. For example, some of these philosophers wondered how all the individual entities we experience with all their differences somehow constitute the unified reality that we call a universe. A typical question for a Pre-Socratic thinker was, "What is everything made of?" Suffice it to say, creative imagination is the real power of philosophy and not calculating

10 The poems attributed to Homer were passed down in an oral tradition. Tradition attributes the poems to a blind bard known as Homer, but we cannot say for sure that the poems we possess were the work of one person much less Homer.

11 M.I. Finley, "Homer and the Greeks" in *The World of Odysseus* (New York: New York Review of Books, 1954), 5.

12 Metaphysics is the study of all theories about the nature of reality. Those theories range from idealism (mind and spiritual forces are ultimately real) to materialism (matter-energy and physical forces are real).

reason. But the truth discovered by the first Western philosophers was not poetic or mythological. It was philosophical.

. *Thales*

Thales is known as the father of Western philosophy. He sought an underlying principle that could account for the nature of the world. His answer was that water was the single causal principle behind the natural world. After all, water is necessary for life. Water is a naturally occurring substance that can take different forms (liquid, solid, gas). For Thales, a cloud was water at low density, and a mountain was made up of higher density water.

. *Anaximander*

For Anaximander, the proper way to judge humans is to see them as creatures who really should not exist at all and who do penance for their lives by their many sufferings (and by dying). Anaximander is a pessimist who tells us that human life is basically the poor existence of a sinner living under the sentence of death.

Anaximander saw what we all see in the world. Individual things come into being and then they always go out of being. Whatever is created or born eventually passes away. Anaximander was gripped by this observation: whenever definite qualities are perceivable, we can prophesy the passing away of these qualities. If something is hot or cold or possesses any other definite quality, then it will at some time go out of existence. Never can a being which possesses definite qualities be the origin of all things. For Anaximander, that which truly is cannot possess definite characteristics. Primal being is devoid of any definite qualities that would lead to its passing away. Ultimate reality, for Anaximander, is the Indefinite—the womb of all things. The birth of individual entities with their definite qualities is always a crime against the Indefinite. Anaximander, when observing the multiplicity of things in the universe, came to an ethical conclusion: How can anything pass away which has a right to be?

. *Pythagoras*

Pythagoras is a familiar name to math students. He was a mystic and maybe even a cult leader. He taught the doctrine of reincarnation and that ultimate reality is number. His school venerated numerical patterns.[13] The number one represented the point. The number two represented the line. The number three represented the surface. Number four represented the solid.[14] The numbers 1, 2, 3, and 4 equal the number 10 when added (which made 10 the perfect number). Whereas other Pre-Socratics were looking for a common substance to account for this universe, Pythagoras posited something intangible. Numbers are real things in a universe that includes matter and immaterial objects.

. *Xenophanes*

Xenophanes is famous for saying, "If horses could draw, they would draw their gods like horses."[15] He criticized Homer for anthropomorphizing the gods. Homer's gods possessed disgraceful traits and were not worthy of veneration. Xenophanes was a cultural relativist. He also thought Pythagoras's notion of reincarnation whereby a human soul could migrate into the body of an animal was ridiculous. He did believe in a deity, but it was a vague monotheism. His god was in no way like humans in shape or in thinking. His legacy is the value of falsification: we may not know the truth with certainty, but we can know with certainty what is not the case. [16]

---

13 Pythagoreans especially admired the tetractys of the decad (a diagram that represents the first four numbers in a triangle of ten dots or points). They worshipped the triangle and the number ten.

14 Philip Stokes, *Philosophy: 100 Essential Thinkers* (London: Arcturus Publishing Limited, 2015), 11.

15 Ibid., 13.

16 Ibid., 14.

. *Heraclitus*

Heraclitus located the first principle of the world in the process of change. Everything is in a state of flux. Reality is not a bunch of objects located in the container of space. Reality is best understood as the process of change. For Heraclitus, the three basic elements were Earth, Water, and Fire.[17] Fire was primary. Picture a small log before you place it in a fire. How does its appearance change once it is in the fire? The shape, size, and texture of the log change. Smoke, heat, and light are created in the exchange process. Heraclitus believed that while we are surrounded by change, there is nevertheless a balance of opposites. It was the eternal condition of the universe to be full of strife and opposition in such a way that no force ever completely vanquishes its opposite. Heraclitus used the term *Logos* to describe the deeper structure of the world. According to McKirahan, Heraclitus's "great discovery is that all things take place or come to be in accordance with a Logos."[18] *Logos* is the general principle that guides all things in the spheres of nature and morality.

II. *The Hellenic Age (475-320 BCE)*

The Hellenic Age extends from the Greeks' defeat of the Persians to the death of Alexander the Great. This was the golden age of ancient Greece, but it did not last long. The hallmark of this period was a "greater and greater humanism" and celebration of human beings.[19]

A. *Greek Tragedy*

Greek tragedy provides the beginning for what we know as drama in our time. However, if you were transported back to the Hellenic Age, you would find Greek dramas to be very different from what

17 Stokes, 15.

18 Richard D. McKirahan, *Philosophy Before Socrates: An Introduction with Texts and Commentary* (Indianapolis, IN: Hackett Publishing, 1994), 133.

19 *Experience Humanities*, 8th ed., Eds. Roy Matthews, F. DeWitt Platt, Thomas F.X. Noble (New York: McGraw-Hill, 2014), 81.

you see on stage or video screen today. Our actors (and actresses) do not typically wear masks.[20] For one thing, there was much less acting in Greek tragedy. Performers would stand still and chant their lines. Additionally, physical action took place off stage and would be reported in the chants. You would also discover that a Greek tragedy has a chorus. A chorus was made up of about twelve to fifteen singers and dancers who would provide a commentary on the play's events. The earliest plays consisted of a single actor who would chant a line and a chorus that would respond. A key development was the addition of a second actor, which made dialogue possible. In addition to wearing grotesque masks, actors wore elaborate costumes. Gestures would have been exaggerated to compensate for the lack of facial expression and the fact that the people sitting far from the stage would have trouble seeing subtle movements. The performance would not feel as natural as we are accustomed to experiencing. Greek plays were almost always performed as part of a religious festival. The production of plays was a way of honoring the gods. For Athens, it was Dionysus, the god of wine, ecstatic religious experience, and theater. Each Dionysia was also a theatrical contest. Each year three playwrights were selected to compete. Competitors were required to submit a cycle of three tragic plays followed by a satyr play. The plays were scheduled for the beginning of the sailing season when favorable winds could bring Greeks from other cities to the festival. Civic pride was at stake. Athens, as the greatest city, would be expected to put on the greatest festival. Attendance may have reached 15,000 people in an open-air theater.[21] What was called the "orchestra" in those days meant "place for dancing."[22]

---

20 Of course, there was Leatherface in *Texas Chainsaw Massacre* (1974), Michael Myers in *Halloween* (1978), and Hannibal Lectre in *Silence of the Lambs* (1991), to name only a few.

21 James C. Hogan, *A Commentary on the Complete Greek Tragedies: Aeschylus* (Chicago: University of Chicago Press, 1984), 2.

22 Ibid., 3.

Any fiction that deals with tragic events may be called tragedy. But for our purposes we will consider tragedy to be fiction inspired by a serious concern for the problem of man's fate. Greek tragedy is serious in that it treats the meaning of human life in a non-superficial way. Reading about a reversal of fortune in a Greek tragedy is very different from reading a newspaper account of a reversal of fortune. Tragedy is not merely about losing money or being treated unfairly or having your heart broken; rather, it treats all suffering from the perspective of the meaning of the human condition.

B. *Greek History*

The whole Greek world was attacked by Persia and Carthage early in the fifth century BCE. The main attacks came under Xerxes, and they failed. The Greeks had solid body armor, longer spears, and better athletic training.[23] The defeats were not serious to the Persian Empire, but to the Greeks these victories were all important.[24] The victory at Marathon was a source of great pride to Athenians. Athenians boasted that they were the saviors of Greece due to their roles at Marathon as well as the naval battle of Salamis.[25] The Athenians organized the Delian League in 478 BCE in order to scale up the ability of the Greek world to prevent further Persian aggression. Cities paid assessments to Athens to maintain the Athenian naval force. The navy had hundreds of ships and needed oarsmen numbering 36,000.[26] Eventually, the Delian League became the Athenian empire. The Athenians built a pair of "long walls" connecting Athens with its harbor.[27] Thus, Athens became a fortified city. Fear of Persian attacks lessened, and military spending was replaced by a building program led by Pericles. In the middle of the

23 John Garraty, Peter Gay, eds. *The Columbia History of the World* (New York: Harper & Row), 172.

24 Ibid.

25 Ibid.

26 Garraty and Gay, 174.

27 Ibid.

fifth century BCE, Athens was at the height of its power. Hundreds of cities (*poleis*) were controlled by Athens. But Athens's prosperity frightened her Greek rivals, especially the Spartans.

No account of Greek history would be complete if it failed to mention that Herodotus is considered the father of history. He hoped to preserve for all time the memory of what people had done by giving an account of the past. For him, the historian records important events as well as providing them with an interpretation. One purpose of history is to preserve glorious memories. Herodotus travelled extensively and visited various cities in Greece, Asian Minor, Babylon, Egypt, and Italy. His exposure to non-Greek ways of doing things expanded the horizons of Greek thinking. He believed in gathering all versions of an event and then arranging this material thematically rather than chronologically. He felt that history showed a repetition of patterns. He also presented historical information in the form of entertaining stories, so his accounts are lively. Even today, Herodotus has the ability to draw you into the events he describes by creating vivid scenes containing interesting personalities.[28]

C. *Sophists: Protagoras*

Protagoras was the first person to proclaim himself a Sophist and to charge fees for his teaching services. He was a cross between a lawyer and a self-help coach, and grew wealthy from his profession. Plato named some of his dialogues after Sophists, but due to his hostility toward them, his information is not reliable.[29] Athenians regarded Sophists much like we regard lawyers. Democracy in Athens opened the door for non-royals to participate in political leadership, which made rhetorical ability an important requirement

28 Thucydides is another important Greek historian of the Hellenic Age and will be discussed later.

29 John Gilbert, "The Sophists" in *The Blackwell Guide to Ancient Philosophy*, ed. Christopher Shields (Malden, MA: Blackwell Publishing, 2003), 27-29.

for worldly success. Protagoras claimed to teach success in life. He claimed to teach excellence (*arete*) so that one could become competent, admired, and even wealthy. He is famous for saying that "Man is the measure of all things," which was the starting point for his philosophy of relativism. Protagoras meant that there is no standard or measure by which to judge things except ourselves. Everything we experience happens inside our consciousness. We can only know reality as it appears to us in our own consciousness.

Sophists were skilled at looking at the opposite side of each argument. For the Sophists, all we have are opinions based on appearances. This led to epistemological skepticism as well as moral relativism. Again, the doctrine most closely attached to Protagoras is relativism. From his time to our own, cultures have struggled with the problems raised by relativism and skepticism.

### D. *The Academics: Socrates, Plato, and Aristotle*

There was a historical Socrates who was executed in Athens in 399 BCE. Socrates did not write anything that has survived. He did not charge a fee for his teaching or organize a school. But the Socrates we meet in Platonic dialogues serves as a mouthpiece for Plato's own philosophy. Most scholars view Plato's early dialogues as resembling the historical Socrates to a greater degree. To the best of our knowledge, the actual Socrates questioned people and challenged the consistency of their beliefs. Socrates asked probing questions.[30] He was a public figure who interacted with individuals by questioning whether or not they really knew what they thought they knew. In this role, Socrates did not teach any positive doctrine. The Socratic method works by posing questions to individuals and then exposing weaknesses in their answers. Quite often conversation conducted in the form of Socratic questioning would terminate in an awareness of a logical fallacy.

30 He was considered a gadfly. He was more than annoying—his conversations stung. In the *Meno* he is compared to an electric eel because a conversation with him could leave you feeling numb.

Christopher Shields explains the six-stage process of the Socratic Method (*elenchus*) as follows:

1. Socrates asks a question of the form: What is F-ness? (What is courage? What is justice? What is virtue?)
2. The respondent answers: F-ness is G. (Courage is standing firm in battle. Justice is helping one's friends and harming one's enemies. Virtue is the ability to acquire good things.)
3. Socrates elicits additional beliefs from his respondent. (Is it possible to stand firm in battle because one is frozen by fear? Is it just to help one's friends if they have been unjust? Is virtue always just if you acquire good things in an unjust manner?)
4. Socrates shows his interlocuters that their views are internally inconsistent.
5. Socrates's interlocuters realize that they have endorsed an inconsistent set of propositions and usually give up on their answer to Socrates's initial question.
6. Socrates professes to share their ignorance and recommends a renewed search for the essence of the moral quality under consideration.[31]

Most people found a discussion with Socrates exasperating. Apparently, all they learned was that they did not know something that they previously thought they knew. Socrates refuted, but he did not replace bad ideas with better ones. His conversations end in puzzlement and the admission of ignorance. Plato's *Euthyphro* is an excellent example of such a conversation. Socrates left an indelible impression on Plato who in turn influenced Aristotle.

31 Christopher Shields, *Ancient Philosophy: A Contemporary Introduction*, 2nd ed., (New York: Routledge, 2012), 37.

Plato founded his school "The Academy" in 387 BCE, and Aristotle studied there for twenty-three years.

E. *Cynicism: Diogenes of Sinope*

A contemporary of Aristotle, Diogenes was a Cynic. His nickname was "the dog" for his vagrant lifestyle.[32] He neglected hygiene and was lewd, crude, and socially unacceptable. Being called a dog was not meant as a compliment, but he embraced his nickname anyway. To him, dogs are superior to most people because dogs are honest. Dogs are transparent with their feelings of approval and disapproval. Most of all, dogs do not need much to be happy. Dogs can live very well on one meal a day and are fine drinking plain water. Basically, dogs have fewer resources than humans, but are happier than humans.

Cynics taught that the less you needed to be happy, the more you were like the gods who were self-sufficient. Cynics appreciated the way Socrates was independent of public opinion and social standards. Socrates was a rugged individualist from their point of view, teaching that you only needed your moral integrity to be happy. Happiness did not depend on material possessions and social status.

Like all ancient schools of philosophy, the goal of their way of life was happiness. For them, traditional ways of life and traditional customs were a waste of effort. While Plato elevated wisdom, Cynics elevated self-sufficiency. After all, being tough (physically and emotionally) is a human virtue. For Cynics the good life amounts to a free life. Cynics were free to speak their minds even if it went against tradition. They were free from material possessions. They were free from ambition, fame, and political power. In fact, Cynics did not believe in getting involved in politics. Cynics ridiculed speculative philosophy and anticipated the Skeptics by harshly judging theoretical and dogmatic thinking. Cynics practiced what they preached. They trained themselves to be happy

32 Stokes, 30-31.

with less. Poverty was not a problem for them, but rather the path to peace and contentment. The Cynics were the only philosophers to actually praise poverty as a blessing.

Cynics were outspoken and even brazen, but they also acted like society's conscience because they exposed hypocrisy and addiction to artificial needs. Cynics want you to know that you have a greater capacity for hardship than you realize. Odysseus was a model for them. They also admired Hercules (not so much for his strength as for his gumption). Apart from these extraordinary examples of human endurance, Cynics viewed humans as a race of moral degenerates who valued prestige and wealth above all else. Most humans are preoccupied with social standing and luxury. Plato allegedly described Diogenes as "Socrates gone mad."[33] He lived in a barrel, wore rags, ate onions discarded from the market and, most importantly, he lived free from social embarrassment.

III. *The Hellenistic Age (323-31 BCE)*

Alexander the Great died in Babylon in 323 BCE. After he died several large kingdoms were created by his generals. There ended up being three large kingdoms as follows: the Ptolemies in Egypt, the Seleucids in Mesopotamia and Syria, and the Antigonids in Macedon. "Culture in the Hellenistic age was cosmopolitan, multicultural, tolerant, and experimental."[34] Two distinct philosophical species of skepticism emerged during the Hellenistic period. One of them developed out of Plato's old Academy and the other from Pyrrho's teaching. Recall that when Plato died Aristotle was passed over with regard to controlling the Academy. Ancient writers assert that the Academy took a sudden and radical turn toward skepticism when Arcesilaus took it over in 272 BCE. The new focus was on examining contrary arguments with a view to suspending judgment (*epoche*). Later on, St. Augustine will attack "Academic Skeptical

33 Qtd. in Stokes, 31.

34 See "Summary" and "Legacy of the Hellenistic World" in *Experience Humanities*, 8th ed., eds. Roy Matthews, F. DeWitt Platt, Thomas F.X. Noble, 101.

Philosophy," which shares a kindred spirit with Pyrrhonism.[35] One of the issues that skeptics bring up is called the "criterion of truth." If someone says that something is true, then a skeptic will ask them how they know it is true. Well, the person says, I have a standard or criterion I used to measure or judge the truth. The skeptic will then ask you how you know that your standard for the truth is true. As you can see, an infinite regress commences since you will need to justify your standard for the truth by a standard for your standard and so on. The skeptical problem of the criterion for truth is a serious one. It will come up again during the Reformation and in Descartes's philosophical project.

### A. *Skepticism: Pyrrho of Elis*

Pyrrho emphasized the fact that Socrates was always asking questions while insisting that he was ignorant. Pyrrho and his students taught that nothing in our lives is certain. Indeed, we can be certain of nothing in the whole universe. We have sensations and opinions, but we do not possess knowledge. The skeptics were hardcore relativists. By examining opposing sides of every argument, it was possible to plunge every perspective into doubt. Given our inability to access objective knowledge, skeptics advocated suspending judgment. The best way to live was to accept the fact that appearances are our reality. As long as you live in doubt, your mind will be perturbed. By suspending judgment, you will gain tranquility of soul, which, for the skeptic, means happiness.

### B. *Stoicism: Zeno of Citium*[36]

Stoics esteem self-sufficiency. They seek to become wise to the point where nothing that happens to them could disturb their peace of mind. The highest wisdom is discerning what is under your control

35 Sextus Empiricus is our best source for the doctrines of Pyrrhonism. He lived in the second century ACE.

36 The founder of Stoicism is not the Zeno of paradoxes. The Zeno of Stoicism was not a friend of Parmenides.

and what is not. Stoics teach that you do not control your circumstances, nor do you control other people. But your own attitude and beliefs are in your control. The key is to keep your will in harmony with nature. And nature should be understood in terms of *Logos*. *Logos* is the divine ordering principle that is immanent in this world. The immanence of the divine is conceived such that everything that is made of matter has a touch of the divine in it. Furthermore, Stoics taught that whatever happens does so out of necessity. You do not control what happens, but your attitude towards what happens provides the condition for your happiness. Try starting your day in Stoic fashion with the thought that no matter what happens to you this day you will not give other people the power to disturb your peace of mind. Someone might say something rude to you, but they cannot make you feel insulted or make you lash out at them. Never say that someone else made you mad or otherwise upset you; take responsibility for your responses. Even if someone tortures your body, he cannot make you hate him or make you feel fear. Such control over your emotions will take practice, but Stoicism promises you a way of life that leads to peace of mind.

## IV. The Rise of Rome

Rome is as old as Athens. But Greek culture reached its height of influence before Rome emerged as a dominant powerhouse. Rome started out as a minor city-state founded by herdsmen and farmers on seven low hills beside the Tiber River. It took centuries, but Rome successfully conquered the various peoples living in what we call Italy. After Italy was conquered, Rome's chief rival in the Mediterranean was Carthage. The Punic Wars were a series of three wars fought between Rome and Carthage between 264 BCE and 146 BCE. The people living in Carthage were of Phoenician ethnicity. The Latinized version of "Phoenician" was "Punic." Punic Wars refer to wars between Carthage and Rome.

At the start of the First Punic War (264–241 B.C.), Carthage was the dominant power of the Western Mediterranean while Rome was in the process of building its power.[37] The Second Punic War (218–201 B.C.) saw Hannibal's crossing of the Alps, but he was not able to conquer Italy. By the end of the Third Punic War (149–146 B.C.), Rome had conquered Carthage's empire and completely destroyed the city. Once Carthage was utterly defeated Roman civilization grew to be the colossus of the Mediterranean world. In fact, Romans would refer to the Mediterranean Sea as *Mare Nostrum* (Our Sea). Eventually the Roman way of life would engulf the peoples and cultures of the ancient Near East, Eastern Mediterranean, North Africa, Western Europe, Central Europe, and England.

## THE WORLD OF POLIS AND COVENANT TEXTUAL GLOSSES

### Homer, *The Iliad* and *The Odyssey*

Whether your professor assigns Homer's *The Iliad* or *The Odyssey*, you should know the legend of the Trojan War, including how the war ended and what happened in the decade following its conclusion. According to legend, Troy was besieged for nine or more years and was eventually conquered by a Greek army led by King Agamemnon. *The Iliad* is an account of only a few days of that war. *The Odyssey* tells the story of a warrior who has a long, difficult journey home after the war and discovers more difficulties when he gets there.

Homer's poetry was meant to be chanted by a bard who had not memorized the lines but composed the poem directly in front of an audience.[38] An illiterate bard would chant these stories for

37 Our expression "pyrrhic victory" comes from the victory of a Carthaginian general named Pyrrhus who defeated the Roman army in a battle in 279 BCE. Pyrrhus's victory was offset by the staggering loss of many of his best officers and soldiers.

38 Finley, 22.

hours, a feat that required concentration. For this reason, Homer's poetry is filled with epithets such as "the wine dark sea" or "rosy fingered dawn." Epithets are repeated phrases necessary for the oral performance of a story that is chanted according to an artificial meter. Almost one third of *The Odyssey* is comprised of epithets. The repeated phrases are important for two reasons: first, they are devices for making sure the pattern of sounds work out properly; second, they help with the oral delivery and aural reception of the story. A repeated phrase gives the audience a chance to rest while giving the bard time to gather resources for the next segment of the story.

The opening lines of Homer's *The Iliad* are famous for getting to the heart of the poem:

> Rage—Goddess—sing the rage of Peleus's son Achilles,
> Murderous, doomed, that cost the Achaeans countless losses
> Hurling down to the House of Death so many sturdy souls,
> Great fighters' souls, but made their bodies carrion,
> Feasts for the dogs and birds,
> And the will of Zeus was moving toward its end.
> Begin Muse, when the two first broke and clashed,
> Agamemnon, lord of men and brilliant Achilles.[39]

The theme of *The Iliad* is rage. Achilles's immoderate and irrational anger (and its consequences) is a story that needs to be sung. The poem celebrates warrior virtues such as strength, courage, and strategic thinking. *The Iliad* also illustrates the importance of honor and its relation to justice. Agamemnon was upset because his honor was offended. Achilles was angry because Agamemnon offended his honor. Justice, for Homer and the Greeks, was giving extraordinary

39 *Homer, The Iliad,* trans. Robert Fagles *(New York: Penguin Group, 1990), 77.*

people the honor that they deserved. Some honor was earned by Achilles for his deeds; some honor was due Agamemnon because of his status. In sum, honor was a significant aspect of justice for both gods and humans.[40]

Like *The Iliad*, *The Odyssey* begins *in medias res*. *The Odyssey* is a return epic in that it recounts a long journey home.[41] A major theme of this homecoming epic is *xenia,* which refers to the guest-host relationship: the way hosts treat strangers. The guest-host relation is not a species of friendship; rather, it is an obligation rooted in the will of Zeus. While Odysseus has been away, a group of men seeking to take Odysseus's place as king of Ithaca have been growing increasingly rude in their behavior toward Penelope and Telemachus. Indeed, these suitors plot to murder Telemachus. These suitors were a rough bunch; they occupied Odysseus's home and plundered its resources while pressuring Penelope toward marriage. The suitors violated the guest-host relationship. The guest-host relationship is also illustrated in scenes where Telemachus is host and other scenes where he is guest. Odysseus experiences multiple hosts on his way back to Ithaca.

Homer describes a time in which men were heroic. In the heroic age, men were stronger and more courageous. There was nothing akin to the Greek polis during the heroic age. There was no universal ethical code or city authority. Indeed, heroes had little social conscience because society had developed only a little. During this period there were families but no government beyond the household. In the Age of Heroes, men were primarily obligated to win battles.

40 Later, in the *Republic*, Plato will describe the timocratic soul as focused primarily on honor. A good example of a timocratic organization is the military. Soldiers salute those of higher rank. Medals are given to honor service. The currency of the military is respected authority. Plato will call a city ruled by one or more honor-oriented individuals (often members of the military) a timocratic city.

41 There are two types of Homeric epic: *kleos* (focuses on glory) and *nostos* (focuses on homecoming).

### Thucydides, *History of the Peloponnesian War*

The Peloponnesus is a peninsula that extends below Athens and juts out into the Mediterranean Sea. Mycenae, Argos, and Sparta are located on the Peloponnesus. It is connected to the mainland of Greece by the narrow Isthmus of Corinth. It was named for the mythical figure Pelops, who was the grandson of Zeus and the grandfather of Agamemnon. In 431 BCE one of Athens's allies came into conflict with one of Sparta's allies. This led to a larger conflict between the forces of Sparta and Athens. The war would last for nearly thirty years and would involve the entire Greek world. The Athenians entered the war with confidence because they had enormous wealth, a superior navy, and the leadership of Pericles. Sparta and its allies could not match Athens's wealth or her Navy. But the Spartans had a well-trained army, and there was tremendous resentment against Athens in many cities on account of Athenian arrogance.

Pericles played to Athens's strengths, and he figured that the longer the war lasted the weaker Sparta would get. Pericles avoided a land war with Sparta. Sparta and its allies invaded Athenian territory but were not engaged by the Athenian army. Sparta was not able to win decisive land battles because the Athenians gathered inside its long walls. The Spartans could not penetrate Athenian defenses. But Athens did send a naval fleet out to make small raids in Spartan-controlled territory.[42] The Athenian raiders would leave by the time the Spartan army arrived. A stalemate developed: Sparta was supreme on the land while Athens ruled the seas. But the crowding of Athenians contributed to the spread of a plague. Over 25% of the city's population, including Pericles, died from the plague. A group of demagogues, including a man named Cleon, stirred up people's emotions. The people were persuaded to switch away from Pericles's strategy. For over a year the Athenians tried

---

42 Gregory S. Aldrete, *History of the Ancient World: A Global Perspective* (Chantilly, VA: Great Courses, 2011), 118.

to take Syracuse. Just as the Athenians were about to give up and go home, all the Greeks soldiers were killed or captured. Athens surrendered unconditionally in 404 BCE. Its naval force was drastically reduced, its long walls were brought down, and its democracy was dismantled as part of the peace.[43] When it was finally over, Athens fell into a period of great disillusionment.

Thucydides lived after Herodotus and took a different approach to recording history. His accounts were rigidly chronological. Thucydides had served as an Athenian general, and his failures caused him to be exiled. He started writing history while in exile. Thucydides wanted indisputable historical facts to be the basis for making conclusions about past events. He stressed the accurate recording of facts and the use of logical analysis to discern why events happened. The most controversial parts of his work are the frequent speeches given by various people. He reports these speeches as if they are quotations, but he admitted to making up much of their content.[44] History is more than a chronicle of events; the speeches provide him with the chance to express his interpretation of events.

Thucydides is considered a political realist because he emphasized conflict and competition in international relations. Realists understand history more in terms of security and power rather than international cooperation. Nevertheless, Thucydides saw politics as involving moral issues.[45] For instance, he questioned whether international relations could be guided by our normal sense of justice. He anticipated Machiavelli and Hobbes as seen in the very first speech in the *History*—a speech given at the debate that took place in Sparta before the war.[46] You can also glimpse his political

43 Aldrete, 120.

44 Aldrete, 110.

45 "Political Realism in International Relations," *Stanford Encyclopedia of Philosophy*, revised May 2017. https://plato.stanford.edu/entries/realism-intl-relations/

46 Ibid.

realism in the way he explains the cause of the Peloponnesian War when the Athenian envoys speak in the "Melian Dialogue."[47]

Thucydides is not so colorful as Herodotus, but he shares with Herodotus an interest in understanding the origins of events. If we understand the past accurately, then we can better predict the future. *The History of the Peloponnesian War* is especially interesting because it is a contemporary history. Thucydides was a living participant in the war of which he wrote.

### Plato, *The Apology, Crito, Republic,* and *Phaedo*

Plato's account of Socrates's trial in the *Apology* is dependable in terms of basic facts. This trial actually happened, and Socrates was really executed. But for all we know, Socrates's defense may have been stronger than how Plato presents it. We do know that the trial would have been conducted in front of a jury of 501 citizens and would have been completed in a single day. There were two phases to Athenian trials: (1) a phase for determining guilt or innocence; and (2) if guilty, a phase for determining an appropriate punishment. Trial procedure required that the prosecutors would propose a penalty and the defendant would offer a counter proposal. The jury was not free to determine the penalty; it could only choose a punishment from among the two proposals. Presumably, this would encourage both sides to suggest reasonable punishments.

According to Thomas G. West, *The Apology* consists of three speeches.[48] The first speech is a formal defense directed to the jury. The second speech comes after the guilty verdict and is a response to Meletus's proposed death penalty. Socrates shares his parting words to the jury in the third speech.

47 "Political Realism in International Relations," *Stanford Encyclopedia of Philosophy*, revised May 2017.

48 *Four Texts on Socrates: Plato's Euthyphro, Apology, & Crito and Aristophanes' Clouds*, trans. Thomas G. West and Grace Starry West (Ithaca: Cornell University Press, 1984), 23.

At the outset, Socrates divides his accusers into two categories. His defense is organized around his classification of accusers. The "old" accusers are people who have spread rumors or falsehoods about him over a period of decades. Socrates was familiar with this slandering. What did Socrates say that his slanderers said about him? Socrates knew that people frequently pigeon-holed him as a natural scientist on par with impious Pre-Socratics. He knew of the rumors that characterized him as a busybody who investigates the things in the heavens and under the earth. He knew that these old accusers also depicted him as a Sophist. Socrates was capable of sophistry; he had the ability to make the weaker argument into the stronger and taught others how to do the same. The old accusers make the case of guilt by association by placing Socrates in the company of Sophists and Pre-Socratics

Socrates denies the charges of the old accusers but still has to account for the fact that he has somehow managed to get himself into deep trouble. Surely, Socrates must have done something criminal or stupid to land himself in this predicament. After all, if Socrates is so innocent, then why do people tell these stories?

In the middle of the first speech, Socrates responds to the "new" accusers who are actually present at his trial. Meletus was one of the new accusers; indeed, he was Socrates's main legal adversary in court that day. Socrates put Meletus on trial by subjecting him to Socratic questioning. Socrates successfully shows that Meletus's charges are inconsistent. For example, Socrates cannot be both an inventor of new gods and an atheist.

After defending himself against both kinds of accusers, Socrates leads the discussion away from the charges and talks about his way of life.[49] Socrates argues that if his way of life is good, then practicing it would not cause Athens any harm. Socrates brings his first speech to a close by putting the city's understanding of impiety and corruption on trial. Socrates proposes a new standard for justice

49 In the *Apology* (38a) we encounter that famous saying of Socrates, "The

by portraying himself as the paradigm of civic virtue. For Socrates, Athenian law has been overly influenced by Homer—especially by an admiration of Homeric heroes such as Achilles. Socrates proposes a new standard for human excellence. He may be guilty of corrupting the youth according to the traditional standard, but not by the better standard that he proposes. Since Socrates was charged with impiety, a part of his revaluation of values must include a redefinition of piety.

After his lengthy first speech, Socrates gives another speech in which he proposes an alternative to Meletus's suggestion of the death penalty. Instead of the death penalty, Socrates tells the jury that he deserves free meals for life in the Prytaneum.[50] No doubt this counter-proposal to the death penalty annoyed members of the jury. But Socrates argued that he was innocent during the first phase of the trial. It would be inconsistent of him to propose a penalty because it would not be deserving. Nevertheless, the jury chose the death penalty.

The third and final speech starts with a prophecy directed toward those who voted for his conviction. Socrates predicts that his followers will continue to question the traditional values of Athens and that they will be much harder on the status quo. Finally, he addresses those who voted for his acquittal. It is a heart-warming speech. He does not want those who supported him to feel demoralized by the outcome of the trial. He tells them that death is a good thing and that the gods take care of good men. Socrates's last words in public were to ask a favor from his accusers: treat my sons as you claim that I have harmed Athens.

Plato's *Crito* is a short dialogue that assumes Socrates's innocence. Crito, the title character, is a close friend of Socrates. He is old, wealthy, and clearly not Socrates's philosophical equal. Unlike

---

unexamined life is not worth living."

50 The Prytaneum was a building maintained by Athens to provide lodging and food for important visitors and particularly deserving citizens such as Olympic victors, military heroes, and others who were great benefactors to the city.

*The Apology*, where Socrates gives a series of public speeches in a formal setting, the *Crito* provides a more intimate and friendly conversation between Socrates and Crito. The dialogue takes place in jail. Crito arrives early to tell Socrates that his execution will be scheduled soon.

Crito is not happy with the outcome of the trial. He still thinks there is time for Socrates to escape his low-security cell and live in exile. Crito argues that since Socrates was unjustly convicted, he has no obligation to remain in jail. If Socrates does not escape, he will be committing suicide with government assistance. Such a death would be dishonorable. Further, Socrates has a duty to his wife and children to remain alive so that he can care for them. Crito also points out that if Socrates is executed, he would lose a dear friend. Crito's reputation will be damaged because many people will say that he was too stingy to pay the bribes that would ensure Socrates's escape. Crito explains that the practical matters have been solved and that the expense of getting Socrates out of jail and to a safe haven in Thessaly is not impossible.

Crito reminds Socrates that it was the opinion of the many (and not expert knowledge) that landed Socrates on death row. But one of Socrates's main principles was never to return a wrong with a wrong. The response to injustice in his case should never be more injustice. Another point that Socrates makes against the escape option is that his escape would have bad consequences for the city. Finally, Socrates tells Crito that the most important thing is to maintain a just soul. It is better to die than do something unjust like bribe guards and defy Athenian law. In sum, two harms would be done if Socrates escaped: Socrates's character would be substantially damaged, and Athenian law would be undermined. As far as the raising of his children, Socrates knows that his friends will fill the gap and care for his children. Even if he escapes to Thessaly, he would not move his children there because they would be foreigners. So, whether he escaped or not, his children would be cared for by his friends and not by him.

The gentle conversation up to this point shifts abruptly when the personified Laws of Athens make a speech to the two men. The Laws argue that by escaping Socrates would destroy the laws by encouraging private citizens to disobey court verdicts. Crito's argument in favor of Socrates's escape loses to the claims made by Socrates and the Laws of Athens.

The ostensible theme of Plato's *Republic* is the nature of justice. The persons in the dialogue are Socrates (who is also the narrator); Glaucon and Adeimantus (the brothers of Plato); Cephalus (a wealthy old man); Polemarchus (the son of Cephalus); Cleitophon (an Athenian politician); and Thrasymachus (a Sophist). The fictionalized conversation of the *Republic* was written around 375 BCE and describes a conversation that took place in 422 BCE.[51] The numbers and letters in the margins of your translation are called Stephanus numbers.[52]

Socrates would have you think about all the good things in the universe. Next, take all good things and separate them into three categories. First, some things are good in themselves. Those are called intrinsic goods. Second, some things are good as means for obtaining intrinsic goods. Those are called instrumental goods. Finally, some good things are both intrinsically good and instrumentally good. An example of an intrinsic good would be the pleasure one gains from reading a book. Money is an example of an instrumental good since money is something we value because

51 Nickolas Pappas, *Routledge Philosophy Guidebook to Plato and the Republic*, 2nd ed. (New York: Routledge, 1995), 16.

52 The numbers that appear in the margins of most editions of Plato's *Republic* are divided into five segments, A to E, to make it easier to find specific sentences. The letters are not supplied in every instance. Just as churchgoers with different versions of the Bible refer to chapter and verse instead of page numbers to locate a passage, so Stephanus numbers can lead those using different translations to a specific passage in Plato's *Republic*. For example, you could be told to go to 509 d in order to find Plato's Divided Line teaching.

it brings us intrinsic goods (such as the enjoyment we receive from a pleasurable book). An example of something that is intrinsically good and has the ability to bring us other good things is health. It is enjoyable to be healthy, and a healthy person would have the power of sight to read books as well as the ability to earn the money to buy books, etc. Of the three categories, which set of goods is supreme? You would probably agree with Plato that things that are both intrinsically good *and* have the power to generate other goods comprise the finest category.

Next, Plato asks, "Where would you put morality?" Before you answer this question, think about every reason you have been given for being moral. From childhood to the present, what reasons have you been taught for being moral? Plato boldly asserts that all teachers of morality have gotten this wrong (even the theologians). Most people teach morality as an instrumental good. For example, "If you want friends, then you should share your toys," or "Honesty is the best policy." Moral teachers often point to social and other benefits of living morally. Even some theologians argue that moral living will benefit you in the next life. Your elders may have told you, "You should please God by following His commands." This would be another example whereby the intrinsic goodness of morality goes unstated. Even if you are moral to avoid the pang of conscience, you are treating morality as an instrumental good (using it to reduce pain). Plato will argue at length to show that being moral (or in his terms "having a just soul") is both intrinsically and instrumentally good.

Do you believe that it is always in your best interest to be moral? We have plenty of opportunities to lie, cheat, or steal without getting caught. In fact, there might be situations where the benefit of what we gain may outweigh the consequences of being judged immoral. Plato's Herculean task is to prove to you that it is always in your own best interest to be moral.[53] He will give

53 Morality typically refers to the way we treat others; a morally good person

you reasons for being morally upright in all circumstances (even if your actions were not visible to God). Plato will argue that justice naturally produces good effects.

The structure of Plato's argument forms around two central questions: "What is justice?" and "What kind of good is justice?"[54] Plato's first task is to show what justice is in its essential nature. Before you can properly evaluate whether or not being moral in all circumstances is in your best interest, you must first know what justice or morality is. Granted, if you lead a just life you can reasonably expect honors and rewards, but justice cannot be defined solely in relation to beneficial consequences. Justice would not cease to be justice if it were not attended by the good consequences it deserves. Second, Plato must show you that justice itself (and not merely having the reputation for being just) is beneficial. Finally, he must show that the intrinsic value of having a just soul is so great that it always and in every circumstance is in our best interest to be just.

The basic outline of Plato's argument is this: justice is an intrinsic good and also an instrumental good. We would expect that the *Republic* would treat justice as an intrinsic good and then show its instrumental value. But after he finishes his argument about the intrinsic value of justice in Book IV, he digresses. The digression is conspicuous and lengthy. In Books V-VII he appears to leave the topic of justice and focuses on the treatment of women and children, property, rule by philosophers, and knowledge of the Forms. In Books V-VII (the big digression), we encounter the Sun Simile, the Cave Allegory, and the Image of the Divided Line. Books VIII-X return to the basic outline of the argument by considering the instrumental value of justice in one's soul. The dialogue ends with the Myth of Er, which teaches us that having a just soul also matters in the afterlife. As you read and discuss Plato's *Republic*,

is considerate of others. But if we are supposed to act for the good of others, then how can acting morally be in our own best interest each and every time?

54 R.C. Cross and A.D. Woozley, *Plato's Republic: A Philosophical Commentary* (London: MacMillan, 1964), 61.

try to figure out why Plato located his most important teachings in the form of a big digression found in its center. Plato's *Republic* is a complex work. Before reading it in your honors seminar, there are multiple things you should know.

Plato conceived of reality in two spheres: what appears to be real, and what is really real. He described the difference between appearance and reality in terms of Becoming and Being. In addition to the ever-changing world that appears all around us (Becoming), there is an unchanging reality (Being). Plato rejected the relativism of the Sophists and anchored truth and morality in the realm of objective, transcendent reality: the world of the Forms.

For Plato, Forms are the cause of every particular thing that exists beneath them. A Form is the essential quality, structure, or essence of a thing. The main features of Forms include the following: Forms are objective (they exist independently of our minds); transcendent (they do not exist in space or time); non-temporal; immutable (not subject to motion or change); intelligible (grasped only by the intellect); paradigmatic (they are the unique models for every kind of thing that exists); and they are perfectly complete (they are fully actualized).[55] The theory of Forms is the belief in a transcendent world of eternal and absolute beings, corresponding to every kind of thing that there is, and causing in particular things their essential natures. Furthermore, Plato called the form of *The Good* the highest Form: the source of all being and all knowledge. The many Forms derive their existence from *The Good* as it illuminates intelligible objects and makes them knowable. Just as the sun sustains earthly life, *The Good* causes the Forms to exist truly. *The Good* is the highest reality and the ultimate object of the soul's progress.

Most students are familiar with Plato's "Allegory of the Cave," which illustrates how the majority of humans are deluded about

---

55 Ed. L. Miller, *Questions That Matter: An Invitation to Philosophy*, 2nd ed. (New York: McGraw-Hill, 1987), 74-75.

reality. Most people mistake their limited world of experience for the only world of experience. Only with great effort can people be turned away from their customary patterns of thinking in the direction of higher awareness. If it takes effort, then we may wonder why we should even bother. Plato's answer is that humans are by nature rational, and our happiness lies in enjoying the fullness of Being.

Plato's *Phaedo* is another significant Platonic dialogue. Phaedo was an earnest follower of Socrates and was present with Socrates when he took the poison. At the beginning of the *Phaedo*, however, the figure Phaedo is no longer in Athens but has traveled to Phlius (which was a polis on the northeastern part of the Peloponnesus). Echecrates and a few others are present and anxious to hear about Socrates's final hours. *Phaedo* is Plato's eulogy to Socrates. According to R. Hackworth, the *Phaedo* shows Plato at the height of his powers:

> That the *Phaedo* is a work of supreme art, perhaps the greatest achievement in Greek prose literature, is something that needs no argument. The serenity of Socrates in the hours before he drank the hemlock, his conviction that the parting of the soul from body is not the death of the soul, his unabated zest in argument, the devotion of his intimate friends, the admiration of the jailer for his prisoner, above all perhaps the moving record of the last few pages, given with inimitable simplicity and restraint of language—all these things contribute to the greatness of a work which for many readers stands, if considered pure literature, even higher than that other literary masterpiece, the *Symposium*.[56]

56 R. Hackworth, "Introduction," Plato's *Phaedo*, trans. R. Hackforth (Cambridge: Cambridge University Press, 1955), 3.

### Aristotle, *Nicomachean Ethics*

Unlike Socrates's method of *elenchus*, Aristotle's thinking does not end in puzzlement or stop at an impasse. Aristotle sought to resolve puzzles by untangling them. The process of untangling commences with a survey of what the brightest people of the past have already contributed. In fact, you should even consider what the uneducated majority has had to say. You should not feel bound by any of these conclusions of the past, but you should regard the opinions of both the wise and the majority as resources.

His father was a physician, and it is likely that Aristotle learned anatomy and dissection before studying at Plato's Academy. Unlike most of Plato's students, Aristotle was something of a dandy who paid a lot of attention to his clothes.[57] Aristotle was the brain of Plato's Academy for almost twenty years. When Plato died, Aristotle was thirty-seven years old. The trustees of the Academy did not choose Aristotle to be the next master of the Academy because they viewed him as a foreigner. Aristotle left Athens and married a woman who died during childbirth. Aristotle later lived with a woman, and they had a son together. The *Nicomachean Ethics* was dedicated to their son, Nicomachus. Aristotle was invited to train King Phillip of Macedon's son, Alexander. Alexander the Great was Aristotle's most famous pupil and ordered his soldiers to bring back specimens of plant, marine, and animal life for his old teacher to study. In 334 BCE Aristotle returned to Athens and started his own school, called the Lyceum, named for the wolf form of the Greek god Apollo. Aristotle's students were known as peripatetic philosophers because they discussed philosophy while strolling along tree-covered walkways called the Peripatos. Aristotle was charged with not respecting the gods of the state and fled Athens, "lest Athens sin twice against philosophy."[58] For hundreds of years,

57 Douglas J. Soccio, *Archetypes of Wisdom: An Introduction to Philosophy* (Belmont, CA: Wadsworth, 1992), 135.

58 Christopher Warne, *Aristotle's Nicomachean Ethics* (New York: Continuum,

educated people have known the man who died in 322 BCE simply as *the Philosopher*. Nature hit the bullseye with Aristotle.

As we have seen, Plato was the great teacher of a beyond world. For him, the material world of our sense experience was the reflection of an invisible, ideal reality.[59] In contrast, Aristotle is a philosophical naturalist who stressed collecting facts and using information to make this a better world. As a naturalist he believed that the natural world was ordered to a degree that allows us to discover laws of nature. He also thought that nature always acts with a purpose.[60] Living things possess an inner urge (*entelechy*) to develop toward a goal. An acorn has the natural, built-in goal of developing into an oak tree, for example. A living thing's goal is determined by its species.

Humans are part of the natural order. This planet is our home. In surveying life on this planet, Aristotle observed three kinds of life that he called souls. The lowest level of living soul is vegetative. The second level is sentient soul or animal soul. The third level is rational or human soul. Like plants, humans convert energy from the environment to sustain their lives. Like animals, humans have conscious experience. But a unique potential of humans is our ability to analyze and reason. A good plant, animal, or human is one that realizes its potential. A good human life would be a life that provides the necessary conditions and opportunities for a person to become fully himself or herself and in which the person has the character to do so. Knowing what is good cannot make you happy unless you have the moral character and habits of acting wisely. Acting wisely means you "hit the mark" of moderation. Living well is having a rationally ordered life in which intellectual, physical,

---

2006), 2.

59 For Aristotle, form and matter may be treated as separate in thought only; formless existence was actually impossible. Things can only exist according to some pattern.

60 Aristotle's form of thinking is called "teleological" because *telos* refers to goal or end.

and social needs are met under the management of reason. Good habits are necessary for living well.

The main goal of the *Nicomachean Ethics* is to describe what it means to live and act well. Answering a series of related questions will give you some sense for Aristotle's approach to human happiness (*eudaimonia*). First, what is the ultimate source of value in your life? Second, what makes it possible for you to perform a meaningful action? Finally, what is it that keeps all of your desires from being empty and futile? For Aristotle, the answer to each of these questions is the Supreme Good. The *Nicomachean Ethics* requires that you think about the ultimate goal of your life.

According to Aristotle, the ultimate goal for all human life is happiness (which is not contentment but rather something that you do). Happiness is not a subjective feeling or emotional disposition; happiness is an activity. Happiness is not based on material possessions. Happiness centers on finding a purpose in order to realize your potential. Happiness includes you working on your behavior to become the best version of yourself. For Aristotle, life is an activity and cannot be reduced to a series of pleasant sensations or happy moods. Life is something that you live. Happiness is inexorably connected to activity (but not just any activity).

Aristotle connects happiness and virtuous action. It would be difficult to achieve happiness without trying to be a good person. In Book IX of *Nicomachean Ethics,* Aristotle insists that people who want to live well and treat others fairly need (at all costs) to love themselves. As Edith Hall explains, "Happiness is not compatible with self-loathing."[61] You have to believe in your own fundamental decency and respect yourself in order to like other people. Criminals and depraved people seek pleasure but fail to seek pleasure in ways that are conducive to their happiness. Aristotle is an advocate of virtue ethics. He thought you should act out of settled dispositions of character, which he called moral virtues. Instead of asking,

---

61 Hall, 34.

"What is the right thing to do?" you should be asking, "What is the right kind of person I should be?" Aristotle developed an agent-centered morality as opposed to an act-centered one.

Aristotle emphasizes moral character. You are responsible for the states of character that you possess. Like Plato, Aristotle considers a virtue to be something that enables you to function better as a person. For example, if you have the virtue of self-control, you will be able to function better at work and at home. A vice, on the other hand, leads you to harm yourself and others. Being moral includes having skill with regard to being human. For instance, a good human would know how to manage his desires. This is why Aristotle taught the doctrine of moderation. Moral virtue is finding the appropriate range of action between two extremes (excess and deficiency). A good person must manage his emotions well. One powerful emotion humans may have to deal with is fear. An excellent human would be one that has developed the power to manage fear. Too much fear and you are a coward; too little fear and you are reckless. Along the same lines, generosity in the appropriate range is a virtue: too much and you are extravagant and wasteful; not enough and you are miserly and stingy.

Aristotle subscribed to the same cardinal (fundamental) virtues as Plato: wisdom, moderation, courage, and justice. For Aristotle, becoming a good person requires practice. Living a moral life involves practicing morality and building good habits. Virtue ethics challenge you to rise above ordinary moral demands. Just because you do not steal or murder does not mean that your moral development is sufficient. Like Plato, Aristotle thinks morality is less about figuring out the right thing to do and more about being the right kind of person.

Being the right kind of person who is predisposed by habit to make rational choices is conducive to your happiness. Aristotle also explained that happiness is something you create over your lifetime. When people approach their last breath on this earth, what do they typically regret most? "I wish I had let myself be happier."[62] "I wish I had made more effort with friendships."[63] "I wish I'd had the courage to live a life true to myself, not the life others expected of me."[64] Aristotle teaches us how to be true to ourselves in terms of realizing our potential. It is never too late to start being true to yourself.

### Aeschylus, *The Oresteia*

Aeschylus's world was more sinister than Homer's. But unlike Homer, he insisted on the justice of the gods. For him there were principles of justice, and there was an order in the universe to which even the gods must adhere. Aeschylus was gripped by the thought of rigid cosmic order and ironclad necessity. The outcomes in all of his plays are fated and inescapable. Only seven out of over seventy plays written by Aeschylus have survived. Not only are we missing many of his plays, we are also missing the broader context of theatrical experience (music, dancing, singing, staging, costumes, etc.). Most of his plays were first performed at the religious festival of the god Dionysus.

Aeschylus's *Oresteia* was originally a set of four plays. The fourth play, which we do not possess, would have been a satyr play. The missing play would have been shorter and would have contained brazen sexuality, drunkenness, and pranks. The surviving trilogy includes *Agamemnon*, *The Libation Bearers*, and *The Eumenides*.

The first play deals with the death of Agamemnon, who was murdered by his wife and her lover (Aegisthus) following his sacrifice of his daughter (Iphigenia). The second play features Agamemnon's son, Orestes, who seeks to avenge his father's death by killing his mother, Clytemnestra. In the third play, Orestes is being pursued by the Furies in punishment for his matricide and takes refuge

62 Hall, *Aristotle's Way*, 38.

63 Ibid.

64 Ibid.

in Athens. The Furies are the three goddesses of vengeance who live in the Underworld and roam the surface of the earth to hunt down humans who had committed certain types of crimes. The Furies are grotesque but never hunt down an innocent person. The Furies point to the rage we feel immediately after witnessing a terrible wrong. They represent the outrage we feel against some types of crime.

But all of the bloodshed in the three closely connected plays follows from the dark history of Agamemnon's family. Robert Fagles provides a succinct outline of this history:

> The house of Atreus is the embodiment of savagery. No other Greek family can rival it for accumulated atrocities. The founder of the line was Tantalus of Lydia, a barbarian whose spirit haunts the *Oresteia.* He offended the gods by feeding them on his own son's flesh, and they condemned him to starve in Hades, 'tantalized' by the drink and luscious fruits just out of reach. But they restored his victim, Pelops, to a new, resplendent life. Later he went to western Greece, where he won the hand of Hippodameia by a ruse which killed her father—a murderous chariot race which may have been the origin of the Olympic games. Pelops had two sons, Atreus and Thyestes. When Thyestes seduced his brother's wife and contested his right to the throne, Atreus banished him and then, luring him back for a reconciliation, feasted him on his children's flesh. Horrified, Thyestes cursed Atreus and his descendants and fled into exile with his one remaining son, Aegisthus. Atreus had two sons, Agamemnon and Menelaus, who jointly inhered the realm of Argos and married two daughters of Tyndareos, Clytaemnestra and Helen. Agamemnon was the commander-in-chief of the Greek forces that attacked Troy to avenge the seduction of Helen by Paris, son of Priam.

> At the outset of the expedition, however, Agamemnon had to sacrifice his and Clytaemnestra's daughter Iphigeneia.[65]

Tragic cycles of bloodshed as described by Aeschylus are older than recorded history. For the greater part of human history, justice was "blood for blood." If you killed one of ours, then justice demands that we kill one of yours. Breaking the cycle of violence and suffering is no small thing. This should help you appreciate Aeschylus's tragic dramas because he celebrates the triumphant struggle of light in its costly defeat of darkness. He celebrates the victory of law courts over vengeance and vigilantism.

### Sophocles, *Oedipus Rex* and *Antigone*

Seven of Sophocles's tragedies have survived: *Ajax, Antigone, Oedipus the King, Women of Trachis, Electra, Philoctetes*, and the posthumous *Oedipus at Colonus.* In 468 BCE he defeated the reigning champion of Greek drama, Aeschylus. The ancients called Sophocles "the most god-fearing of mankind."[66] Sophocles is mentioned in Book I of the *Republic* for enjoying old age and its relief from male sex drive. He was the supreme artist of Greek tragedy, representing its apex. If you think you can improve one of Sophocles's plays, you can be sure that you are only trying something Sophocles rejected.[67] Sophocles's plays show us Homeric figures like Ajax. Ajax was a hero at Troy, and in Sophocles's play (*Ajax*), Ajax cannot live with disgrace and so kills himself. Aristotle credits Sophocles with introducing a third speaking actor. Sophocles's plots are usually more intricate than those of Aeschylus. He uses the chorus less than Aeschylus. His genius was in showing us the depth of human psychology. He offers

65 Robert Fagles, "The Serpent and the Eagle," Aeschylus' *The Oresteia: Agamemnon, The Libation Bearers, The Eumenides*, trans. Robert Fagles (New York: Penguin Classic Books, 1975), 14-15.

66 Herbert J. Muller, *The Spirit of Tragedy* (New York: Washing Square Press, 1965), 66.

67 Ibid., 66.

us the drama of the human soul. Sophocles especially celebrates humans with strong wills. In sum, he developed Greek tragedy to a higher level by adding depth of character.

*Oedipus the King* (also known as *Oedipus Rex*) tells a story that may be familiar in outline. Oedipus will kill his father and marry his mother as predicted. In neither case is he adequately aware of what he is doing. However, the audience will know his fate from the beginning. This makes for a story rich in irony. This is not a play in which a hero's tragic flaw brings him down. This is not an account of how pride gets punished. Nevertheless, Oedipus's personality seems to contribute to the unfolding of the story. For example, his admirable character traits include a passion for the truth. His fierce insistence on finding out the truth has him digging into the past. Every episode shows us a new helper that aids Oedipus in that digging. His helpers even include his mother, Jocasta (who is also an innocent victim).[68] Oedipus gains clues until he fully realizes what his fate had been the whole time. In the end, Oedipus's personality traits are used by Sophocles to bring Oedipus to the fulfillment of his fate. *Oedipus the King* shows us the power but never the justice of the gods. The theme of the play is that the suffering of the innocent is shocking.

*Antigone*, unlike *Oedipus the King*, does not require that the audience know the story. In fact, the contrast between *Antigone* and *Oedipus the King* is significant. This is not a story that opens our eyes to events that have already happened. Rather, it is a story that moves forward relentlessly to a tragic ending. The tempo of the action is remarkable. Sophocles uses the choral odes to magnify the tension that builds among the characters. Creon is king of Thebes who exercises political authority (for the sake of the common good) by commanding that Antigone's brother be denied a proper burial. Antigone defies political authority out of a strong moral sense. In

68 David Greene and Richard Lattimore, eds. *Greek Tragedies, Volume I* (Chicago: University of Chicago Press, 1960), 108.

her conscience, she knows the right thing is to see that her brother receives proper burial rites. The conflict between ruling authority and private conscience is the theme of the play. Sophocles sets up a series of encounters in *Antigone* that once again showcase irony: "[...] Creon, acting always in the belief that he is sacrificing himself for the good of the community, gives way, but too late to save Antigone, Haemon, and Eurydice, who need not have died at all; and [...] Antigone dies thinking that Haemon has deserted her, when in fact he was faithful.[69] Irony for Sophocles is not merely a literary device; it is his way of viewing life. But Sophocles also teaches that while you can view life with ironic detachment it is not possible to live that way.[70]

## Epicurus, *Selected Writings*

Epicurus ran his school out of a residential compound in Athens called the "Garden." His followers were considered friends and included men as well as some women and slaves. All the ancient schools of philosophy viewed philosophy as a way of life that aimed at happiness. For Epicurus that meant freeing one's mind of frets: the best way to be happy is to live without fear. He lived during a time when stories about the afterlife terrorized many people. His answer was to replace superstitions about suffering in the next life with science. Scientifically speaking, we are made up of atoms, and death is nothing to fear. Technically, we will never actually experience death because "we" will not exist at the point when the unity of our atoms is lost. Consequently, the afterlife is nothing to fear. Distress comes from false beliefs whereas happiness comes from pleasure.

Epicurus understood that there are bodily pleasures and that there are higher pleasures such as friendship and writing poetry, etc. For him, the happy life is a pleasant life in which you live free

69 Greene and Lattimore, 179.

70 Muller, 81.

from fear and spend time with friends enjoying pleasure. Epicurus taught a pleasure-seeking philosophy known as hedonism; however, he was not a crude hedonist. Seeking sensual indulgence will sabotage your happiness; you are much better off controlling your desires and living a simple life. Epicurus thought that the best way to live was to go through life unnoticed.

## The Old Testament and the Biblical Metanarrative

When we refer to the Christian scriptures as "the Bible," there is a subtle invitation to perceive the biblical canon as a monolithic artifact. The Bible, however, exhibits a spectrum of genres, and the assembly of its contributing authors and editors represents an amazing diversity of ethnicities and nationalities, languages, experiences, theological perspectives, and motivations for writing. As a literary project spanning centuries, the Bible is a collage of texts. To say what the Bible is "about" in anything but the broadest terms, then, runs the risk of oversimplifying the greatest collection of writings in history.

At the same time, many who make a habit of exploring these sacred texts detect a common pulse beneath its pages – a narrative strand that threads throughout all sixty-six books. This idea, that the Bible is a composite of many voices telling a singular, overarching story, is what interpreters usually call the "biblical metanarrative." Broadly speaking, the biblical metanarrative is the story of the divine-human relationship. Having noted above the inherent risk, we will hazard a more specific explanation from the New Testament: "All this is from God, who through Christ reconciled us to himself and gave us the ministry of reconciliation; that is, *in Christ God was reconciling the world* to himself, not counting their trespasses against them, and entrusting to us the message of reconciliation" (2 Cor. 5:18-19). The idea that "in Christ God was reconciling the world" certainly wields some explanatory power with regard to the Bible's take on the divine-human relationship.

But something is missing. Expressed in these terms, the biblical metanarrative would seem to preclude any meaningful contribution from the Old Testament. If the Bible is about Jesus, what do we really need to know about Moses, Abraham, or David?

As it turns out, our excerpt from Paul's letter to the Corinthian church depends on some rather dramatic assumptions. What is it, exactly, that needs reconciling in the first place? The divine effort to patch things up with humanity takes for granted that there was something going on between them in the first place. How was that relationship established? What was it like? How did it ever come to be in need of repair? There are a hundred details to unearth here, but there are still more pressing issues to consider. Why would God *ever* care to be reconciled with the world at all? This divine posture toward humanity simply has no merit, as the Bible itself testifies to humans repeatedly making their relationship with God into something of a dumpster fire. But the most perplexing matter is this: how does the birth, life, ministry, death, and resurrection of Jesus do *anything* to accomplish the business of reconciliation? Even if we account for the biblical confession that Jesus is in fact God, present among the people, why would we expect that divine presence to effect any sort of reconciliation?

Without the Old Testament, Jesus is a riddle. But set within the Old Testament's narrative and theological context, these quandaries start to make sense. God's redeeming presence among the people, accomplished in Christ as an expression of God's unyielding faithfulness toward creation, is the pitch-perfect zenith to a story that begins in Genesis.

The Old Testament's account of ancient Israel forms the backdrop for the New Testament's Jewish identity – both in terms of its characters and the authors who portray them. In particular, New Testament authors source their terminology and concepts from the Old Testament in order to portray Jesus. The Hebrew term *mashiach*, which refers to an "anointed one," translates into the New

Testament as *christos* – Jesus is "the Christ" (that is, the "Messiah" or "Anointed One"). The sacrificial system in Leviticus provides a conceptual basis for the atoning effect of Christ's suffering on the cross. The key connection, however, is the identification of Jesus as "the new covenant." This language connects Jesus to a covenantal ancestry that stretches back millennia (to Abraham, Moses, and David). But the hope for a new covenant was also explicitly anticipated by the prophet Jeremiah:

> Behold, the days are coming, declares the LORD, when I will make a *new covenant* with the house of Israel and the house of Judah, not like the covenant that I made with their fathers on the day when I took them by the hand to bring them out of the land of Egypt, my covenant that they broke, though I was their husband, declares the LORD. For this is the covenant that I will make with the house of Israel after those days, declares the LORD: I will put my law within them, and I will write it on their hearts. *And I will be their God, and they shall be my people.* And no longer shall each one teach his neighbor and each his brother, saying, "Know the LORD," for they shall all know me, from the least of them to the greatest, declares the LORD. For I will forgive their iniquity, and I will remember their sin no more. (Jer. 31:31-34)

At critical junctures throughout the biblical metanarrative, we find remarkably similar language describing the divine-human relationship. The Old Testament is the historical, literary, and theological framework for the New Testament, and so is foundational to any formulation of a biblical metanarrative.

## Genesis

### *The Shape of a Beginning*

Genesis is the Bible's origin story. Like any such account, it curates from the whole tapestry of tradition those definitive threads that, when traced from the beginning, allow the reader to make sense of her own world and its current state of affairs. To be sure, Genesis achieves this effect through its principal characters and the interactions between them. But the literary structure of Genesis is just as freighted with the interests of the storyteller. To appreciate this design, the reader needs to develop a sense not only for the broadest movements in the narrative, but also the literary pattern that binds them together.

Genesis is comprised of two major sections: the primeval and ancestral narratives:

**Primeval Narrative (Gen. 1-11)**

1. Creation (1-2)
2. Sin's Entry (3)
3. Cain and Abel (4)
4. The Flood (6-9)
5. The Tower of Babel (11)

**Ancestral Narrative (Gen. 12-50)**

1. Abraham (12-25)
2. Isaac (25-26)
3. Jacob (27-36)
4. Joseph (37-50)

These two narrative arcs differ in scope, content, and style. The primeval narrative maintains a more universal focus – it is concerned with the origins of all creation and the whole of humanity. It employs a kind of "exalted prose" to illuminate the most fundamental attributes of divine character and human nature, as well as the relationship that develops between them. There is no inkling of "Israel" at this point in the story, and likewise the LORD remains unbound to any particular people. Long before the complicated evolution of the Abrahamic, Mosaic, and Davidic covenants or the storied times of the Israelite *polis*, there was God and humanity alone together on the stage of creation.

Those who become engaged in this story and accustomed to its manner can find themselves nearly stumbling over Genesis 12:1: "Now the Lord said to Abram, 'Go from your country and your kindred and your father's house to the land that I will show you.'" The careening speed of the primeval narrative pauses for a more patient study, and its universal perspective telescopes to a single individual and his family. The poetic inclinations of the narrative give way to a more "legendary epic" style that is well-suited for the portraits of Israel's patriarchs and matriarchs.

However distinct the primeval and ancestral narratives may be, to regard these accounts as autonomous is to misunderstand the story. Sewn throughout Genesis is a series of genealogies that name descendants and selectively recount the events of their lives. Throughout the narrative expanse between Adam and Joseph, the storyteller remains tethered to one familial line. The relationship that transpires between God and Abraham is inextricably bound up with the universal divine-human relationship. The implication for readers of this origin story is that the remarkable relationship God cultivates with Abraham's family reveals God's intentions in the world.

*The Heart of the Matter*

The storyteller's narrative design invites readers to look beyond a mere explanation of how things came to be; the horizons of Genesis plainly reach further. But situating Israel's ancestors within God's grand design for the world likewise falls short of capturing what Genesis is "about" as a whole. Indeed, Genesis has a way of frustrating any attempt to define its thematic center of gravity. Readers can perhaps find better footing in the book's central character.

While popular discussion has focused attention on how creation in Genesis 1-2 relates to history and science, these matters are candidly of less interest to the storyteller. What happens–and how–are narrative materials selected and consumed in the effort to introduce God. In the first chapter of Genesis readers encounter an all-powerful *Elohim* (the Hebrew term for "God"), whose voice compels order from chaos and animates creation into being. A second creation story in Genesis 2:3-25 provides a more intimate portrait of *Yahweh* (the Old Testament's personal name for God, usually translated "Lord"). In this account the Lord is like an artist, forming human figures from clay. Together Genesis 1-2 present a God who is wholly distinct from but nonetheless present with creation.

These two attributes–divine transcendence and immanence–are the fundamental building blocks for the biblical story. The Bible makes little sense without them. When human mistrust ruptures a harmonious divine-human relationship, the swell of evil that follows simply cannot exhaust God's enduring partiality toward humans. Only God is capable of the recovery that follows, and only a God genuinely engaged with humanity would care to undertake the effort. The extraordinary thing, however, is the nature of God's involvement with those whose lives are troubled by evil.

In the closing chapter of Genesis, readers witness an emotional scene between Joseph and his brothers. Joseph's brothers are terrified, and understandably so. The little runt Joseph, whom they abandoned to slavery as a child, had become one of the most powerful men in the world. In any other story, their doom would be all but certain. Rather than focusing on the cruelty of his brothers, however, Joseph saw the storehouses of grain in the midst of famine – a circumstance of his command over Egypt. "As for you," Joseph concludes, "you meant evil against me, but God meant it for good, to bring it about that many people should be kept alive, as they are today." At the heart in Genesis is God, the catalyst throughout the primeval and ancestral narratives, who works through unlikely individuals to reconcile the divine-human relationship. In this way Genesis determines the trajectory for the biblical metanarrative that follows.

## Exodus

### *An Occasion to Remember*

The exodus from Egypt is the signature event in the Old Testament story. That observation can sometimes surprise readers, who would understandably choose some other noteworthy candidate: the creation of the man and the woman, sin's decimating entry into the world, the giving of the law at Sinai, the dynasty of King David, Solomon's temple, even the Babylonian exile. But the very identity of the Israelite people – inseparable from its relationship with the Lord – is forged in the exodus event. "I will take you to be my people," God declares, "and I will be your God, and you shall know that I am the Lord your God, who has brought you out from under the burdens of the Egyptians." The effect reverberates throughout the Old Testament, as the exodus is reenacted in Israel's festivals, reprised in its songs of worship, and remembered in times of national crisis. If you could ask the Old Testament, "Who are the Israelites?" it would undoubtedly reply, "The people whom the Lord delivered from bondage in Egypt."

As much as the exodus event stands out, the book of Exodus

does not stand alone. Genesis concludes with the death of Joseph, who reveals to his brothers, "I am about to die, but God will visit you and bring you up out of this land to the land that he swore to Abraham, to Isaac, and to Jacob." Exodus picks up where Genesis leaves off, with Israel's descendants situated in Egypt. The story first accelerates, advancing a few hundred years in just a few verses, but then slows to chronicle the early life of Moses and the exodus itself. Likewise the end of Exodus flows into the following book of Leviticus. The final scene in Exodus depicts the Lord inhabiting the tabernacle (a mobile temple of sorts). In the opening lines of Leviticus, the Lord summons Moses to the tabernacle in order to relay the details of the law. In similar fashion Numbers and Deuteronomy continue the story of Israel in the wilderness, with the tabernacle (and so divine presence) in the midst of the people. In sum, Genesis 12–Deuteronomy 34 comprise a continuous narrative, and it is therefore best to see Exodus as "Volume II" of a five-volume *Torah*.

### *A Man to Lead*

Moses is arguably the most iconic human figure in the Old Testament and one of the most famous people in human history. Perhaps it is no surprise, then, that he should lead the Hebrews out of Egypt (notably, along with a "mixed multitude" of other peoples as well; see Exo. 12:38). His grand destiny only makes sense in hindsight, however, as a naïve reader of the story would not likely assume Moses was cut from such cloth. The infant of an enslaved woman, Moses was fated to become a discard at the end of a most fleeting existence, altogether anonymous to history. Instead he floats into the hands of the Pharaoh's daughter, who ironically employs Moses's own mother to nurse him until he is old enough to be taken into Pharaoh's household. From the courts of the Egyptian king, Moses is afforded a rare glimpse into all Egyptian society, presumably learning its language, culture, and religion. As a grown man, Moses kills an Egyptian guard and is forced to flee into the wilderness. There he will learn how to sustain life by the desert's rules. In these ways the storyteller labors to show that peril is providence in the life of Moses. Destiny could not have afforded better preparation for the one who would helm the exodus from Egypt.

*A Law to Follow*

Even someone who has never seen the inside of a Bible can ordinarily name at least one detail from the Old Testament, and "the Ten Commandments" is a usual suspect. The Decalogue, however, does not establish the relationship between the Israelites and the LORD so much as it defines the terms of a relationship already in progress. In this sense the Mosaic covenant (yet another way to refer to the Ten Commandments) begins the transformation of the Hebrew refugees into what will eventually become the nation-state of Israel.

The laws that follow and expand upon the Ten Commandments do indeed bear some similarities with the legal traditions of other ancient nations. A common example in this discussion is the so-called Code of Hammurabi. This artifact, a seven-foot tall finger carved from basalt, was recovered by French archaeologists in 1901. Inscribed on the finger are over two hundred laws addressing scenarios from everyday life, describing conditions and consequences not unlike those registered in Exodus and Leviticus. Carved into the fingernail is a relief of Babylon's most famous ruler, Hammurabi, who reigned in the first half of the 18th century, BCE (centuries before the most common dates for the exodus). How the Code of Hammurabi and Israel's legal material actually relate is the subject of ongoing study, but the similarities at least suggest that the pressures of survival in the wilderness were beginning to shape them into a civilization.

*A Place to Dwell*

When asked what happens in Exodus after Moses receives the Ten Commandments, most readers will draw a blank. Is that not the end of the book? In fact, Exodus continues for some fifteen chapters, which portray the LORD taking up residence in the midst of the people. The salient feature in this narrative is the construction of the *mishkan* (a Hebrew word meaning "dwelling," usually translated "tabernacle"). This portable sanctuary is where the LORD would dwell, where Moses and the people would worship, and where these two parties in the divine-human relationship would meet. Admittedly, the account of the tabernacle's construction can seem to over-indulge in detail, but the storyteller's approach is nonetheless fascinating:

| **Creation of the World (Genesis)** | **Construction of the Sanctuary (Exodus)** |
|---|---|
| And God saw everything that he had made, and behold, it was very good. (Gen. 1:31) | And Moses saw all the work, and behold, they had done it. (Exo. 39:43) |
| Thus the heavens and the earth were finished. (Gen. 2:1) | Thus all the work of the tabernacle of the tent of meeting was finished… (Exo. 39:32) |
| God finished his work which he had done… (Gen. 2:2) | So Moses finished the work. (Exo. 40:33) |
| So God blessed the seventh day… (Gen. 2:3) | So Moses blessed them. (Exo. 39:43) |

By using creation in Genesis as a literary model, the storyteller invites readers to see the divine "dwelling" in Exodus as a mini-creation – a kind of scaled-down cosmos. The analogy has some purchase, as both the creation and tabernacle narratives envision the same thing: God's presence among the people. The tabernacle will eventually take a more permanent form in Solomon's temple, but the concept of divine presence persists. The garden, tabernacle, and temple all represent this core theological metaphor in the Old Testament, which will finally be perfected in the New Testament gospels. Jesus is, quite literally, God present among the people.

**Isaiah**

Encountering a text like Isaiah for the first time can leave readers feeling a little like Alice, tumbling down the rabbit hole. Anchored to literary and cultural conventions that are largely unfamiliar to a present-day, Western audience, taking Isaiah out of context is easy. While Isaiah's literary craftsmanship manages to send even the most temperate interpreter into raptures, its expansive, multi-faceted scope can also intimidate any reader. Likewise, generations of scholars have labored to untangle the multilayered history of the text itself–a matter that still does not enjoy consensus. After rehearsing a long history of scholarship, one well-regarded expert finally concedes that Isaiah is "one of the most complex literary structures of the entire Old Testament."[71] These challenges are compounded by Isaiah's colossal footprint in the Bible. In sheer size, Isaiah is second only to the Psalms. New Testament authors, who undertake little without first consulting the Old Testament, quote Isaiah more than nearly any other biblical book (again, second only to the Psalms). Compared with the broader corpus of ancient Near Eastern prophetic literature, Isaiah stands out again as a singular achievement. So even while Isaiah clearly conforms to its ancient roots, there is really nothing else like it.

All of which makes this *gloss* a delicate maneuver. Our aim is therefore not so much to explain Isaiah in brief, but to identify the basic ingredients necessary to beginning one's own inquiry. Crucial to finding one's bearings in Isaiah are 1) situating prophecy within its socio-historical context and 2) acclimating to the prophetic

71 Roland E. Clements, *Old Testament Prophecy: From Oracle to Canon* (Louisville: Westminster John Knox, 1996): 81.

genre. Resting on this basic foundation, we may better observe the features and leitmotifs of Isaiah.

*Prophet Life*

The primary word for a prophet in the Old Testament is *navi*, which in its most basic sense denotes a "speaker" or "spokesperson." In the orbit of this central term are a variety of ancillary titles: "man of God" or "man of the spirit," "messenger," "seer," and even "watchman." This nomenclature highlights the key attribute of the ancient Near Eastern prophet: an *agent* who addressed a people on behalf of a deity. Today prophets are often perceived as essentially "foretellers," clairvoyant windows into an otherwise shrouded future. Their ancient function, however, had more to do with representing divine interests–God's perspective on and evaluation of the people's present circumstances. Certainly, the prophet was sometimes tasked with declaring the long-term effects of the people's current state of affairs, and so the prophet's gaze would turn to the future's distant horizon. Even so, our popular sense of the ancient prophet could benefit from some recalibration, as they were less like a personal fortuneteller and more like a divine attorney.

Given this divine-human intermediary role, it is not surprising that prophets constituted a distinct class of religious specialists who wielded incredible social and political power. Consider the character Samuel, the prophet who is responsible for hiring (and firing) Israel's inaugural king. The prophet Nathan, who appears in the narrative almost as if he had been standing there all along, unflinchingly castigates a very royal King David for murdering Uriah and taking his wife, Bathsheba. The prophet Amos, who hailed from the southern kingdom of Judah, reprimands the northern kingdom's wealthy elite so severely that a local priest (Amaziah) tells Amos, "O seer, go, flee away to the land of Judah, and eat bread there, and prophesy there." Such examples of prophetic influence are not limited to the land of Israel, but extend throughout the ancient world. In the ancient Mesopotamian city of Mari, among the ruins of the king's palace, archaeologists have unearthed hundreds of prophetic texts that read like this:

> The prophet of Addu, God of Halab, said to me: "Am I not Addu, God of Halab, who has raised you [...] who helped you regain your father's throne? I never ask too much of you. Respond to the appeals of your people when they experience injustice and give them a just verdict. You are to do what I ask and what I write you to do. You will obey my word and keep watch over this land continually."[72]

Ancient prophets advised and even regulated monarchs concerning matters of worship, war, justice, famine, civil administration, and the like. If today we were to observe, for example, a law-enforcement official, in the span of an instant glance we would recognize and assume a very complex set of social rules. In a similar fashion, the "office of the prophet" in the ancient world was an immediately recognizable role, as they represented the divine authority that ordered the world and determined its course. No wonder their lives and writings have reached so far beyond the circumstances of their origin.

*Greatest Hits*

The book of Isaiah is not really a book. Readers instead discover within its sixty-six chapters a collection of prophetic oracles, interwoven with narrative interludes. These oracles are typically composed in verse; readers of modern translations do not always recognize that much of Isaiah is poetry (as is the case with most prophetic texts). As a poetic anthology representing a prophet's rhetorical performances, the literary nature of Isaiah has more in

72 Victor Matthews and Don Benjamin, *Old Testament Parallels: Laws and Stories from the Ancient Near East* (Mahwah, New Jersey: Paulist Press, 1991); 109-110.

common with your favorite album than with the book you are currently reading.

It is important to register how this "literary nature" affects the way interpreters make sense of Isaiah. The Old Testament storyline does of course provide some fundamental orientation, but interpreters are more keenly attuned to the themes and motifs threading their way through the text, playing the load-bearing roles that ultimately shape what Isaiah is "about." Here the brilliance of Isaiah is on full display, somehow managing to orchestrate a litany of elements into a multivalent but coherent theological vision.

Theology really is the essential property that governs the assembly of oracles toward a whole. Isaiah rests on the underlying conviction that divine character is the catalyst for how things ultimately play out on the stage of history. God's superior *trustworthiness* is therefore a constant refrain in Isaiah. All human power is tentative, while God's will is an immutable force. God's people should place their bets accordingly.

Readers who explore Isaiah with any sensitivity to literary patterns will discover a robust supporting cast of motifs. One may note, for example, Isaiah's frequent use of light, or the way Isaiah reprises the exodus story to adopt a posture of hope toward the future.[73] The effort to give a full account of Isaiah's literary artistry (and theological insight) no doubt remains unfinished.

73 For examples of Isaiah's use of "light," see Isa. 2:5; 5:20, 30; 9:2; 10:17; 13:10; 26:19; 30:26; 42:6, 16; 45:7; 49:6; 50:10, 11; 51:4; 58:8, 10; 59:9; 60:1, 3, 19, 20. For an explanation of the exodus motif in Isaiah, see Rikk Watts, "Echoes from the Past: Israel's Ancient Traditions and the Destiny of the Nations in Isaiah 40–55," *Journal for the Study of the Old Testament* 28 (2004), 481-506; Bernhard W. Anderson, "Exodus Typology in Second Isaiah," in *Israel's Prophetic Heritage: Essays in Honor of James Muilenburg* (Eugene, Oregon: Wipf and Stock, 2010), 177-95; Anthony R. Ceresko, "The Rhetorical Strategy of the Fourth Servant Song" (Isaiah 52:13-53:12): Poetry and the Exodus-New Exodus" *Catholic Biblical Quarterly* 56 (1994): 42–55.

## Wisdom Literature

### *From Whence It Comes*

The Bible's wisdom-literature tradition is comprised of three books: Proverbs, Job, and Ecclesiastes. While this explanation seems simple enough, what actually constitutes a "wisdom text" and from what context such traditions derive are subjects of surprisingly intense debate. Some interpreters reject the "canonical" definition of wisdom literature (that it consists of the three books listed above) as arbitrary–a complaint that is not without merit. Instead, these interpreters approach wisdom more explicitly as a literary genre, and so include *any* text that bears a comparable generic profile. From this perspective, the wisdom tradition encompasses many psalms and deuterocanonical texts as well.

On one hand, wisdom literature clearly testifies to having folk roots–a tradition born from life lived by everyday people. Proverbs, for example, frequently preserves insight as advice from parents to their children. On the other hand, wisdom literature is among the most "literary" kind of writing in the Bible. Some interpreters, for example, will regard the poetry of Job as the Bible's finest literary achievement. Given that few in the ancient world could read or write with any proficiency, the notion that Job is somehow the result of a soldier's or farmer's pastime seems dubious. Whether wisdom is ultimately a phenomenon of tribe or scholar is difficult to determine, but we can at least hazard the suggestion that both have left their fingerprints on the books we have received from antiquity.

### *To the Beat of a Different Drummer*

How many times, might one venture to guess, does the book of Job recall the likes of Abraham, Moses, or David? The fact that these names do not appear in Job illustrates just how fundamentally different wisdom literature is from anything else in the Old

Testament. In order to understand this difference, readers need some familiarity with the Old Testament's ideological background.

Interpreters will often employ the German term *heilsgeschichte* to describe the theological underpinnings for much of the Old Testament. The word literally means "help-history" and is usually translated as something like "salvation history." It is a shorthand way to refer to the so-called covenantal metanarrative, in which God repeatedly intervenes in history in order to reconcile a divine-human relationship that sin has made derelict. The flashpoints for this divine inbreaking into history are the four major covenants of the Bible (Abrahamic, Mosaic, Davidic, and the New Covenant in Jesus).

Underpinning wisdom literature, however, is not covenant but *creation*. In short, wisdom literature shifts one's gaze from the heavens in order to consider one's own feet and the path they travel. The wisdom authors devote less attention to the properties of the special relationship between Israel and her God, in order to document the natural order of life in the human community and describe, quite simply, the way the world works. Wisdom literature is therefore primarily concerned with the principles that govern the cosmos, the nature of the human experience, and how to navigate these realities skillfully. While the wisdom tradition unequivocally situates these concerns in the orbit of divine sovereignty, Proverbs, Job, and Ecclesiastes nonetheless betray a distinctly human focus.

In addition to this distinction, wisdom literature is also the most "international" sort of writing in the Old Testament. Wisdom literature was a largely ubiquitous phenomenon in the ancient world, and there seems to be some measure of exchange between the sages of the Old Testament and those of other ancient societies. One of the earliest examples is the "Teachings of Ptahhotep." Ptahhotep was one of Egypt's high-ranking political advisors during the twenty-fifth century, BCE. His writings frequently bear a likeness to Proverbs:

> If you are fortunate enough to sit at table with someone greater than yourself, take graciously what is offered to you. Do not become envious and greedy, always wanting more.[74]
>
> When you sit down to eat with a ruler, observe carefully what is before you, and put a knife to your throat if you are given to appetite. Do not desire his delicacies, for they are deceptive food. (Pro. 23:1-3)

One finds more conspicuous examples in the "Teachings of Amenemope," a thirteenth-century Egyptian wisdom text:

> Guard yourself from robbing the poor, from being violent to the weak. Do not associate with the rash man nor approach him in conversation.[75]
>
> Do not rob the poor, because he is poor, or crush the afflicted at the gate, for the LORD will plead their cause and rob of life those who rob them. Make no friendship with a man given to anger, nor go with a wrathful man, lest you learn his ways and entangle yourself in a snare. (Pro. 22:22-25)

Other Egyptian texts, such as "The Tale of the Eloquent Peasant," "The Song of the Harper," and "The Dispute over Suicide," have been linked to passages in Ecclesiastes. Wisdom parallels may be found in the Mesopotamian world as well. Scholars sometimes refer to the "Dialogue between a Man and his God" as the "Sumerian Job," and likewise the "Dialogue about Human Misery" is nicknamed the "Babylonian Job."

Wisdom literature's inattentiveness to matters of covenant, its

---

74 Translation from Bill T. Arnold and Bryan E. Beyer, *Encountering the Old Testament* (Grand Rapids: Baker, 2015), 396. See also Bill T. Arnold and Bryan E. Beyer, *Readings from the Ancient Near East* (Grand Rapids: Baker, 2002), 182-84.

75 Translation from Andrew E. Hill and John H. Walton, *A Survey of the Old Testament* (Grand Rapids: Zondervan, 2000), 312.

human focus, and the common literary space it shares with other cultures all serve to illustrate its distinctive nature in the Old Testament. To regard these books as theologically independent from the rest of the Old Testament, however, would misjudge them. In fact, the driving theological thesis within Old Testament wisdom actually derives from the *Torah*–specifically the book of Deuteronomy. The so-called "doctrine of the two ways" maintains that seeded within any given deed is a corresponding consequence. The wise choose the righteous path, leading to blessing. Fools take the wicked route, which leads to cursing. (For a good example of this doctrine in context, see Deu. 28.) As the author of creation, God has ordered the world according to these two paths, and fidelity to God ultimately determines the way of the wise and righteous. Proverbs generally embodies this retributive theology, while Job anxiously chips away at its immutability.

So it would seem that there are actually two different types of wisdom in the Old Testament. Interpreters usually refer to these types as *practical* and *speculative*. Practical wisdom preserves the insight gleaned from generations who have tried to navigate life toward blessing. It assumes the doctrine of the two ways as a matter of orthodoxy (even while hinting at its limitations). Proverbs is far and away the best example of this type. Speculative wisdom, on the other hand, takes more interest in asking probing questions than finding useful solutions. Adopting a skeptical posture toward the assumption of a well-ordered reality, speculative wisdom is vulnerable to–and often vexed by–life's uncertainty. Job is the obvious example here. Ecclesiastes is harder to categorize; some interpreters regard it as a savagely skeptical treatise, while others detect a kind of seasoned acceptance of the struggle to navigate life.

## Proverbs

In the strictest sense, Proverbs is not really a book. The designations "index" or "archive" probably stretch the truth too much as well, since those terms imply an ordered subject matter–a feature that Proverbs does not exhibit. So, Proverbs is most aptly described as a collection of, well, *proverbs.*

What exactly is a proverb, then? A generic definition reads something like, "a short pithy saying stating a general truth or piece of advice."[76] Fair enough. A more precise definition, however, might be "a concise statement of apparent truth that has currency."[77] By *concise,* we mean that it is packaged for easy human transmission. Nobody would remember a saying like, "a healthy and balanced diet maintained regularly over the course of a human life will most likely lead to longevity, decreased health issues, and reduced private and public expenditures on health care." Yet we can all recite "an apple a day keeps the doctor away" without even really knowing where we heard it. By *apparent* we mean that their truth is readily observed; proverbs tell you what you already know. Of *course* a healthy diet leads to healthier bodies; such knowledge does not require a medical degree. Finally, *currency* means that proverbs are useful; they prefer to circumvent philosophical quandaries in favor of "getting things done right."

Though collected in random fashion, Proverbs does frequently address topics such as money, relationships, and communication. These subjects are hardly surprising, given that Proverbs belongs to the "practical" species of wisdom. Proverbs 15:17 is a typical example, which happens to remind readers about the value of a good relationship: "Better is a dinner of herbs where love is / than a fattened ox and hatred with it." There are several hundred such

76 See, for example, *Oxford English Dictionary*, s.v. "Proverb."

77 See Wolfgang Mieder, *Proverbs Speak Louder than Words: Folk Wisdom in Art, Culture, Folklore, History, Literature, and Mass Media* (New York: Peter Lang, 2008), 11.

examples, making Proverbs a treasure trove of advice for life. But anyone who has done much living knows that the "wise path" really depends on the circumstances, and this fact is not lost on Proverbs:

> *Answer not a fool according to his folly, lest*
> *you be like him yourself. (Pro. 26:4)*
>
> *Answer a fool according to his folly, lest he*
> *be wise in his own eyes. (Pro. 26:5)*

Should one answer a fool? It depends. The application of proverbs therefore requires a measure of skill and experience–*wisdom*–to know the right path in any given situation: "Like a thorn that goes up into the hand of a drunkard / is a proverb in the mouth of fools." (Pro. 26:9)

Consuming this collection of wisdom provides readers with the means to observe, understand, and successfully navigate life along a course that leads to peace, prosperity, and success. Proverbs tends to regard life's adversity optimistically, as constructive trials that spur new growth. To borrow a coined phrase, proverbs are all about "the art of living well."

Within Proverbs, there is one section that differs from the rest. Proverbs 8 contains an extended personification of wisdom. "Woman Wisdom" is represented as one who stands "upon the way" and calls out to anyone who would pay attention enough to receive the blessings she naturally affords. She declares that she existed before the creation of the world, and–remarkably–was a kind of master architect who assisted the Lord in the work of creation. (This passage is probably the theological backdrop for the "Hymn to the *Logos*" in the opening chapter of John's gospel.)

## Job

Job is probably one of the more misunderstood books in the Bible. Popular sentiment (and a long history of interpretation) heralds Job as a man of exemplary piety. According to this reading, Job is a wisdom hero who patiently and faithfully endures severe misfortune only to emerge victorious and receive the spoils of blessing. Unfortunately, one must avoid actually reading Job in order to maintain this impression.

To be fair, the text of Job does include a narrative introduction and conclusion that, when juxtaposed with one another, comprise a fairly complete folk-hero story like the one suggested above. Between these narrative sections, however, are some thirty-nine chapters of poetry in which Job is anything but patient or pious. The following excerpt is an instructive example:

*What is man, that you make so much of him,
and that you set your heart on him, visit him
every morning and test him every moment?*

*How long will you not look away from me, nor
leave me alone till I swallow my spit?*

*If I sin, what do I do to you, you watcher of man-
kind? Why have you made me your mark? Why
have I become a burden to you? (Job 7:17-20)*

Interpreters widely recognize this passage as a parody of Psalm 8, a hymn of thanksgiving:

*When I look at your heavens, the work of your fin-
gers, the moon and the stars, which you have set in
place, what is man that you are mindful of him,
and the son of man that you care for him?*

*Yet you have made him a little lower than the heavenly beings and crowned him with glory and honor. (Psa. 8.:3-5)*

The gravity of Job's language truly gives one pause. An analogy would be something like recomposing the beloved hymn "Amazing Grace" with heated accusations against God. Job the patient and pious? One could almost fear a strike of lightning just for reading such poetry out loud. Yet in his pursuit, Job is as unflinching as he is relentless.

The literary structure of Job, which links the narrative and poetic sections together, is also telling:

| Job's Tribulation \| | ---------- Job's Protest ---------- | \| Job's Restoration |
|---|---|---|
| 1:1-2:13 | 3:1-42:6 | 42:7-17 |

As we have observed above, simply deleting the lengthy poetic section in the middle would leave readers with a traditional story that goes just how a patron of conventional wisdom would expect. But Job's poetic discourse interrupts this classic tale and brazenly–even shockingly–challenges that orthodoxy. Just as suffering disturbs Job's life, so his protest disturbs the narrative. *How* Job tells its story conveys *what* Job is about.

The poetic section itself is comprised of an extended dialogue between Job and his friends. The debate centers on human suffering and the limits of orthodox (practical) wisdom. To understand the conversation, the reader needs some familiarity with the prevailing views about justice:

1. God was the source of justice in the world.
2. The righteous-wise were blessed; the wicked-foolish were cursed.
3. Justice was only possible during one's lifetime. There was no afterlife in which God could mete out ultimate blessing or cursing, only a common "nonexistence" in *Sheol.*

4. The presence of blessing or cursing in one's life, therefore, was evidence of a person's righteousness or wickedness.

Job's dialogue partners repeatedly assert this logic, pressing Job to search inward and find the error that led to his suffering. Job refuses. Instead he turns outward, accusing God of causing his suffering, even though Job had steadily followed the wise and righteous path. To the astonishment of his friends, Job demands a court hearing with God. In this way Job rebuffs the authority of his own tradition and appeals to his experience, which finds him innocent and assigns culpability to God's administration of justice in the world.

And therein lies the rub. On one hand, Job rejects the conventional wisdom of his day. At the same time, Job's unyielding quest for an audience with God actually *assumes his conviction* that God is just. In short, Job believes precisely what he cannot believe. This insoluble conflict gives the book its potency and inoculates the Old Testament wisdom tradition against any naiveté about the human experience.

In the end, Job gets his wish. From a "storm wind" God answers Job. For many readers, the divine response is perplexing. In a nutshell:

Job's Question: *If you are just, then why has my wise and righteous path led to cursing?*

God's Answer: *I created the world.*

So far, we have taken for granted that the book of Job is an example of "theodicy"–a discourse concerned with the justice of God. Indeed, the whole dialogue between Job and his friends assumes that justice is the central principle of reality. God's response (however frustrating) seems to challenge that assumption, as the fundamental categories in God's response are not justice and injustice, but order and chaos.

**Ecclesiastes**

Early rabbinic tradition associates Ecclesiastes with Solomon, but for more than a century the majority of interpreters have identified the book as an example of postexilic wisdom (400-200 BCE)–a conclusion confirmed by more recent linguistic analysis. Among interpreters, Ecclesiastes solicits some of the most varied reactions across the entire field of biblical studies. While the book eludes precise definition, we may tentatively group it with Job as an example of speculative wisdom. What stands out in Ecclesiastes is *how* it manages to speculate.

Ecclesiastes identifies its speaker as *Qohelet*, a Hebrew term that refers to a "speaker in an assembly" and is usually translated in Ecclesiastes as "Teacher" or "Preacher." This *Qohelet* is an experienced individual, well-versed in the lessons of conventional wisdom. But he does not actually espouse that orthodoxy. Instead, he utilizes the methods of traditional wisdom to deconstruct its own conclusions. It is a stunning move, and a feature that probably accounts for the book's wide-ranging interpretations. The Teacher seems frustrated with conventional wisdom's easy answers that oversimplify life. By observing the cosmic order of things, the Teacher establishes principles that upend proverbial thinking:

1. Divine reason is inaccessible. God orders creation, and therefore humans cannot fully discern that order.
2. The human experience is unpredictable. As a result, the wise and righteous path guarantees nothing.
3. Human life is finite. One's capacity to navigate life for blessing is likewise restricted, as is the consistent expression of the doctrine of the two ways. Death can effectively sever the deed-consequence link.

These conclusions sink in the hearts of interpreters, leaving some to regard the Teacher as a brutal cynic: "Meaningless! Meaningless!" says the Teacher. "Utterly meaningless! Everything is meaningless." (Ecc. 1:2) Yet as the Teacher continues on his course, he does not actually appear to despair. What proves "meaningless" (the basic sense of the Hebrew word here is "vapor") are the artificial maxims about the way the world works. The Teacher's alternative is not cynicism, but something more like an existential resignation toward life. Life is not fair or even coherent, the Teacher acquiesces, but one can nonetheless experience life as it comes and make a reasonable effort to choose the right path–perhaps even finding enjoyment along the way. This assessment compels the Teacher to favor a quiet and simple life, to maintain a healthy respect for the mystery of divine prerogative, and to limit his concern for both virtue and vice.

**Psalms**

Peering inside a traditional church, one is likely to find a hymnal. As a collection of the community's shared, lyrical confessions about the pilgrimage of faith, the hymnal is the closest contemporary analogy to the book of Psalms. The word "psalm" actually derives from a Greek word (*psalmos*) that means "hymn," and the corresponding Hebrew word (*mizmor*) meaning "melody." When the Jerusalem temple was destroyed in 586 BCE – and again in 70 CE –there was of course no "pew" on which to shelve a hymnal. As a result, the Psalter (another name for the book of Psalms) historically transitioned from lyrics sung in worship to poetry read in devotion. Even as we focus on reading psalms as poetry, however, one should also keep in mind its musical roots.

The salient feature of Hebrew poetry is called *parallelism.* In simplest terms, parallelism denotes two poetic lines that are juxtaposed, prompting the reader to draw a connection:

*For the Lord knows the way of the righteous,*
*but the way of the wicked shall perish. (Psa. 1:6)*

*The heavens declare the glory of God*
*the skies proclaim the work of his hand. (Psa. 19:1)*

*Come and see what God has done:*
*he is awesome in his deeds among mortals. (Psa. 66:5)*

To those more accustomed to rhythm and rhyme, parallelism may not seem very "poetic." But parallelism has a way of bringing to life the intrinsically poetic potential of language. In addition to its pervasive parallelism, psalms employ poetry's usual suspects: imagery, repetition and patterns, figures of speech, and other literary constructs such as tone, motifs, and themes.

Over three-quarters of the psalms bear superscriptions, titles that give attributions, name melodies and instruments, or provide other liturgical details. In rare instances superscriptions note the psalm's occasion, and from the contents of a few psalms we can also infer a historical setting. Otherwise, the psalms are conspicuously absent of historical detail. Interpreters refer to this characteristic as the "ambiguity of the Psalter." It is most likely the result of an intentional editorial process, designed to make the psalms adaptable to a variety of life circumstances and so allow them to speak into the hearts of future generations.

More precisely, the psalms speak *for* the hearts of generations. While Christians generally regard scripture as "God's word to humanity," psalms work explicitly in the opposite direction: they are humanity's words to God. This feature captivated the great fourth-century theologian Athanasius: "In the Psalms we are instructed how one must praise the Lord and by speaking what words we properly confess our faith in him. And in the case of each person one would find the divine hymns appointed for us and our emotions and equanimity."[78]

78 Athanasius, "Letter to Marcellinus," in *Athanasius: The Life of Antony*, ed. Emilie Griffin; trans. Robert C. Gregg (San Francisco: Harper San Francisco, 1980), 93-94.

## CHAPTER TWO

# THE WORLD OF CAESAR AND CHRIST

GARY R. POE AND FRANCISCO PLAZA[1]

This course introduces honors students to one of the most significant periods in Western history. Rome grows from a small settlement of farmers and shepherds along the Tiber River to rule the entire Mediterranean world and beyond. Rome was the dominant military, social, political, and economic power of its age. The Romans were responsible for many important elements of the Western world and European traditions, such as the Julian calendar, Romance languages, a republican form of government, and the love of formal spectacle sports. Virgil in the *Aeneid* summed up what would be the contributions of the Romans:

Others, I have no doubt,

Will forge the bronze to breath with suppler lines,

Draw from the block of marble features quick with life

1 The historical overview, New Testament glosses, and Augustine gloss were written by Gary Poe. All other glosses were written by Francisco Plaza.

Plead their cases better, chart with their rods the stars,

That climb the sky and foretell the times they rise.

But you, Roman, remember, rule with all your power,

the peoples of the earth – these will be your arts:

to put your stamp on the works and ways of peace,

To spare the defeated, break the proud in war.[2]

The Romans themselves were never great innovators, but made use of earlier ideas and traditions, translating them into a new age and ensuring that these ideas and traditions persevered and spread. In the midst of Rome's rule we also have the beginnings of Christianity and its early developments, a movement that will also shape much of the Western world. Much of who we are and the values we hold were shaped by the developments of this period.

*General Roman Characteristics*

The values of the Roman people were very much shaped by how they ruled and acted. In general, the Romans were a practical people.[3] Unlike the Greeks, who explored philosophy and created a vast treasury of plays and statues, the Romans were more interested in the practicalities of life. They were more concerned with how to get fresh running water and flushing toilets than with philosophical flights of fancy. Three main values shaped the Roman psyche: agriculture, family, and religion. Founded on a community of farmers and shepherds, the ideal Roman man was the farmer-soldier. If you have ever seen the movie *Gladiator*, you will remember that throughout the movie, anytime Russell Crowe's character dreamed

2 Virgil, *Aeneid*, trans. Robert Fagles (Viking Penguin: New York, 2006), 6:976-984 [emphasis added].

3 Ralph Mathisen, *Ancient Mediterranean Civilizations: From Prehistory to 640 CE* (Oxford University Press, 2015), 329-31.

of a better life, he had a vision of life back home on the farm with his family. Family was held in high regard in Roman society. Divorce was very rare until late in the Roman Republic. The *paterfamilias*, or head of the family, had the power of life and death for all in the family. Whether one wanted to get married, or was trying to acquire land, or even to secure a loan, one needed the approval of the *paterfamilias*. This is not to say that women did not also play a significant role in the Roman family. The matron in a Roman household wielded much more influence than her contemporary in Greek culture. Finally, religion also was an important factor in Roman life. Every Roman household kept a fire burning on its hearth for the goddess Vesta (goddess of the home and family) to insure the family's prosperity and continuity. All houses had niches where they kept the family gods. Often there was a statue of Penates (the protector of the cupboards and food storage) along with a pantheon of symbols for other gods and goddesses.

*Assimilating with Other Cultures*

As practical people, the Romans were quick to assimilate the ideas and practices of other peoples they believed could help them. The two main cultures that greatly influenced the early developments of Rome were the Etruscans and the Greeks. The Etruscans were a late seventh-century B.C. people who ruled over the Romans for a time. The Etruscans were a people from the region north of Rome known as Etruria; they were considered more developed than the Romans at this time. It is from the Etruscans that the Romans learned the ins and outs of trade and travel on the Italian peninsula and beyond. Because they already had well-established markets, Rome benefitted from their rule. The Etruscans also helped the Romans better manage their businesses and record keeping. One of their legacies to the Romans was the development of Roman numerals for keeping track of business transactions.[4]

The Etruscans also gave the Romans an origin story in the account of Romulus and Remus. This is the story of how King Numitor of Alba Longa (ruled by Aeneas of the *Aeneid* and a later neighbor of Rome) is usurped by his brother Amulius. In order to ensure the end of Numitor's lineage, Amulius commits Numitor's daughter Rhea Silvia to the community of the Vestal Virgins. The god Mars visits Rhea, and she conceives the twin boys Romulus and Remus. Usually death of offspring would be the punishment for pregnancy for a Vestal Virgin, but instead Amulius sentences the boys to be abandoned in the wilderness to die of exposure. As the legend goes, they are discovered by a she-wolf and nourished by her until a shepherd discovers and raises the boys. In the end, they grow up along the Tiber River which flows in and around the seven hills of Rome. Eventually the boys grow to manhood and seek to establish their own city. In a heated argument over which hill to build their city (Romulus favored the Palatine Hill and Remus the Aventine Hill), Romulus kills his brother Remus. He then goes on to found his city called Rome in 753 B.C., and becomes the first king of the city. This story supplies the Romans with a lineage that connects them to both the Latin peoples of the central Italian peninsula and to the Greeks, as Numitor was descended from Aeneas who had survived the destruction of Troy.

This leads to the description of how the Greeks became an important influence on the Romans. The Greeks were a people of a highly artistic culture. From the Greeks, the Romans learned philosophy, poetry, arts, and architecture.[5] There is a bit of irony here, though. The Etruscans had conquered and ruled over the Romans for a time and influenced the Romans in many ways. The Greeks,

4 Mary Boatwright, Daniel Gargola, & Richard Talbert, *The Romans: From Village to Empire* (Oxford University Press, 2004), 28.

5 Ibid., 26.

on the other hand, were conquered militarily by the Romans and ruled by them. And yet, it is Greek cultural forms that became the goal and norm for much of the Roman world. The Romans even coined the term "humanities" to refer to the artistic, literary, and philosophical activities of the Greeks; the humanities eventually became the standard for civilized life. So in the end, it could be said that culturally the Greeks conquered the Romans! We have Virgil to thank for introducing us to how the Greeks came to influence the Romans through his epic poem *The Aeneid*. It is in this story that we are told of the journey of Aeneas after the fall of Troy. Driven by Fate and directed by the gods, he seeks out a new land promised to him and his followers in Italy. In this story, Virgil demonstrates how the rule of the new Roman Emperor, Augustus, was foretold well before the founding of Rome. The poem illustrates how Augustus is the chosen ruler of Rome and that his ancestry goes all the way back to Aeneas and his journey from Troy. Therefore, once again the dominance of Rome is all part of the gods' plans and has been in the works for a long, long time.

*Roman History*

Roman history is usually divided into three main periods associated with the various political systems by which Rome was structured. First, Rome was a monarchy. From 753 B.C. until 509 B.C., Rome was ruled mainly by Etruscan kings. With the overthrow of the last Etruscan king in 509 B.C., Rome established the Republic. The Roman Republic expanded and developed from 509 B.C. until 31 B.C. when the first official Roman Emperor came to power. In 31 B.C. with the rise of Octavian (Julius Caesar's adopted nephew) as the sole ruler of the Mediterranean world, we have the beginnings of the Roman Empire. This vast Empire went through many different rulers and changes until its final fall in A.D. 476. This fall begins the Medieval period of Western Europe.

### *The Monarchy*

While Rome was ruled by kings during this first period from 753-509 B.C., many of the developments of later political values were established during this time; already, a balanced system of government existed. Even with a king, there was also a council of elders from amongst the landowners. This body was known as the *Sens* (elders) and became the forerunner of the Roman Senate. While it had limited powers during this time, we begin to see the origins of this powerful legislative body during the period of the kings. At the same time, we also see another important element develop that will plague Rome from then on. Early class struggle began during the period of the monarchy.[6] As Rome began to expand, urban dwellers who were not landowners but who began to prosper were cut off from any political power or influence. In this "conflict of the orders," we see the development of two rival classes in Roman society. Amongst the landed aristocracy, you have the patrician class, which was often at odds with the developing and now more prosperous plebeian class. While the monarchy was able to keep this conflict in check, it established long-standing conflicts that would play a much bigger role in the period of the Republic. The monarchy came to an end with the overthrow of the last Etruscan king, *Tarquinius Superbus* or Tarquin the Proud. His reputation of acquiring the throne through murder, along with his expenditures and expeditions, made him a very unpopular ruler. Legendarily, those tensions all came to a head when the wife of one of the leading families had her reputation ruined by Tarquin's son and committed suicide. As a result, senators Lucius Collatinus and Lucius Brutus led an uprising, defeating Tarquin and expelling him from the city.

---

6 Robin Winks & Susan Mattern-Parkes, *The Ancient Mediterranean World: From the Stone Age to A. D. 600* (Oxford University Press, 2004), 123-26.

*The Republic*

With the overthrow of the Etruscan king in 509 B.C., the Romans needed to develop a new system of government. Rome established its Republic based on a system of representative government and separation of powers that would last almost five hundred years.[7] This system ensured that no one individual could ever rule over others as a king again. The Republic can best be understood when divided into three periods. The first period, known as the Early Republic, was from 509-264 B.C. and can be characterized by the establishment of the republican form of government and the subsequent expansion into the Italian peninsula. The second period, referred to as the Middle Republic, ran from 264-133 B.C. and involved the expansion of Rome beyond the Italian peninsula and the conflicts with the Carthaginians. The last period, the Late Republic, was from 133-31 B.C. and saw the ultimate demise of the Republic and the move toward the Empire.

The Early Republic dealt with both internal crises and external crises. Internally, the struggles between the patricians and the plebeians intensified as the new government formed. In an effort to prevent any single man from control, the patricians sought to create a system of checks and balances. The chief position was that of consul, and there were always two, each with veto power over the other. In addition to the consul, the Republic still had the *sens* or what was now known as the senate. This is where the real power rested, and it was this body that chose the consuls. Early on, the plebeians were given no part in this system. It was all in the hands of the patrician class. Clashes between the two classes continued with various uprisings until 287 B.C. when the senate agreed to the creation of the Citizens' Assembly (also known as the Plebeian Council, a development from the earlier Assembly of the Tribes), a legislative body comprised of the plebeians. With the creation of this assembly, there were now two legislative bodies and two

7 Boatwright, *The Romans*, 48-51.

consuls, additions that enfranchised more of the population and maintained some checks and balances in the system. This is all described in detail by the Greek writer and Roman slave Polybius in his *Histories* in the mid-second century B.C.[8]

The external crises of the young Republic came from the threat of nearby peoples on the Italian peninsula. Several wars during this time led to the final defeat of the Etruscans as well as the defeat of the Samnites, Lucanians, and Volscii; the Romans also drove the Greeks out of the south of Italy. This is when Rome developed its strategy that would help them conquer the then-known world. As they defeated these people, the conquered were allowed to self-govern and keep their religions as long as they contributed men for the army and paid taxes. The Romans also developed a system of enfranchisement in terms of who became full citizens. Some people were only allowed to trade economically with Rome but not given any other rights. Other conquered people whom Rome deemed superior were allowed the rights of citizens, and some were given the right to vote.[9]

With the conquest of the Italian peninsula, Rome turned its attention to the western Mediterranean. This was the beginning of the Middle Republic in 264 B.C. and lasted until 133 B.C. Rome especially had its eyes on the islands of Sicily, Corsica, and Sardinia. Conquering these lands brought Rome into conflict with Carthage, the main naval power of the western Mediterranean. The Romans eventually fought three wars against Carthage, wars known as the Punic Wars.[10] The first Punic war compelled Rome to build a navy and take the three islands from Carthaginian control. The second Punic war from 218-202 B.C. saw Carthage go on the offensive.

8 Found in the Perseus web page at Tufts University. "Polybius, *Histories*." http://www.perseus.tufts.edu/hopper/text?doc=Perseus%3Atext%3A1999.01.0234. (Accessed May 21, 2019)

9 Winks, *The Ancient Mediterranean World*, 127.

10 Punic is from the Latin *poeni*, which was the Latin name of the Phoenicians where the Carthaginians had originated.

Hannibal, the Carthaginian commander in Spain, decided to take the war to the Romans. He marched on the Italian peninsula, but took a difficult route over the Alps and down into the Po River Valley of north central Italy. In doing so, he lost many men and animals (particularly war elephants) but still was able to defeat the Romans in three consecutive battles. Most significantly, in 216 B.C., he destroyed a Roman army of about 80,000 men at the battle of Cannae. This was the largest defeat ever suffered by a Roman army and would remain in the collective memory of Rome for the rest of their history.[11] From that point on, the Romans would not face Hannibal in open battle, and he was able to march all over Italy for ten years doing as he pleased. He drove many people off their land and into the cities as they sought refuge. The dislocation of the local small farmers and shepherds transformed the distribution of land after the war and was partially responsible for the move from a Republic to an Empire. Eventually the Romans found a way to cut off Hannibal's supply routes and proceeded to attack the city of Carthage itself. This attack led to Hannibal's departure from Italy to return to Carthage and defend the city which eventually led to his own defeat and the defeat of Carthage. In 149 B.C. there was one last attack on the city of Carthage, but that was more of an act of revenge than anything else, and it gave Rome the chance to complete the destruction of Carthage. With this final victory, Rome had full control of the western Mediterranean. The impact of the Punic Wars included enlarging Rome's imperialistic ambitions. More importantly, most of Italy's small family farms were replaced by large farms owned by the richest of Rome, cultivated by a growing slave force. The displacement of the peoples to the cities transformed Roman society and brought a new set of challenges to the city.

The Late Republic ran from 133 B.C. to 31 B.C. and was a period marked by growing civil strife and expansion into the east-

11 Boatwright, *The Romans*, 114.

ern Mediterranean. Rome is best described as an oligarchy during this time. The patrician families now owned most of the land and continued to dominate the senate. The developing inequality in society created a mass of landless citizens, slaves, and foreigners in the city. Trying to provide for this growing mass of people led many politicians to propose a variety of ways to feed and entertain them. In response to this crisis, we see the development of what was called "bread and circuses." By the first century A.D., about one-quarter to one-third of the population was being fed by the state, hence the "bread." But to try and keep these masses more subdued, Rome provided entertainment as well. This led to the development of the "circuses," best represented by gladiatorial contests and chariot racing. In the midst of this internal turmoil, there came a rise in politicians who built their success on populist appeals to these landless masses of people; very powerful charismatic leaders gained the support of the masses. Cicero was especially troubled by this development and warned the people in his *On Duties* of the dangers to the Republic from these demagogues.[12] Ultimately, Julius Caesar used this kind of popular support to solidify power and control; Caesar appeared to be the singular ruler the senate had always feared. On the Ides ($15^{th}$) of March in 44 B.C., the senate, led by Marcus Junius Brutus and Gaius Cassius Longinus, assassinated Caesar by stabbing him outside the senate building. This event threw the Republic into turmoil and civil unrest that was not fully settled until Octavian defeated Mark Anthony and Cleopatra at the battle of Actium in 31 B.C.

### *The Empire*

The rise to power of Octavian marks the beginning of the Roman Empire and the end of the Republic. Now Rome and the entire Mediterranean world were under the control of one man as he led

12 Cicero, *On Duties*, eds. and trans. M. T. Griffin & E. M. Atkins (Cambridge: Cambridge University Press, 1991).

the entire Roman army. When Octavian returned to Rome after Actium, he promised to restore the Republic. He was a politically astute individual and was careful to accept titles that appeared to make him out to be a king. He maintained the senate and other government offices, but power was moving more and more to him alone. While accepting a number of titles, the one he chose to emphasize was that of *Princeps Civitatis*, or the first citizen of the state; this was an adept populist move. He was careful not to be seen as a monarch but wanted instead to be recognized as one who was committed to the people of Rome and the ideals they represented.

With Octavian's rise to power, his efforts initiate the *Pax Romana*, or the Peace of Rome. While there was some reduction in the freedoms of the Republic, the people of Rome were ready to give up some freedoms for more stability and peace. Octavian's authoritative military title of *Imperator* gave him control of the entire Roman army, allowing him to utilize these forces to maintain peace throughout the Mediterranean world. In recognition of his leadership, the senate bestowed upon him a new title in 27 B.C. From this point on, he was known as Caesar Augustus, a title suggesting that, because of his greatness, they bestowed even more authority on him. With this event, Octavian, grandnephew of Julius Caesar and adopted son, became the first Roman Emperor and the first to be called Augustus.

Caesar Augustus proceeded to build upon his popularity and success in a variety of areas. Toward the end of his life, he proclaimed that he had "found Rome of brick and left it of marble."[13] While this quote may be more legend than reality, the truth is that he did expand on the building projects within the city of Rome, making it a city of extravagant grandeur. He built a new palace, new temples to Vesta and Apollo, as well as a new forum near the old forum of Julius and the Pantheon. Another important

13 Suetonius, *The Twelve Caesars, Augustus,* trans. Robert Graves (New York: Penguin Classics, 2007), XXVIII, 3.

part of Augustus's controlling and maintaining the Empire was the building of roads. Used not only for trade and commerce, roads were needed to move armies around the Empire. One of the most important developments to the Roman Empire—and later for the growth of Christianity—was the building of an Empire-wide network of roads. The efforts of Augustus to build infrastructure and roadways made for an Empire that would last for another four centuries. Additionally, Caesar was known for his patronage of literature. This period of writings is often referred to as Rome's golden age of literature. First and foremost came Virgil's *Aeneid.* In this work, Virgil made the connection between Augustus and the Trojans, and demonstrated that Caesar's reign had been fated since before the city of Troy fell centuries earlier. It was also during this time that the writer Ovid published his *Metamorphoses.* This wild collection of bodily transformations was the source of many Greek and Roman myths for centuries to come.

Caesar Augustus lived to the age of seventy-five, dying in A.D. 14 after ruling for forty-five years. By this time, he restored the peace to Rome, transformed the Republic into a vast Empire, and put in place the infrastructure that would help Rome thrive in its control over the Mediterranean world.

The political and social structure that Augustus left to Rome was immediately tested by his successors, the Julian emperors. These rulers—who included the likes of Tiberius, Caligula, Claudius, and Nero—were remembered as being tyrannical, vicious, and demented individuals. One of the weaknesses of Augustus's government was that no provisions were made for choosing successors. This lack of direction would plague the Empire for most of the rest of its history. Nero particularly is noted for his cruelty and is blamed for the burning of Rome in order that he might build a new and better palace. In the aftermath of this tragic fire, he used the new Christian sect in Rome as his scapegoat. He then initiated one of the first persecutions of Christians in A.D. 70 in Rome, persecutions that are still remembered by Christians today. With the end of his reign and with each of his successors, the challenges of choosing an heir to the throne were cause for tension in the Empire, a tension that tested the stability of the kingdom each time.

The period from A.D. 96-180 came to be characterized as the period of the five good emperors.[14] These were men who, first and foremost, established successors well before their deaths. They worked to prepare those who would lead after them, whether it be their own sons, or if not, through the adoption of men they thought suitable for the position. In this period we see the reign of Nerva, Trajan, Hadrian, Antoninus Pius, and Marcus Aurelius. Nerva (A.D. 96-98) was remembered for his efforts to relieve the suffering of the poor and his promotion of education for all citizens. Trajan (A.D. 98-117) expanded the Empire to some of its farthest boundaries. He too was known to be a generous patron of education and literature as well as of many great public works in the city of Rome and around the Empire. Hadrian (A.D. 117-138) slowed the expansionist policies put in place by Trajan. He was more interested in improving what Rome had at the time than in adding to it. Hadrian also demonstrated much more concern for the provinces of Rome and actually traveled far and wide in the Empire. No other emperor traveled as widely as he did. He even spent time along the wall named for him in the North of England. Finally, the last of these great rulers was Marcus Aurelius (A.D. 161-180). Marcus was an adopted son before becoming the ruler of Rome. He is most remembered for the stoic philosophical ideals of his *Meditations.* It was during his reign that we begin to see the attacks and invasions from some of the Germanic tribes from the North; these attacks and invasions mark a decline in the Empire from which it had a hard time recovering.

With the death of Marcus Aurelius and the reign of his son Commodus, the Empire entered a bleak period. (Think of the

14 Boatwright, *The Romans*, 364-65.

movie *Gladiator* and the Joaquin Phoenix character.) Commodus ruled from A.D. 177 until his assassination in A.D. 191. Due to his ego and self-promotion to godly heights, his reign cannot be seen as a success. With his death, the Empire was plunged into civil war and unrest. The period from A.D. 191 to 284 was one of serious decline. The rulers of this period are referred to as the barrack emperors because so many of them came from the military. Of the twenty-seven rulers during this time, only four died of natural deaths.[15] All the others were either assassinated or killed in battle. The historical records of this time contain very little positive reports; they mainly consist of accounts of the declining government and the ever increasing attacks along the borders in the north and east. The Gauls, the Sassanids (Persians), the Goths, and even the Franks began to put a lot of pressure on the borders around the Empire. Trade was restricted, and the armies usually had to forcibly requisition food and supplies to survive. Even the economy suffered greatly in the midst of this unrest with rampant inflation and a continually debased currency. In many provinces the economy resorted to bartering rather than trying to use coins.

There was little hope for recovery until the reign of Diocletian (A.D. 284-305) and his reforms. Coming from the eastern part of the Empire, he styled himself along the lines of an Oriental monarch, a figure which was much more powerful, regal, and semi-divine than Romans usually thought of their rulers. He centralized authority like no other emperor but with a twist. He recognized that the Empire was too large for any one man to rule it and repel invaders on all the borders. He created what came to be known as the tetrarchy. In this system he divided the Empire in half, east and west. Over each region there would be an *Augustii*, or ruler. To each *Augustii*, an assistant/successor known as a Caesar would be assigned. This meant there was an Augustus of the east with a Caesar as assistant, and an Augustus of the west with a

15 Ibid., 432.

Caesar as assistant. The provinces were then divided up amongst these four rulers to better manage the affairs of state. This central organizing was successful for a while and temporarily slowed the decline of Rome.

The other memorable event with Diocletian was his effort to restore Rome to the traditional worship of the gods of their ancestors. In calling all citizens to offer sacrifices to Jupiter, he put the growing Christians in his Empire in a bind. When many Christians refused to offer this sacrifice, Diocletian cracked down on them. He knew from past experience that he did not want to create martyrs and tried to find ways to influence Christians by such means as confiscating property and books and arresting leaders. In the end, his efforts were unsuccessful and he unleashed what came to be known as the Great Persecution from A.D. 303-311. In light of his failed efforts, Diocletian backed away from the persecution, and finally in A.D. 311 he abdicated his throne, being one of the only late Roman Emperors to retire peacefully. His successor Galerius issued the Edict of Toleration in A.D. 311, noting that the persecution had not been successful in making Christianity a tolerated religion in the Empire. This marked a real turn in Christian history because the Edict of Toleration ensured that Christians were no longer a persecuted people in the Empire, but free to pursue their faith openly.

After Diocletian's abdication, the Empire was thrown into turmoil once again as his hope that his Tetrarchy would establish a clear line of succession failed. Consequently, civil war erupted, and the armies put forth their champions. After a period of unrest and with a series of victories, Constantine became the new Emperor in A.D. 313. His final victory that same year was at the battle of the Milvian Bridge. The legend is that he had a vision in which he heard a voice saying, "By this sign conquer."[16] The sign he saw was the cross. According to his biographer, Eusebius, he accepted the

16 Ibid., 451-52.

Christian religion and adopted the cross as his battle standard. With the assurance of his victory, Constantine fully embraced Christianity and came to favor Christians in the Empire during his reign. Most importantly, he called the first ecumenical council of the church in which all the leaders of Christianity were summoned to his summer palace in Nicaea in Asia Minor. In an effort to settle the issue of the divinity of Christ, the council affirmed that Christ is fully divine and developed the Nicene Creed to make this belief official. For the first time a Roman Emperor played a role in the life of the church and the making of religious decisions. He also issued the Edict of Milan in A.D. 313 that confirmed the Edict of Toleration as well as provided funds to build churches and gave tax breaks to church leaders in the Empire. Life as a Christian in the Empire changed drastically after the reign of Constantine. The other important event in Constantine's reign was the establishment of his capital in Constantinople. He built a new capital in what was the city of Byzantium and then renamed it after himself! This began a shift in power in the Roman Empire away from Italy and the city of Rome and to the eastern part of the Empire. All of this signaled the decline of the western portion of the Empire and further division between the east and the west.

The reign of Theodosius (A.D. 379-395) completed the divide between east and west, and confirmed the triumph of Christianity in the Empire. He greatly favored the eastern half of the Empire, but more significantly he recognized Christianity as the only religion needed in the Empire. In A.D. 390 he proclaimed that Christianity was the only true religion and outlawed all other religions in the Empire. With this proclamation, Christianity grew from a small Jewish sect in Judea to the dominant faith Empire wide. With his death in A.D. 395 the Empire was fully divided between east and west. He gave his two sons, Arcadius and Honorius, control of the Empire. The younger, Honorius, was unable to hold his kingdom together, and the west began to unravel. It fell to various kingdoms, starting with the invasion of the city of Rome in A.D. 410 by the Goths. This cataclysmic event, which a mere fifty years earlier would not have been thought possible, began the decline of the western half of the Roman Empire. The eastern half of the Empire continued, being ruled from Constantinople, until the city fell to the Ottoman Turks in 1453. Historians refer to this eastern Roman Empire as the Byzantine Empire. The west continued to be invaded by other forces including the Vandals, the Huns, and again for the final time by the Goths. In A.D. 476 Odoacer, leader of the Gothic army, deposed Romulus Augustulus, the last ruler of the city of Rome. Odoacer sent the symbols of Romulus's office to Constantinople, signaling the end of the Empire in the west. This left the western remnant of the Empire open to settlement by Lombards, Vandals, Visigoths, Goths, Franks, Angles, and Saxons. The west, never to be united again, entered the Medieval period.

*Early Christianity*

In the midst of the Roman Empire, a new movement began to develop. During the first century A.D., we see the birth and development of Christianity. This movement would grow quickly as it progressed from a small sect within Judaism in an obscure part of the Empire to becoming the official religion of the Empire in a little less than four centuries. When tracing the development of Christianity, we can divide its history during the Empire into two distinct periods. The first period, from the beginnings in the first century A.D. up to Emperor Galerius issuing the Edict of Toleration in A.D. 311, is characterized by martyrdom and persecution. Christianity during this period was shaped by the ever-possible threat of violence and suppression. The second period, from A.D. 311 until the fall of Rome in A.D. 476, was a whole new experience for Christianity. Since the church was no longer facing the threat of persecution, we see explosive growth along with new types of literature and movements.

*First Christian Period A.D. 100-311*

In this first period from the first century until A.D. 311, martyrdom shaped Christian activity and writings. Persecution against Christians can be divided into three main periods. The first was mainly at the hands of Jewish mobs as was the case with Stephen (Acts 7:54-60). The second period was focused more on interactions between Christians and Romans. These events were spasmodic and localized in scope; there was no real state-organized persecution early on. Even when the state sought out Christians, it was only at a regional level. These included the persecutions by Nero in Rome around A.D. 68-70, and the emperor Domitian in Rome and Asia Minor between A.D. 91-96. During this persecution, the apostle John was exiled from Ephesus to the isle of Patmos. In the period of the five great emperors, Trajan, Hadrian, Antonius Pius, and Marcus Aurelius particularly, Christians were not to be harassed unless they had actually broken laws or incited incidents against the state. The main policy of Rome was more of a "don't ask, don't tell" policy under these emperors.[17] Finally, the third period of persecution is characterized by deliberate, intensive, and organized persecutions on the part of the Roman state. The first of these was under the emperor Decius. The year A.D. 247 marked the supposed millennial celebration of Rome's foundation. Decius saw this as a great opportunity to call everyone to offer sacrifices to Jupiter in an effort to reinvigorate the Roman state. This ended up being the last great pagan festival of Rome unchallenged by Christianity. The bishops of Rome, Antioch, and Jerusalem, along with the apologist Origen, lost their lives. The bishops of Alexandria and Carthage survived, but were sent into hiding by their congregations. The emperor Valerian also sponsored an empire-wide persecution in A.D. 257 that lasted for three years. The final persecution is known as the Great Persecution and impacted the largest number of Christians. This was the persecution instituted by the emperor Diocletian as part

17 Ibid., 425-30.

of his reform efforts in the beginning of the fourth century. This persecution went through several phases in an attempt to wipe out Christianity. The first phase involved the destruction of property and the confiscation and burning of sacred books. Christians who held public office were dismissed from their posts, and those in the upper classes of society lost all of their privileges. The idea was that if the infrastructure was undermined the religion would fall apart without creating martyrs. When this effort failed, a new phase was begun that involved the arrest of all church leadership. These leaders were then expected to offer sacrifices to the gods. When these individuals refused, many of the imprisoned church leaders were executed. In the end Diocletian grew frustrated by his inability to impact the church, and he abdicated his throne to Galerius. Galerius tried some half-hearted attempts to continue the persecution, but in A.D. 311 he called a halt to all persecution of Christians and issued his Edict of Toleration, which allowed Christians freedom to "live as Christians."[18] The end of this period of persecution brought an end to martyrdom and the beginning of a new period of interactions between the Roman state and the church.

Christian writings during this period were either the story of martyrs or arguments making the case for Christianity in a hostile world, otherwise known as apologetics. The martyr literature took on a form all its own as it sought to preserve the heroic victory of those Christian leaders who had given their lives for the faith.[19] These martyrs were men and women who could literally bear witness to Christ's resurrection by their own experiences. Their stories had more influence in constituting Christian spirituality during the period after the New Testament than any other event or writing. By the second century, martyrdom was the ideal for a

18 Found in the Fordham University Internet Ancient History Sourcebook. "Galerius and Constantine: Edicts of Toleration 311/313." https://sourcebooks.fordham.edu/source/edict-milan.asp. (Accessed May 21, 2019)

19 The Greek word *martyr* literally means "to witness," according to Boatwright, *The Romans*, 429.

Christian. Persecution affected the spirit of the church more by its continually immanent threat than the actual numbers would suggest. Through martyr stories, a type of theology of martyrdom developed. The martyr was thought to have received a special dispensation of the grace of God given not to everyone, but only to the martyr. There was a sense of being chosen in some random way. It was also believed that the martyr was imitating and participating in the suffering of Christ. This was often spoken of in images of the new birth that the martyr experienced. Finally, it was believed that the Holy Spirit was present with those martyrs who had confessed their faith in Christ publicly before the magistrates. Therefore, they believed these martyrs had special spiritual powers. This began the tradition that the remains, or relics, of a martyr still contained this special power of the Holy Spirit and, therefore, must be preserved and cherished.

The other writers during this period were the apologists. These writers were busy trying to make a defense of the Christian faith in a hostile world. Apologies were often written as responses to the intellectual challenges that were brought against Christianity. These writers wanted to show that Christianity was logical, viable, and reasonable. What were some of the charges being brought against the Christians? First, they were charged with immorality and degrading practices. They were considered cannibals who had orgies at their nightly meetings held in secret. Of course, these charges were in reference to the Eucharist and the kinds of love feasts spoken of in the book of Acts. Christians were also accused of atheism because they did not believe in the Roman gods. For this reason, they were charged with treason. Other charges included withdrawal from societal expectations, theological absurdity, and responsibility for the calamities that were befalling the Empire. The apologists answered these charges in a number of ways. One of my favorite responses comes from the apologist Tertullian who, in response to the charges of immorality, pointed out that the only reasons the Romans thought Christians were behaving in these ways (cannibalism, orgies, etc.) was because those were the kind of things they were doing![20] The apologists also pointed out that Christians actually made good citizens because of their efforts of prayer on behalf of the rulers of the Empire. In many ways the apologists were able to counter many of the arguments that Christianity was somehow a detriment to society.

*The Second Christian Period A.D. 311-476*

With the Edict of Toleration in A.D. 311 followed by Constantine's Edict of Milan, persecution of Christians ended. The church was now not only tolerated, but at times favored by the state. In response to these changes, we see the development of a new type of spirituality that developed in the monastic tradition along with different emphases in Christian literature. As Christianity became more and more accepted in the late third and early fourth centuries, it was becoming more closely tied to the culture and society of the Roman Empire. More rigorous and sensitive Christians were threatened by this easy assimilation of culture and Christianity; they withdrew from society and culture, first as individual hermits, and then later forming separate communities. In doing so they also embraced a more ascetic or disciplined lifestyle. The word *ascesis* is a Greek word that literally means "to practice" and is often used in terms of the rigors of athletic training. Philosophers and religious sects often used the word metaphorically to refer to the rigors of their lifestyles that were often quite austere and disciplined. Christianity had its "athletes" as well. In fact, Paul refers to the Christian life being like athletics in 2 Timothy 4:7, "I have fought the good fight, I have finished the race, I have kept the faith." The goal was holiness before God. These Christian ascetics disciplined them-

20 Tertullian, "The Apology." http://www.tertullian.org/works/apologeticum.htm. (Accessed May 21,2019)

selves through the practices of fasting, prayer, meditation, celibacy, food restrictions, service, and often some form of manual labor.

These Christian ascetics believed that this kind of spirituality was really only possible in the wilderness or deserts of the world. What was the source of this idea? Those who withdrew in the wilderness were shaped by a number of powerful biblical examples. There were numerous Old Testament antecedents including Elijah, Jeremiah, and the Nazarites. The concept of "the desert" also held significance in Jewish spirituality in both a negative and a positive way. On the negative side, it was the land cursed by God as evidenced by the absence of water and life and therefore thought to be the home of the demons. But the desert also has a positive spiritual notion. This is the place where Jacob and Moses encountered God. It is also the place where the Law was presented to the people and the place they wandered for forty years waiting on God. This active kind of spiritual geography was on the minds of those first Christian ascetics who had their own desert experiences. The New Testament also has some ascetic wilderness features. John the Baptist came from the wilderness and was a desert dweller. Jesus was called out in the wilderness where he was challenged by the devil before he began his own ministry. All of these biblical examples played a part in shaping the new ascetic movement in Christianity.

As Christianity appeared to be more accommodating to more and more persons, and as it became less a religion of the persecuted, these ascetics thought that the church was losing its rigorous counter-cultural edge. Since spiritual warfare was no longer happening in the arenas and amphitheaters around the Empire, early Christian ascetics decided to take the offensive in spiritual warfare. In this way they believed that they were keeping alive the radical faith of the martyrs and maintaining the intense nature of the Christian faith. These early monks and nuns did not see themselves as innovators, but as individuals trying to keep alive the idea of a close community of faith by taking on the same spiritual powers the martyrs had faced during the periods of persecution. They saw themselves keeping alive the spirit of the martyrs by dying daily through the rigors of their ascetic disciplines. Here we see the beginnings of a simple movement that would grow to be a very powerful force in the Christian church in the centuries to follow.

The ascetic or monastic (coming from the Greek term *monos* for "solitary one") tradition took on several forms, but is best characterized by looking at two variants. Some of the first monks were hermits who went into the wilderness or desert to live alone for years. One of the first of these we have on record is Antony of Alexandria, Egypt. In the year A.D. 270 after hearing a sermon on Mat. 19:21 to go and sell all of his possessions, he took this call literally. He sold all of his family's belongings and found a place for his sister in a religious community (possibly the first Christian community for women?). He then pursued his call in the Egyptian desert. We hear of this legend in the famous *Life of Antony* by Athanasius, the bishop of Alexandria.[21] This work was an influential force in the conversion of Augustine a century later.

At the same time that we see the flourishing of the monastic tradition, Christianity devoted more time to self-definition and explanation of its beliefs. With Constantine's rise to power, the church challenged those who they believed had heretical views while refining their own understandings of the faith. Some of the greatest theological writers of the church now had time and support to develop their ideas. In response to heresy, the church began to call ecumenical councils, bringing together leaders from all across the Empire to hammer out orthodox views. One of the biggest challenges to the church at the beginning of the fourth century was the threat of Arianism. This was a movement that had started in Alexandria, when an elder (Arius) in the church there proposed the notion that Jesus was not fully divine. This idea took hold

---

21 Athanasius, *The Life of Antony*, Trans. Robert Gregg (Mahwah, NJ: Paulist Press, 1980).

in a number of churches around the Empire. When Constantine sought unification in the church to help with the Empire, he found a divided church. In May of A.D. 325 he called the first church council to meet at his summer palace in Nicaea. The church leaders debated there for several weeks before affirming the concept that Jesus was fully divine and co-eternal with God the Father. This was affirmed in one of the first creeds developed for the entire church. The Nicene Creed, the conclusion of this council meeting, became the defining statement of Christian belief. There would be several creeds after this, but this was the creed that most Christians point to when looking for a complete but concise statement of Christian beliefs.

This was a time when theological speculation and exploration were expanding. Some very significant writers published their ideas during this second period of Christian history. These are often referred to as the Church Fathers, and their writings would have impacts on the church that lasted for centuries. While there were numerous writers during this time, we will only recognize a few. In the east you have the fullest explanation of the doctrine of the Trinity by a group of three men known as the Cappadocian fathers. Cappadocia was a region in central Asia Minor (Turkey today) where Christianity had great success. Three very important bishops there spent much of their time shepherding their flocks partly through their theological writings. Basil of Caesarea (A.D. 330-379), his school friend Gregory of Nazianzus (A.D. 329-389), and Basil's young brother, Gregory of Nyssa (A.D. 335-395) worked out a way to articulate an understanding of the doctrine of the Trinity that has stood the test of time. Their ministry and writings were foundational to the ideas and concepts promoted in the church from that point forward.

Augustine, bishop of Hippo in North Africa, becomes *the* theologian for western Christianity. Before Thomas Aquinas in the thirteenth century, no other Christian writer came close to rivaling his literary output and influence. Augustine, born in A.D. 354 in Thagaste, North Africa, grew up exposed to the best education the classical world could offer. He studied most of the greats but was especially influenced by Cicero and Virgil. He eventually became a teacher of rhetoric and lived for a time in Carthage, Rome, and Milan before returning to North Africa where he became the bishop of Hippo in A.D. 391. Over the course of his life, he embraced Manichean philosophy, astrology, and Neo-Platonism, along with other practices before his eventual conversion to Christianity. This journey was chronicled in his famous *Confessions*, written in A.D. 400. His eventual conversion after the prayerful efforts of his mother Monica and the preaching of Ambrose, bishop of Milan, was forever memorialized in this work. As bishop, Augustine is remembered for his many sermons, letters, and theological works. Besides his *Confessions*, he is remembered for his expansive work, *The City of God*, an apologetic for Christianity in response to the criticisms after the sack of the city of Rome in A.D. 410. Many in the Empire blamed the Christians for this devastating attack on the eternal city. Augustine gave a thorough historical and theological overview to demonstrate that Rome had problems long before this attack and that Christianity is actually the one real hope the world has.

With the deposing of the last ruler in Rome, Romulus Augustulus, in A.D. 476, we see the end of Roman rule in the West. And while that had a significant impact on much of society in Western Europe, the church persevered. In fact, the church became the sole social institution from the Roman period to continue into Medieval Europe. While the political entity of Rome came to end, much of its influence was carried on through the institution of the church. As we see the development of the Middle Ages, there was a growing synthesis of the Roman, Germanic, and Christian elements that shaped and defined the Medieval world.

## The World of Caesar and Christ Textual Glosses

### **Polybius (c. 200 – 118 B.C.), *Histories***

Born in Megapolis, Greece, Polybius spent most of his life in Rome. Although very active in politics, and well-acquainted with the leading politicians of the day, his main interest was the study of Roman history. In particular, Polybius was interested in exploring the reasons for Rome's unprecedented success, as evidenced by its progress from a city-state to a world empire in less than fifty-three years. But like the great Greek historian Thucydides before him, Polybius also went beyond a mere description of events in search for a pattern or form to historical change. The task of the historian, Polybius believed, is to provide a general and comprehensive scheme of events in order to enlighten current and future officials regarding the best courses of action to take under given circumstances.

Focusing on the characteristics of the Roman state during the second Punic War against Carthage (218-201 B.C.), Polybius looked for ways that would prevent Rome from following the fate that had destroyed the powerful civilizations of Troy, Assyria, Persia, Greece, Macedonia, and Carthage: Would Rome ultimately collapse as well? Are dissolution and destruction, and not continuity and political stability, the dominant forces in history? History, Polybius concludes, exhibits an inescapable cyclical pattern. Its movement is always toward change and instability. The political search for order, therefore, is ultimately fruitless.

Following closely the works of Plato and Aristotle, Polybius distinguished between three legitimate forms of government and their corresponding corrupted counterparts. The legitimate forms of government were kingship, aristocracy, and democracy. Their corrupted counterparts were tyranny, oligarchy, and ochlocracy or mob rule. For Polybius, it is possible to identify a general pattern in the movement of history since these different forms of government always follow one another in the same predictable sequence. The historical cycle begins when kingships arise as a response to chaos. Natural disasters and other threats to social existence force the strongest to impose their will to restore social order. In time, monarchs abandon the demands of justice and become tyrants: rulers who no longer govern for the sake of the common good but rather seek their own particular good. As tyrants become increasingly ruthless and their rule intolerable, a small group of enlightened individuals rises up against the tyrant and establishes an aristocracy, or rule by the wise. In time, however, aristocracies also begin to degenerate when the pursuit of wealth replaces the order of justice as the overriding goal of leadership. Gradually, then, aristocracies degenerate into oligarchies, or rule by a few. A time eventually comes when the abuse perpetrated by the wealthy few to increase their privileges reaches a point where the people have no other option but to rise up and establish democracies in order to pursue freedom and restore equality. Yet, democracies are also unstable. Ultimately, the masses resort to violence and rioting to prevent the wealthy from recovering their previous dominance. Gradually, democracy degenerates into ochlocracy or mob rule, producing a situation of generalized chaos, and thereby bringing the historical cycle once more to its starting point.

In light of this analysis, why was Rome so uniquely successful? What stage of the historical cycle did Rome occupy? Polybius argues that beyond military or economic power, the real source of Rome's strength lay in its mixed political regime. Rather than a pure form of government, the Roman constitution contained elements of each type: the monarchic element through the Consuls; the aristocratic element through the Senate; and the democratic element through the Assembly. This mixed regime allowed the representation of all social classes and provided a mechanism of checks and balances to prevent any social group from unduly extending its power. Through this mixed regime, Rome had managed to create a relatively stable society and postpone the inevitable changes of history. The mixed constitutional system allowed Rome to delay the disastrous fate that befell other civilizations. But in the end, no society can endure forever. Rome, in Polybius's view, would also eventually succumb to the movement of history. Polybius already witnessed symptoms pointing to the decline of Rome.

From an anthropological perspective, Polybius's philosophy of history raises crucial philosophical questions: Is human history governed by fate? If so, what is the relationship between fate and human freedom? Is human freedom reduced to just postponing or delaying what fate has already decreed as inevitable? Are instability and chaos the dominant forces of history and not order and justice? Does evil, then, ultimately prevail? Are there laws that govern the movement of history? If so, are these laws immanent or do they have a transcendent origin in the mind of God? If God has a plan for his creation (providence), which ends in the reign of truth, goodness, and justice, what role does human freedom play in His ultimate victory over the forces of evil and injustice? What is the relationship between God's providence and human freedom?

These are just some of the questions that Polybius's philosophy of history invites us to consider. These questions also were at the center of Augustine's thought, an author we encounter in The World of Christendom and Islam. In the *City of God*, Augustine provides an answer to these issues that will greatly impact the subsequent development of Western thought: Christ is the center of history. The significance of human events, therefore, is measured from their movement toward or away from Christ (*ordo amoris*–the order of love).

**New Testament**

The concept of "new" implies an old. The twenty-seven books that comprise the New Testament depend upon the history and traditions of the Hebrew Scriptures or what Christians call the Old

Testament. This "new" collection of Scripture tells of the life, death, and resurrection of Jesus of Nazareth along with the beginnings of the first Christians. While the sixty-six books of Scripture are divided into these two parts, both are still necessary to the biblical metanarrative and how God is at work "reconciling the world." (2 Cor. 5:18) These twenty-seven books are made up of a variety of different genres. Within these twenty-seven books, written in *Koine* Greek, the reader finds Gospels, history, epistles, and even apocalyptic literature.[22] The entire focus of these writings is on Jesus and how to live a life following Jesus.

The question of how we have these twenty-seven books, no more or less, is an intriguing discussion to say the least. In an effort to safeguard the Christian faith, there was an effort to delineate a list of writings to be considered inspired and therefore authoritative. The development of the New Testament canon (from a Greek word literally meaning "measure" or those books that "measured up") was a process that lasted for several centuries.[23] Shortly after A.D. 100, the fourfold Gospel, Acts, and ten of Paul's letters were used almost universally in public worship. Works that were disputed for a time included Hebrews, II Peter, II and III John, James, and Jude. In Athanasius's Easter letter, addressed to the churches in his Alexandrian diocese in A.D. 367, we see for the first time a church official listing the twenty-seven books to be used by the churches for teaching and edification. While this process appears rather random, there had been many discussions that led up to this final list of twenty-seven that was then confirmed at several church councils after 367.

In all of these discussions, there was a common core of criteria used in determining which books to include and which ones to exclude. First and foremost was the apostolicity of a text. Was

22 Stephen Harris, *Understanding the Bible* (Mountain View, CA: Mayfield Publishing Co., 2000), 351.

23 Ibid., 34.

it written by an apostle? This immediately gave credibility to a writing. Next was the question of antiquity or age. When was the text purported to have been written? Texts written earlier had a better chance than later writings. Anything written after the first century did not stand much of a chance. Third was the concept of catholicity. Was a text found to be widely circulated and used throughout the churches? Did this text prove to be useful in teaching the churches in which it was read and studied? Did it have universal appeal in the churches? Last was the idea of orthodoxy. Did a text teach in accord with the basic beliefs of the church, especially related to the teachings about Christ, or did it prove to be divisive? Works that created more friction than harmony in Christian communities were not acceptable for the canon. So the twenty-seven books that we now know as the New Testament were thought to be apostolic, antique, catholic, and orthodox.[24] This twenty-seven-book canonical collection was confirmed at a council in Rome in A.D. 382, a council in Carthage in A.D. 419 as well as the Council of Trent in 1545.

## Gospels

The Gospels are the only real sources for the life, death, and resurrection of Jesus. But why four books by four different authors? Would a singular authoritative text make more sense for such an important historical figure? Each of the Gospels was written to a particular audience and to emphasize different ideas. The early church recognized the diversity of these Gospels and left them unique to better relate to the diverse world where they were being read. The Gospels, while similar to some of the historical works in the Old Testament, are composed in a rather distinctivee style. There is nothing similar to these in the ancient world. They are a rare combination of history, polemic, and biography. The first

24 Ibid., 41-44.

three Gospels are much closer in content than the Gospel of John. For this reason, they (Matthew, Mark, Luke) are referred to as the synoptic Gospels. Synoptic is a Greek word that means "to see together."[25] Because they are so similar and share so much of the same material, they are joined together. The book of John on the other hand presents things in a completely different way and even changes the chronology of some of the events to emphasize different ideas.

Mark is the first Gospel written. It was written around A.D. 70, and because it appears to be first it is thought that Mark created the Gospel genre.[26] Biblical scholars consider it the first written Gospel since it is shorter than all the others, and both Matthew and Luke use it as a source. In fact, it appears that all of Mark is found in both Gospels, implying that they were already aware of Mark when they wrote their Gospels. Mark was thought to be a close companion of Peter, and while not an apostle was considered a good source representing Peter's perspective as an eyewitness to Jesus's life. Mark is most noted for what is called the "Messianic secret."[27] Mark portrays Jesus as keeping his messiahship a secret. Whenever he heals, he warns those he healed not to tell anyone. Mark portrays Jesus as gradually revealing who he is, culminating with Peter's confession.

Matthew was written in A.D. 85. Matthew uses Mark as a source along with other shared material from Luke that is not found in Mark. In addition to these two sources, Matthew also has his own material. The author is believed to be the apostle Matthew. This Gospel is written for a Jewish audience. This can be seen in a number of ways. The ancestry of Jesus is traced back to Abraham, father of the Jews, whereas Luke traces Jesus back to Adam. Matthew often uses the title "Son of David" for Jesus as

25 Ibid., 355.

26 Ibid., 364.

27 J. Benton White & Walter Wilson, *From Adam to Armageddon: A Survey of the Bible*, (Belmont, CA: Wadsworth, 2001), 147.

well as presenting him as the new Moses. Matthew also utilizes Old Testament prophecy more than the other Gospels in his effort to demonstrate that Jesus is the fulfillment of those prophecies. Matthew also structures his book into five divisions to match the five books of Moses in the Torah.

Luke was written around A.D. 90. Luke also depends on Mark as a source as well as sharing some material with Matthew while also having his own material. Many traditions believe that Luke was a doctor and a companion of Paul on some of his journeys. The Gospel of Luke is the most Gentile of the Gospels; it was clearly written for a non-Jewish audience. He dedicates his Gospel to a Theophilus, (Luke 1:3) a name that could be a reference to a particular person by that name, or can be simply translated as "one who loves God." In this vein Luke focuses more on humanity as a whole, tracing Jesus's lineage back to Adam, the father of all humanity. Luke also seems to have a more social focus on the ministry of Jesus, reflecting his work with social outcasts. He particularly emphasizes the role of women like no other Gospel writer. There is a greater interest in children also. Luke is the only Gospel to refer to the childhood of Jesus and John the Baptist. This Gospel also is concerned more with the issue of poverty and wealth than the other Gospels.

John, the fourth Gospel, was written around A.D. 100. It is clearly different than the three synoptic Gospels. The pattern of events and the chronology of events in Jesus's life differ from what is found in the first Gospels.[28] The beginning prologue is more of a philosophical statement about the origins of Jesus with the concept of *logos*. In the Greco-Roman world, and particularly in Stoicism, the *logos* is thought to be that rational force that created and orders the universe. Here John appears to be identifying Jesus with a concept that would have deep meaning in the first century Roman world. John continues his Gospel by making use of great

28 Harris, *Understanding the Bible*, 413.

themes such as life, light, and love rather than following a narrative like the other Gospels.

### The Acts of the Apostles

The Acts of the Apostles tells the story of the apostles and their ministries after Christ's resurrection. Luke, the author of the Gospel, is considered the same author of the book of Acts as he makes mention of his earlier book (the Gospel of Luke) and the dedication to Theophilus. While this book is not exactly history, it is closer to this genre than any other book in the New Testament.[29] Acts is considered an important source for the early Christian church and its growth and expansion. It starts with the story of Pentecost when the Apostles received the Holy Spirit's anointing, empowering them to begin their ministries. Acts is also the source for the early back-story on Paul, who had been known as Saul. After Paul began his ministry, we are introduced to a transformative event in regards to the interaction between Peter and Paul. In Chapter 15 the two disagreed over the place of Jewish practices in the new faith and the requirements for new converts from the Gentile world. The debate was settled in Paul's favor: Gentiles were not required to be circumcised, nor abide by Jewish requirements. The book of Acts also traces the various missionary journeys of Paul, first to Asia Minor, then to Europe as he journeys to Greece on his second trip. His travels finally concluded in Rome where he traveled as a prisoner for his faith. The book ends with Paul preaching to all those he encountered during his last two years while in prison in Rome.

### The Letters of Paul

Several of Paul's letters or epistles are actually the earliest written Christian texts. Paul wrote his letters to various communities and persons even before the Gospels appeared in written form. His

29 Ibid., 447.

letter to the Galatians, most likely his earliest, was written around A.D. 49. Next were his two letters to the Thessalonians written in A.D. 51 and A.D. 52, respectively. His later works include the letters to Titus in A.D. 65 as well as his two letters to Timothy written in A.D. 65 and A.D. 67.[30] His letters were all written in the style of an epistle, a formulaic style that letters in the first century followed. Paul wrote some to entire faith communities, and some to individual persons.

Who was Paul? Paul, or Saul (his name before his conversion), was originally from Tarsus, a town in southern Asia Minor. He traveled to Jerusalem around the age of fifteen to be trained as a rabbi. This would have placed him in the city at the time of Jesus's crucifixion. Shortly after that, he took up the crusade against the Christians and was on a journey to Damascus to persecute Christians when he had a transformative experience with Christ. He was a well-educated, practicing Jew before his conversion. After his conversion he spent some time in Arabia in preparation for his ministry.[31] No details of this are provided anywhere, but it appears it was an important preparation time for him (Galatians 1:16-17). Paul's ministry then began in Damascus as he returned there briefly before going to Jerusalem to spend time with the apostles, especially Peter. After winning the approval of the church in Jerusalem to preach to the Gentiles, he went to Antioch where he ministered for a time before being sent on to Asia Minor and his first missionary journey. In the midst of his travels, he wrote and received letters from the various communities where he had visited and spent time. It is widely accepted that he wrote 1 Thessalonians, Galatians, 1 and 2 Corinthians, Philemon, Philippians, and Romans. Other letters attributed to him but with some questions over his authorship include 2 Thessalonians, Colossians, Ephesians, 1 and 2 Timothy,

30 Ibid., 465-66.

31 White & Wilson, *Adam to Armegeddon*, 119.

and Titus.[32] Hebrews is also a book he is credited with writing by some early sources, but this view has fallen out of favor.

**Romans**

The letter Paul wrote around A.D. 56 to the church in Rome was directed to a community he did not found. It appears that this community had reached out to him, and he was responding to their request. This letter is considered to be the best and fullest representation of Pauline theology. The community in Rome, having likely been founded by Peter, had a strong Jewish influence in its membership. Paul spends a good deal of the early part of the letter discussing Judaism and the Law as they related to the church. He acknowledges the place of the Jews in God's grand plan for redemption while stating why he believes that many of the traditional requirements of the Law were not binding on Gentile Christians.[33] The views he presents here in the first few chapters of the book become the basis for much of how Christianity thinks about its relationship to the Jews for years to come. In the end Paul seems to affirm that God has not rejected the Jews, and that he still loves them as his chosen people. But it remains a bit of a mystery in Paul's writings. Around the twelfth chapter of the book, Paul takes up the issue of ethics and the character and behavior of the Christian believer. For Paul, the overall guiding principle for the Christian should always be love. In Rom. 12:9-10 he says, "Let love be genuine; hate what is evil, hold fast to what is good; love one another with mutual affection; outdo one another in showing honor." He concludes the letter by stating his desire to come and visit them personally. He then singles out several persons for praise in the final chapter—most notable are several exemplary women whom Paul encourages the church in Rome to welcome and support. In the first verse of chapter sixteen, he mentions Phoebe, whom he

32 Harris, *Understanding the Bible*, 465.

33 Ibid., 481.

calls a "Deacon of the church at Cenchreae." This is the only place any person is mentioned with a church title in this way in Paul's writings, and he gives her high praise in suggesting the church help her in her ministry. He closes this letter with his customary benediction blessing of encouragement.

## I Corinthians

The city of Corinth was an important crossroad on the isthmus that connects the Peloponnesus of Greece with the mainland. It was a very cosmopolitan city with lots of different cultures. The Romans had actually destroyed Greek Corinth in 146 B.C., but it was rebuilt by Julius Caesar in 44 B.C. The church in Corinth credited Paul with its founding. He had a much more personal bond to this community and knew the people there much better than those in the Roman church. Based on internal evidence in both 1 Corinthians and 2 Corinthians, it appears that there were other correspondences between Paul and the Corinthian church. This first letter was probably written around A.D. 53, between his first and second visits to the church. The overall intent of the letter was to unify a church full of strife and division. Paul was aware of several very particular issues that were causing contention, and he answered these directly. He takes on such issues as the division over who should be the leader in the church, sexual immorality, and lawsuits against other Christians.[34] After addressing these concerns, he responds more directly to questions being asked of him on topics like the eating of meat offered to idols. He also is concerned with some very practical matters like marriage, how one acts and dresses in worship, and how to respect the gifts of the Holy Spirit. Much of what he has to say at this point is predicated on his belief that the second coming of Christ is immanent. Therefore marriage is discouraged, along with having children. In his mind the time

34 Ibid., 472.

is growing short, and therefore Christians need to be preparing for this coming event. His goal of unity is best expressed in the thirteenth chapter where he develops his famous "love" poem. In this chapter he states that in the end nothing Christians know, say, or do matters if they are not doing it out of love. He then tries to settle the debate over the place of tongues in the church at the expense of other gifts. Finally he concludes in a similar fashion as all his letters. He mentions several persons of importance whom they should look for and help whenever they can, concluding with another prayerful benediction.

Many of the other letters of Paul deal with similar issues. The challenge with reading these Pauline letters is how to interpret them. On the one hand, they are written to very specific audiences and circumstances. Yet on the other hand, they are meant for all of the church. When we read them today, do we see them simply as admonitions to a particular place and time, and look for general principles? Or do we try to apply the very specific statements found in these works to our own situations? I think it has to be a bit of both. In some statements, I believe Paul is speaking to a very particular place. Yet in other places, he seems to be speaking to all Christians. The church has wrestled with these questions for centuries and will continue to do so. Do we not allow women to speak at any time? Do we restrict the wearing of makeup, jewelry, and lace? Should we require slaves to obey their masters? In the end I think we have to consider these statements in their context first before we try to find ways to apply them in our own day and time. As Preben Vang, a friend and fellow educator once said, "Let's talk about Jesus first and then understand Paul and the rest of the New Testament in light of Him and the Gospel stories about his life and teaching." I believe this is a helpful hermeneutic as one begins to read and study the letters of Paul.

**Lucretius, *On the Nature of Things***

Lucretius (91-51 B.C.) was the leading Roman Epicurean philosopher. Since most of the voluminous work of Epicurus (342-270 B.C.) is lost (excluding selected fragments and letters), it is through Lucretius's *On the Nature of Things* (*De Rerum Natura*), written some two hundred years after the death of Epicurus, that we have a complete and orderly exposition of the Epicurean system. Written as a philosophical poem, *On the Nature of Things* is also one of the greatest monuments in Latin poetry.

The main goal of the Epicurean system is to lead human beings from emotional distress to peace of mind. For this philosophical school, this indispensable goal of human happiness can only be achieved through a correct understanding of physics which, in turn, unveils the true nature of gods and human existence. Epicurean physics, therefore, has a practical aim as it not only seeks to provide an understanding of physical reality but also to disprove those ideas about gods and the immortality of the human soul that stand in the way of human happiness. Lucretius, indeed, follows closely his mentor Epicurus in blaming religious belief and fear of eternal punishment for the psychological distress that impedes the serenity that human beings need for their happiness.

Based on the atomistic theories of Democritus, originally developed in the fifth century B.C., Epicureanism argues that all reality is reducible to simple matter or matter-in-motion. Everything we find in reality is composed of little seeds or atoms of homogeneous matter and empty space. The world came into existence after an accidental collision of atoms. Human beings, therefore, are not parts of a created or purposeful order caused or ruled by God but are rather, like everything else that exists, the accidental product of the collision of atoms. Since all phenomena—including the soul—can be explained through the mechanical motions of atoms, there is no need to have any recourse to divine intervention. In the Epicurean materialistic conception of nature, there is no room left for the activity of gods: "This terror then and darkness of mind must be dispelled not by the rays of the sun and glittering shafts of day, but by the aspect and the law of nature; the warp of whose design we shall begin with this first principle, nothing is ever gotten out of nothing by divine power."[35]

While not denying the existence of gods, Epicureans believed that gods, by their very nature, cannot have their blessedness marred by trouble. Gods live in eternal peace, completely untroubled by human affairs and without any interest, therefore, to intervene in them. The evil that afflicts human life is simply irreconcilable with any idea of divine guidance in the universe. The only function of gods is to serve as model for peace of mind.

For the Epicureans, this materialistic conception of reality combined with their description of the gods provides a truly liberating ethical doctrine insofar as they dispel the chief obstacles to peace of mind: fear of death, fear of gods, and fear of eternal punishment. Fear of death disappears as death is nothing but the cessation of physical motion. Fear of gods disappear since, even though they may exist, they are neither interested in nor do they interfere with the affairs of men. And fear of eternal punishment also vanishes since there is no spiritual life after death. With the death of the body, human life simply ceases to exist: "Death therefore to us is nothing, concerns us not a jot, since the nature of the mind is proved to be mortal[36] [...] Why bemoan and bewail death? [...] Why not then take thy departure like a guest filled with life, and with resignation, thou fool, enter upon untroubled rest?"[37]

Liberated from these fears and informed by the truths of materialism, the wise man can achieve that state of serenity and peace

35 Lucretius, *On the Nature of Things* (Book I, lines 149-152) in Whitney J. Oates ed., *The Stoic and Epicurean Philosophers – The Complete Extant Writings of Epicurus, Epictetus, Lucretius, Marcus Aurelius* (New York: Random House, 1940), 71.

36 Ibid., Book III, lines 831-32, 131.

37 Ibid., Book III, lines 931-35, 133.

which is most conducive to his own happiness. Pleasure, which consists in the absence of pain, is the beginning and end of living happily. This pleasure is to be found preeminently in serenity of soul, a pleasure that endures throughout a lifetime. Happiness, therefore, resides not in the bodily pleasures of the moment but in a life of serenity free from fears and anxiety. For Epicurean ethics, human beings need to scale down their desires, overcome useless fears and, above all, turn to the pleasures of the mind, which have the highest degree of permanence. The simple life, devoid of political involvement and excessive passion, is the highest good and the path that leads from emotional turmoil to peace of mind. The wise man will avoid participating in politics since such participation can only disturb his peace of mind.

Many key ideas in Epicureanism have remained influential throughout the course of Western history. In our own days, once again we witness a widespread understanding of reality that focuses exclusively on material causes, dismissing as irrelevant questions about purpose or *telos*. Also, there is a prevalent understanding of human fulfillment that emphasizes individual autonomy, while seeking to exclude any relationship with or dependence on a Transcendent Being. In particular, many people in our days tend to agree with Lucretius's indictment of religion as the source of violence, ignorance, fear, and human suffering: "Again and again our foe, religion, has given birth to deeds sinful and unholy[38] [...] So great the evils to which religion could prompt![39] In this light, it is important to ponder on the spiritual void that Epicureanism leaves in the human heart, an emptiness that Christianity came to fill with its promise of redemption, salvation, and hope.

38 Ibid., Book I, lines 82-83, 70.

39 Ibid., (Book I, line 100), 71.

**Cicero (106-43 B.C.), *On Duties***

Cicero was Rome's finest orator, one of its greatest philosophers, and a leading statesman. Cicero lived during the last years of the Roman Republic. After Caesar's rise to power, which Cicero vehemently opposed, he retired from politics and wrote most of his treatises and letters. One of his greatest skills as a writer was his ability to present the moral doctrine of the Greeks to Roman readers in a clear style. When Caesar was murdered in 44 B.C., Cicero briefly returned to politics and denounced Marc Anthony, one of Caesar's successors. Marc Anthony ordered his soldiers to kill Cicero in 43 B.C.

Much of Cicero's writings were driven by his concern for the Republic and his desire to salvage it from the rise of despotism, which he thought would destroy the civic virtues and the rule of law. *On Duties* is the philosophical treatise on moral duty that Cicero wrote in the last year of his life as a letter in three parts to his son Marcus, who lived in Athens and studied philosophy at the time. This letter, although addressed to his son, appeals to a much wider audience as it is intended for all those with governmental responsibilities. Its overriding theme is how to protect and preserve civic virtues against the rise of an autocrat who puts his self-interest above the interests of the common good. In this text, Cicero looks to reconcile our duty to ourselves with our obligations to faith, family, fellow citizens, and homeland.

In *On Duties*, Cicero explores the dynamics of inner struggle in our moral experience, recalling the "civil war" image that Socrates uses in his response to Glaucon's challenge against the notion that virtue leads to happiness (Plato, *The Republic*, Book II). Ultimately, therefore, the overriding question in *On Duties* is "Why be good?" In our moral experience, we are torn between opposite poles. On one side, a part of us pulls us toward our desires, passions, fears, drives: in sum, toward what seems desirable, beneficial, or advantageous. At the same time, however, we also experience a counter-pull, something in us that pulls us in the direction of what is true, toward a reality that transcends our passions, our physical needs, and desires. This counter-pull draws us toward what is honorable, toward what is morally right.

We could interpret our moral struggle as the duty to renounce the beneficial—that which seems more attractive or desirable—for the sake of choosing what is right. Cicero, however, argues that this is an erroneous perspective: what is honorable (morally right) is always what is most beneficial. In other words, there should be no opposition in our moral deliberation between the beneficial and the honorable. This argument applies to our moral life as individuals, but Cicero was particularly thinking about politics. Some fifteen hundred years later, Machiavelli gave philosophical expression to the opposite argument: in politics, the ends justify the means. Although this is an over-simplification of Machiavelli's thought, nowadays many people agree with the Machiavellian notion that a ruler must be willing to do whatever it takes (even if dishonorable) in order to preserve order (the beneficial). *On Duties* is one of the greatest texts to challenge Machiavelli's position. Cicero's main argument is that the dishonorable can never be beneficial.

Every honorable action, Cicero argues, is always related to the virtues (perfections) that correspond to our human nature. These virtues are practical wisdom (prudence), justice, fortitude, and temperance: "Everything that is honorable arises from one of four parts: it is involved either with the perception of truth and with ingenuity; or with preserving fellowship among men, with assigning to each his own, and with faithfulness to agreements one has made; or with the greatness and strength of a lofty and unconquered spirit; or with order and limit in everything that is said and done (modesty and restraint are included here)."[40]

For Cicero, the nature of a being derives from its *telos* (end). Hence, "natural" is the most accomplished and perfected state of a

40 Cicero, *On Duties*, ed. M.T. Griffin and E.M. Atkins (New York: Cambridge

being. An action is honorable or morally right when it reflects the virtues (perfections) that belong to our nature as human beings. Conversely, to act dishonorably is to choose contrary to nature—unnaturally—insofar as such an act is destructive of our very being. The person whose reason is perfected through the practice of virtues lives the best possible life for a human being. Anything dishonorable falls short of what corresponds to our nature as human beings. Nowadays, people often say things like "it is only 'natural' for teenagers to be messy." But Cicero argues the opposite. A dishonorable action reflects an absence of being, a lack of a perfection that ought to be there given our human nature, that is, given the perfections we ought to have in light of our *telos*. Hence, the truly beneficial is that which is in conformity with the perfection of our being. Something apparently beneficial but dishonorable can only be destructive of our being. Cheating, for instance, may appear beneficial to a student who wishes to obtain a good grade with minimum effort. Cicero, however, would argue that such benefit is only apparent since by cheating a student destroys his or her own self: he or she moves further away from what belongs to a human being by its very nature, by what a person is meant or called to be in accordance to his or her *telos*. For Cicero, therefore, following nature is to embrace the path of virtue as the truly beneficial.

The classical notion of "nature" as *telos* is radically opposed to the way in which the modern world understands this word. For modern thinking, "nature" conveys the idea of something primitive, raw, undeveloped, and innocent: in sum, the initial stage of being. In moral action, "natural" therefore is what comes easily and spontaneously, almost without reflection. For a modern thinker like Rousseau, moral goodness comes from what is "natural" in this way: evil comes from reflection and goodness from impulse. This notion is also at the core of a statement that many young people repeat today: "I have learned to accept myself the way I am." As

University Press, 1991), 7.

Christians, however, we are called to imitate Christ, to be Christ-like—*alter Christus, ipse Christus*. The classical understanding of nature as *telos* helps us realize (in a way that the modern definition of this concept does not) that to be like Christ is not the obliteration of ourselves but, rather, the full actualization of our very being. When we follow Christ, we are not surrendering our self-identity. By virtue of that great mystery of human existence, Christ is the realization and fulfillment of our very being since, as Augustine explains: "Christ, you are more inward than my most inward part and higher than the highest element within me."[41]

### Stoicism: Epictetus, Marcus Aurelius, and Seneca

For the Greeks, the individual was inconceivable apart from the life of the *polis*, the city-state. For both Plato and Aristotle, for instance, it was in the *polis* that the individual attained his end and lived the good life. As the former city-states were merged in a larger world, first through the reign of Alexander the Great and later as provinces of the Roman Empire, cosmopolitanism or the ideal of citizenship of the world came to the fore. But closely bound to the ideal of cosmopolitanism is individualism. As the life of the city-state broke down, the individual was cast adrift in an impersonal, unfamiliar, and unpredictable environment, alienated from those community attachments that had given people a sense of belonging and shared purpose. Stoicism looked to provide an answer to the problem of community and alienation that resulted from the decline of the city-state by offering an avenue to individual happiness in a world characterized by uncertainty. At the core of Stoicism is the belief that underlying the whole of reality in the universe there is a Divine Reason (*Logos*) that acts as a principle of order and goodness. As part of the universe, every human soul, free and slave, rich and poor, Greek, Roman and barbarian, shares in this *Logos* and is there-

41 Augustine. *Confessions*, trans. Henry Chadwick (Indianapolis: Hackett, 2006), Book III, Chap. VI, 11.

fore able to distinguish between moral and immoral acts. Through natural law, human beings have an awareness of what is and is not morally right, and can recognize and respect the dignity of others. To obey and live in accordance with natural law is the path to virtue and happiness. All human beings are fellow citizens of a cosmopolis and, thus, subject to the same moral obligations. To live in harmony with the *Logos* would give individuals the self-mastery and inner peace to resist life's misfortunes, the injustices inflicted by others, and the torment of their own passions.

Among the late Stoics, the most important were the slave Epictetus, the Spaniard Seneca, and the Roman Emperor Marcus Aurelius. For these thinkers, who witnessed how the moral degradation of the Roman Empire was gradually erasing all vestiges of the former ideals and traditions of the Republic, the primary task of the philosopher was to provide moral guidance so that individuals could achieve a certain spiritual and moral independence, and escape the horrors of worldly existence through an act of the will.

### Epictetus (A.D. c. 55- c. 135), *The Encheiridion* (The Handbook)

Epictetus of Hierapolis was at first a slave in the court of the Emperor Nero. When he became a freedman, he continued to live in Rome until Emperor Domitian expelled the philosophers around A.D. 90. It was then when Epictetus moved to Epirus and founded a school where he taught until his death.

The following passage from Epictetus's *Handbook* provides a succinct statement of his moral philosophy: "Do not seek to have events happen as you want them to, but instead want them to happen as they do happen, and your life will go well."[42] This passage comprises the two elements that Epictetus develops in his *Handbook* as essential to the moral growth of an individual: (i) to

42 Epictetus, *The Handbook*, trans. Nicholas P. White (Indianapolis: Hackett Publishing Company, 1983), 13.

trust the divine will as reflected in the order of "nature"; (ii) to learn to distinguish between things in our power and things not in our power. To enjoy health, to ward off death or disaster from himself or his loved ones, to acquire wealth and honors, to avoid injury from others or injustice from government—all this does not depend on the efforts of any individual man. We must accept all events of this kind without rebellion as being the expression of the Divine Will: "Remember that you are an actor in a play, which is as the playwright wants it to be: short if he wants it short, long if he wants it long. If he wants you to play a beggar, play even this part skillfully, or a cripple, or a public official, or a private citizen. What is yours is to play the assigned part well. But to choose it belongs to someone else."[43]

Indeed, for Epictetus, "Just as a target is not set up to be missed, in the same way nothing bad by nature happens in the world."[44] Hence, in the drama of our lives, it is God or the principle of reason (Logos) who determines how each individual is situated in history. Wisdom, therefore, consists in recognizing one's role in this drama and then performing the part well. As individuals, Epictetus insists, we must develop great indifference to those things over which we have no control. This applies even when a loved one dies: "Did your child die? It was given back. Did your wife die? She was given back."[45] Thus, Epictetus continues, "Death is nothing dreadful (or else it would have appeared dreadful to Socrates), but instead the judgment about death that it is dreadful—*that* is what is dreadful."[46]

As actors in a play, we have no control over the story or its plot. But the one thing that the actor can control is his own attitude and emotions. If a person manages to resist sadness, frustration, anger,

43 Ibid., 16

44 Ibid., 19

45 Ibid., 14

46 Ibid., 13

and other emotions regarding events that are outside his power, and rather retains that serenity and inner peace that can always remain under his control, the individual reaches a state of *apathy* which, far from indifference, is the mark of a wise and pious man.

From a Christian perspective, there is something ultimately unfulfilling about Stoic philosophy, despite its valuable ethical advice. Christ, we recall, cried when Lazarus died. Can we ever attain that state of apathy which Epictetus recommends? Is it even desirable? And yet, as Christians, are we not called to remain joyful and trust the will of God? What does Epictetus miss about the human condition?

**Seneca (4 B.C. – A.D. 65), *On Mercy***

Born in Cordoba in southern Spain, Seneca served as tutor and minister to the Emperor Nero. After Nero accused him of participating in a conspiracy against the throne, Seneca was forced to commit suicide.

Like other Stoics, Seneca focused on the practical side of philosophy and ethics rather than with theoretical investigations. For Seneca, philosophy should serve as the means to the acquirement of virtue. A central theme in his moral theory is that every man has the power to be virtuous if he only *wills* to do so. Compared to other Stoics like Epictetus and Marcus Aurelius, however, Seneca does seem to offer less strict, more tempered ethical advice. Seneca recognizes that moral virtue comes after much effort and struggle, and, thus, it is not likely to come by a sudden conversion. Typically, therefore, there are three preparatory stages in the path toward virtue: (i) abandoning some—but not all—sins; (ii) renouncing all evil passions, but admitting that one is still prone to occasional relapse; (iii) escaping the possibility of relapse, but still lacking confidence or trust in one's own wisdom.

Seneca wrote *On Mercy* for the young emperor Nero at the start of his principate. In this text, Seneca tries to admonish Nero on how to conduct his rule, underlying the need for mercifulness in all his dealings. This fact is significant because it introduces a concept that is quite unique in the history of political thought. Seneca says that a ruler must guarantee "security deep and abundant," "law raised above all violations of law," and "supreme liberty in want of nothing save the license to ruin itself." [47] In other words, Seneca begins by identifying three functions of government that are widely regarded as essential: order, justice, and freedom. However, Seneca goes one step further and argues that mercy stands above these three goals as the highest moral obligation for a ruler.

This argument calls for reflection. Although mercy is not an obligation that comes immediately to mind when we think of temporal rulers, it is one of the highest attributes that we recognize in Christ as king of kings. For Seneca, the way in which the gods govern their creation is the model for temporal rulers. According to Seneca, the importance of mercy derives from what truly constitutes the common good. Obviously, the common good demands from government the guarantee of order and justice, as well as the protection of individual freedom. But the promotion of the common good, Seneca argues, demands much more: the ideal community is characterized by the greatest possible concord among its citizens or, in other words, by relationships of friendship and by solidarity. The ruler, says Seneca, "is the bond which holds the commonwealth together."[48] There cannot be friendship among citizens who see each other with suspicion, derision, or even fear. Goodness is the only ground for friendship. Mercy, therefore, is the essential quality of a ruler because it is the virtue that brings people together: "*Give the city an idea of itself as innocent, and it will be*. It will be the angrier with departures from the common sobriety, if

47 Seneca, *On Mercy*, eds. John M. Cooper and J.F. Procopé (New York: Cambridge University Press, 1995), 130.

48 Ibid., 133.

it sees that they are few. *It is dangerous, believe me, to show the city how great a majority the wicked are.*"[49]

In our days of information technology, we have instant news about events from every corner of the world. Most of the news we receive, however, describes horrible deeds. Higher ratings for news agencies seem to correlate with their ability to showcase what is most abhorrent, cruel, and despicable about human action. Seneca's reflections on the requirements of the common good invites us to ponder the factors that are perhaps contributing to the dissolution of community life and to the proliferation of crimes that were even unimaginable just a short time ago.

**Marcus Aurelius (A.D. 120-180), *The Meditations***

Roman Emperor from A.D. 161 to 180, Marcus Aurelius composed his *Meditations* (in the Greek language) in twelve books. Like Epictetus, Marcus Aurelius believed that an individual was not to be disturbed by any failure, provided the failure was due to circumstances beyond his control. As servant of the *Logos* or Reason which governs the universe, the goal in life is to attain an inner state of mind that allows us to live in accord with nature. An individual, therefore, must be eager to do his duty, yet remain indifferent to results beyond his control, while distrusting all those passions and emotions that may disturb his inner poise.

*The Meditations* is a noble book, but it has a certain sadness about it. The theme of death is pervasive throughout the book: "Death is not only a function of nature but beneficial to it."[50] For Marcus Aurelius, to gain the proper moral outlook on life, we must live under the perspective of death. The following passages are illustrative: "It is possible to depart from life at this moment.

49 Ibid., 153-54 (emphasis added).

50 Marcus Aurelius, *The Meditations,* trans. G.M.A. Grube (Indianapolis: Hackett, 1983), 15.15.

Have this thought in mind whenever you act, speak, or think"[51]; "The life of every man is short and yours is almost finished while you do not respect yourself but allow your happiness to depend on the souls of others"[52]; "You are a little soul carrying a corpse, as Epictetus says"[53]; "Altogether, human affairs must be regarded as ephemeral, and of little worth: yesterday sperm, tomorrow a mummy or ashes."[54]

Ultimately, Marcus Aurelius argues, we must have the humility to recognize our very small, almost insignificant role in the order of creation. Individuals try to change history, accomplish great deeds, "make a difference" as young people often say and, yet, the same reality always persists: "Consider, for the sake of argument, the times of Vespasian; you will see all the same things: men marrying, begetting children, being ill, dying, fighting wars, feasting, trading, farming, flattering, asserting themselves, suspecting, plotting, praying for the death of others, grumbling at their present lot, falling in love, hoarding, longing for consulships and kingships. But the life of those men no longer exists, anywhere. Then turn to the time of Trajan; again, everything is the same; and that life too is dead."[55]

This perspective, Marcus Aurelius argues, which focuses on the brevity of life and recognizes our insignificant role in the order of creation, is what allows us to grasp with humility the real value and worth of our individual moral actions. In his view, we must learn to accept our present lot with affection, and live piously and justly without thinking about the past and leaving the future to Providence: "[If] you prize only your directing mind and the divine within you, and are not afraid of ceasing to live, but are afraid of

51 Ibid., 14

52 Ibid., 13

53 Ibid., 34

54 Ibid., 35

55 Ibid., 31-32

never beginning to live in accord with nature, then you will be a man worthy of the universe which created you."[56]

Like Epictetus, Marcus Aurelius emphasizes the need to trust the *Logos*: "Everything which happens, is right."[57] But this willingness to place ourselves under the divine will remains incomplete unless it is animated by love: "There remains as characteristic of the good man that he loves and welcomes whatever happens to him and whatever his fate may bring, that he does not pollute the spirit within his breast or confuse it with a mass of impressions and imaginings, but preserves it blameless, modestly following the divine, saying nothing but what is true, doing nothing but what is just."[58]

As was the case for Epictetus, there is something lacking in Marcus Aurelius's moral philosophy from a Christian perspective. Marcus Aurelius focuses on self-examination and self-exhortation. However, perhaps this search for happiness within the individual's own soul leaves a void too wide between each individual and the all-pervading *Logos* or Reason. Man needs fellowship, and our need to seek fulfillment through the gift of ourselves to others is also at the very core of our humanity. Marcus Aurelius spoke of the brotherhood of man, but "brothers cannot live unto themselves alone and remain brothers."[59] It is interesting to reflect on the texts of Epictetus and Marcus Aurelius to find those elements of Stoic philosophy that were not rejected by the Christian tradition but rather developed and perfected.

56 Ibid., 122

57 Ibid., 27

58 Ibid., 24

59 See G.M.A. Grube, Introduction, xxii

## Publius Ovidius Naso, *The Metamorphoses* (circa 8 CE)[60]

Ovid was a few decades younger than Virgil. Ovid's life and works (like Virgil's) were influenced by the reign of Augustus, the first emperor of the Roman Empire. While Virgil's *Aeneid*, presumably commissioned by Augustus, established a mythology for the origin of the Roman Empire to equal the mythic origins of Ancient Greece, the tales of Ovid's *Metamorphoses* are a collection of fifty longer and approximately two hundred shorter tales; they all include changes or transformations of shape: people (mythical or human) change into animals, or trees, or flowers, or stones. The tales range from satire or parody to heroic saga to grotesque fantasies.

Ovid has had an outsized influence on literature and culture. Many people who don't know his name still know his plotlines. Of all the stories illustrating the fate of "star-crossed lovers," Shakespeare's *Romeo and Juliet* is probably the most well-known; Ovid's "Pyramus and Thisbe" provided a model. Furthermore, the meaning of words like "echo," "narcissus," and "nemesis" is enriched by the stories Ovid wove from the mythological personifications of these words. In addition to exerting tremendous literary influence, Ovid's stories also provide terminology for psychology and anthropology.

While the stories of his *Metamorphoses* are mostly adaptations of many of the myths the Romans borrowed from the Greeks, Ovid's versions provided the most important source of classical mythology for centuries. The work has been the source for many influential works of Western culture, inspiring artists, poets, and musicians. Writers and artists drawing from Ovid include the following: Dante, Boccaccio, Chaucer, Bruegel, Titian, Milton, Shakespeare, G. F. Händel, Kafka, and George Bernard Shaw.

But *The Metamorphoses* is an opportunity to discuss much more than the recurrence of plots or the relatedness of Western literature across time. In Ovid's writing, relations between and among humans and gods are driven by base instincts, and plots are driven

60 This gloss was written by Beate Rodewald and Elizabeth Stice.

by violence, very often rape. Sex is about power more than pleasure, and the enjoyment of it is almost exclusively the privilege of gods and men. These stories about the nature of the world, and how things came to be, treat injustice and abuse very routinely. But precisely because of his influence and the nature of his writings, Ovid provides the opportunity for worthwhile discussion.

Critics of the canon often accuse it of perpetuating outdated or offensive ideas and privileging the voices of dead, Western male authors whose writings center on the importance and perspective of people like themselves. This is indeed the nature of *The Metamorphosis* and its unvirtuous worldview.

However, it is important to note that the vast material's subsequent writers and artists spun off Ovid's stories provide more than simple repetitions of the same stories; for a long time, adaptations have engaged in critical re-castings of the old myths. Shaw's play *Pygmalion* (1914), for example, ends with a "Sequel" Shaw felt compelled to write after the first theatre productions of his play ignored his intention of having Eliza walk away from Professor Higgins's household. Professor Higgins taught Eliza–a simple working-class girl who sold flowers for a living–to speak "proper" English, or rather, the English spoken by the upper classes. Combining his views concerning class and gender, Shaw, who supported the suffragists movement, radically transforms the ovidian story of an artist who falls in love with the "ideal woman" he sculpted; Pygmalion's (the artist's) wish of having her come to life is granted in Ovid's version, and the story ends with the sculptor and his "artwork" as a couple.

*The Metamorphoses* invites us to reflect on what it means to read the canon. Reading the canon need not be the same as celebrating every book in it. Historians often say that history is about understanding the past, not excusing it. The same is true with the "great literature" of the past. Some books are in the canon because of their impact or because of their insight into the culture of their time. We do not have to embrace every author or every value we come across in the honors sequence. *The Metamorphoses* is also an opportunity to discuss the role of violence and misogyny in Western literature and culture. We can better understand the place of these things in the present if we have some awareness of their cultural origins and legacy.

### Virgil (70-19 B.C.), *The Aeneid*

At the request of Augustus (63 B.C. – A.D. 14), the first Roman Emperor, Virgil wrote the epic poem *The Aeneid* to glorify the Roman Empire and exalt Augustus's role in the creation of a world empire that would secure peace, security, and the rule of law. It was also Virgil's mission to tie the origins of Rome to Greek culture so that Romans would find a shared sense of identity and purpose in assimilating, preserving, and transmitting the Greek intellectual heritage. This propagandistic objective is undoubtedly a major characteristic of *The Aeneid.* Through Virgil's poem, Augustus hoped that Romans would learn that he was not just another victorious warlord but a man of destiny, fulfilling the divine mission of bringing peace and justice to the world.

*The Aeneid* is indeed an epic of national glory. Rome has a unique mission to fulfill, even greater than the great intellectual accomplishments of the Greeks since only Romans knew how to govern an empire: "Your mission, Roman, is to rule the world. / These will be your arts: to establish peace, / To spare the humbled, and to conquer the proud."[61] And Augustus is the divinely appointed ruler who brings Rome's mission to fulfillment:

> And here is the man promised to you,
>
> Augustus Caesar, born of the gods,
>
> Who will establish again a Golden Age

---

61 Virgil, *The Aeneid*, trans. Stanley Lombardo (Indianapolis: Hackett Publishing Company, 2005), Book VI, lines 1016-1018.

In the fields of Latium once ruled by Saturn

And will expand his dominion

Beyond the Indus and the Garamantes.[62]

*The Aeneid* recounts the tale of Aeneas and the founding of Rome. The first six books describe Aeneas's journey from Troy to Italy, in a manner reminiscent of Homer's *Odyssey*. The last six books deal with the wars and conquests in Italy, and are close to *The Iliad* in theme and style. *The Aeneid* is an epic poem of extraordinary literary beauty, but perhaps it would not have reached its status as a masterpiece in the canon of the Western tradition had it not transcended its political purpose. Virgil, indeed, does much more than provide a glorified mythical account of Roman history. By raising and exploring timeless questions about the meaning and purpose of human existence, *The Aeneid* is a work that invites and challenges us to deepen our own quest for answers. This is already evident from the very first lines of the poem, where Virgil invokes the muse and asks why sacrifice adds to the value of our moral deeds, and whether suffering is an inevitable experience in our relationship with the divine:

Muse, tell me why the Queen of Heaven

Was so aggrieved, her godhead so offended,

That she forced a man of faultless devotion

To endure so much hardship. Can there be

Anger so great in the hearts of gods on high?[63]

One of the most important anthropological themes in *The Aeneid* is the relationship between fate and freedom. The Latin word for fate (*fatum*) means "that which is said." *Fatum* is close

62 Ibid., Book VI, lines 939-944.

63 Ibid., Book I, lines 12-16.

in meaning to the Greek word *logos*, understood as order, intelligence, and purpose. A divine power informs the world and gives it structure and meaning. Jupiter is the *fatum/logos* of divine order. He has decreed that Aeneas will reach Italy and lay the foundation for Roman power. The triumph of Rome is the unfolding of divine will through the actions of human beings.

If everything is fated, what is the role that human beings play? What is the significance of our freedom if God's plan will come to completion regardless of our choices? A central theme in Stoic philosophy is that human beings can only find fulfillment by submitting to *Logos*, to the divine will. Aeneas's great virtue is his unrelenting determination to obey Fate. Human freedom, therefore, is understood in terms of our choice to accept or resist the divine will. Metaphorically, by means of analogy, we can think about the relationship between a puppeteer and his puppets. The puppeteer controls the plot, provides structure, and directs the movements of the puppets in accordance to his plan. The puppets find themselves with different characteristics, abilities, and circumstances of life. They do not control when they enter or exit the story. Their role in the plot is also decided by the puppeteer. Yet, there is something that puppets can still control: they can surrender to the movements of the puppeteer, contribute to his movements, and ultimately love what the puppeteer wills. But they can also choose to resist, resent, attempt to thwart, and even detest what the puppeteer wants. In his *Epistles*, the Stoic philosopher Seneca explains this relationship between fate and freedom through the following maxim: "Fate leads the willing man and drags the unwilling."[64]

*The Aeneid* is also the story of what a pious man must do to fulfill his duty to the divine command. While other characters represent the moral failings of self-pride and broken faith, Aeneas shows the path to piety. Constantly tempted to turn against Fate, he

64 Lucius Annaeus Seneca, *Moral Epistles*, Volume III, trans. Richard M. Gummere (Cambridge, Mass: The Loeb Classical Library, 1917), Epistle CVII.

must purge himself of passions and material excess. Also, he must learn to trust and obey, even when he does not know or understand what the divine will demands.

Aeneas must also gather the necessary strength to overcome despair, particularly in those moments of hopelessness when extreme suffering puts his faith and determination to the test, and doom seems unavoidable. Through Aeneas's journey, Virgil describes the moral qualities necessary for the foundation of empire. For Rome to rule and fulfill its divine mission, Romans had to cherish and guard the virtue of *pietas* and, like Aeneas *the pious*, place their duty to parents, country, and God above themselves.

### Augustine of Hippo, *Confessions* (400)

Augustine's *Confessions* is a significant work that bridges the Roman Classical world and the Medieval world. It is a work that has continuing influence well into our own age. Augustine traces the development of his own thought as he moves from a skeptical pagan to a powerful apologist for the Christian faith. In this work he wrestles not only with the external challenges to his life, but more importantly focuses on the internal struggles he faces. His descriptions of his inner motivations have led some to describe this text as more of a modern work of psychological catharsis than simply a journal of his spiritual pilgrimage. The work can be divided into two parts. In the first part he narrates his life leading to his eventual embrace of Christianity as the one true faith. The second part of the book is a theological and philosophical explanation of his thoughts on memory, time, and creation.

In the first portion of this book, Augustine traces his development through various pagan philosophies and religions on his way to embracing Christianity. We learn of Augustine's time as a Manichean, a dualistic variant form of Christianity that posited equal forces of good and evil at work in the universe. He also entertains the practices of astrology for a time. Neo-Platonism is an underlying element of his thought, shaping his thinking even after his conversion to Christianity. Much of his journey relates to evil and his personal struggle with sin. He tells the famous story of stealing pears and wrestling with why he and his friends would want to do something simply because they were not supposed to. He is also consumed with the question of lust and the power it seems to hold over him. After the death of a close friend, he grapples with evil and why bad things happen. In his struggle with his own desires and the evil around him, he comes to the realization that evil has no existence at all. As he comes to understand it, evil is simply the privation of good. If God created everything that exists, and all he creates is good, then evil cannot exist because that would mean God had created evil. This understanding is part of the reason he rejects Manichaeism and its belief that evil exists as a counter-force to the good in the universe.

Augustine is also hesitant to fully embrace the Christian faith of his mother due to his perception of it being only for the simple-minded. As he understood it, Christianity was a very simple religion built on faith with little serious reflection and thought. It was not until his encounter with Ambrose, the bishop of Milan, that this perception changes. Once he began to hear the preaching of Ambrose, and after spending time having conversations with him, he came to realize there was a much deeper strain of Christianity that he had not experienced. In the midst of these encounters, he comes to fully embrace the Christian faith, an experience he describes in Book Eight. He is then baptized in 387 in Milan and commits himself fully to the Christian faith.

The second portion of the *Confessions* is focused on philosophical ideas as they intersect with his Christian faith. In his first discussion, he introduces the idea of memory as it relates to all that we know. The real question for him is that while we know many things from earlier memories and experiences, how do we know things we have not experienced, particularly God? This is where his Neo-Platonic background begins to influence his Christianity. He talks about memory more in the vein of Plato, that there are things our souls know based on their recollections of their origins in God. In this way knowledge of God and our coming to know God are really recollections of memories. Augustine then turns to the discussion of time. In this conversation he wrestles with how God knows all. In trying to describe the differences between past, present, and future and how we understand them, he discusses how God experiences all three at once. God, being outside of time, does not experience past, present, and future as we do. While words cannot really describe how this works for Augustine, he notes that the best way we can understand it is that God experiences all three as one point. He thus has foreknowledge as he already has the experience of what will happen. He wants to make a clear distinction between foreknowledge and predestination as they pertain to God. We still are responsible for our actions even if God already knows what will happen. This does not mean God "makes" things happen; he is not manipulating history in a particular way. God has already experienced what will happen and thus knows ahead of time.

*Confessions* becomes a very influential work beyond the time of Augustine. It is considered one of the first autobiographies in Western history. It is read and used widely during the Middle Ages. As honors students move through the curriculum of honors readings, they will continue to see references to this work. Authors including Dante, Chaucer, More, Erasmus, Luther, Calvin, Rousseau and many others will know this work. Henry Chadwick, Oxford historian and translator, believes that it will "always rank among the great masterpieces of Western literature."[65]

65 Chadwick, Introduction to *Confessions* (Oxford: Oxford UP, 1989), 4.

# CHAPTER THREE

# THE WORLD OF CHRISTENDOM AND ISLAM

JENIFER ELMORE AND JORDYN PATRICK

*Introduction*

The classical world has been idolized and romanticized since it ended, but doesn't everyone reflect on the "good ol' days"? Perhaps it has blinded scholars from its raised marble pedestal, casting an undeserving shadow on the transitional period which followed. The era succeeding the fall of Rome has been misbranded as "the Dark Ages"—a term made famous by Petrarch in the fourteenth century. However, some scholars would argue that this label provides a sense of false advertisement of the world which followed.

Before we go any further, let's define our terms. Phrases and words such as "Dark Ages," "pagan," and "barbarian" have heavily negative connotations. To some medieval scholars, regularly coming across these words can cause us to wince or cringe a little, like nails on a chalkboard. As mentioned earlier, the term Dark Ages came about as a result of Petrarch's comparison of the depraved darkness of the early medieval era to the sophisticated light of classical antiquity. Many saw the period as one of an intellectual depression under the rule of the barbarian. Well, we are here to dispel Petrarch's rampant myth! The late Iron Age cultures that surrounded and interacted with Rome were no more barbarian than you are. The term "barbarian" derives from the Greek *barbaros,* often referring to a foreigner or someone whose language and customs differ from those of the Greeks. While this is true at the term's core meaning, as the Germanic tribes were foreigners to Rome, the word barbarian leaves an unpleasant taste in the mouth. When people hear this term, images of wild naked men, tattooed with unkempt hair, yelling and brandishing weapons, often come to mind. However, the truth is that most late Iron Age cultures were civilized with complex societal organizations. Similarly, the term "pagan" conjures up images of the heathen: evil witches, dancing druids, human sacrifice, and the like. The term itself is a reference to any who participate in a religion outside of the main world religions, though it is mostly used to reference non-Christians. The modern word stems from the Latin *paganus*, meaning a rural area, village, and later a civilian. Some feel that the modern take on the term is too broad and with its negative connotation, outdated for use in academia. Therefore, in place of "Dark Ages," the term medieval or Middle Ages will be used. The terms pagan and barbarian will also be excluded from this section due to their misleading connotations.

It is also helpful to identify what we mean by referring to the early medieval period. While scholars may disagree on the specific beginning and ending dates of this era, the following can be used as a basic guideline:

*Early Medieval Era-500 CE-1000 CE*

*High Medieval Era-1000 CE-1300 CE*

*Late Medieval Era- 1300 CE-1500 CE*

This periodization allows scholars to easily identify and study trends and evolving social and political structures. Once Rome's vast empire collapsed, a power vacuum was created. The Early Medieval Era is marked by the various tribes developing into petty kingdoms which then battled one another to fill this void. The High Medieval Era saw the rise of the victors into strengthening kingdoms establishing political and international recognition, as well as relative stability as Christianity spread, and leaders swore fealty to the pope and Church in Rome. By the end of the High Medieval Era, established kingdoms with borders similar to our modern countries today had emerged.

An excellent example of this pattern of development is the Scottish Picts. The term *Picti* was first recorded by the Romans, though it is unknown whether this name was given to various tribes or whether they were a homogeneous or heterogeneous people in ethnicity and identity. The descendants of these northern Iron-Age tribes appear to have developed ethnic solidarity and single *gens*[1] by the eighth century with the creation of several petty kingdoms, all identifying as part of a Pictish nation. These petty kingdoms have left their mark in the form of ruins of hillforts and brochs, power centers, scattered across Scotland. The basis for their society was a gift-giving economy, in which gifts were dispersed by the clan noble or chieftain to those who tended the land in his care. By the ninth century, the petty kingdoms had been conquered and merged to create the Kingdom of Alba, known today as Scotland, ruled by a single king.

The rest of the Western world evolved similarly. The ninth century saw the rise of monarchies, growth of the Church's power, and feudalism. Historians observe the rise of feudalism first within the Carolingian Empire, the predecessor to the Holy Roman Empire. The Carolingian Empire united the kingdoms of Gaul

1 A group of people related through common ancestry, whether female or male lineage.

in modern-day France and extended as far as modern-day Germany, Austria, Slovenia, Croatia, and south into parts of Italy. In the eighth century, Charles Martel was a Frankish statesman who ruled without the title of king. He was well known for his military exploits, increasing the Franks' power and influence. While his grandson Charlemagne, the first Holy Roman Emperor, has been credited as the "father of Europe," Charles Martel could be considered the father of feudalism. With the kingdom's expansion, Charles Martel furnished parcels of land for the nobles. This act created a relationship between the ruling leader or monarch and the nobles, establishing loyalty and the promise of able-bodied men to fight should the king require it. The nobles then would subcontract the land to be worked by vassals, or serfs. The vassals would pay homage or tribute (a special kind of tax) to the noble, thus providing a source of income as well as military service when called upon. The social organization of feudalism continued through the Middle Ages, eventually declining and giving way to a new class system in the fifteenth century.

The social strata during the Middle Ages were as such: at the very top, you had the Church, headed by the pope who was God's voice on earth. Then came the aristocracy, your heavenly appointed Kings and Queens. Next are your nobles and bishops, vassals to the crown. The working class consisted of vassals to the nobles, peasants, and the serfs. The Church was the surviving social institution from the Roman Empire, and by the end of the twelfth century, the papacy had more vassals than any traditional ruler, essentially dominating Western society.

Literary sources from the period tend to discuss the elite and historical events, written by those who had access to education, mostly male clergy and some aristocrats. So how can we better understand how the majority of the population lived at this time? Not surprisingly, the medieval period had high infant mortality rates as well as common childhood deaths. The burial population suggests, however, that if a male were to survive childhood, the average life expectancy would be forty to fifty years. If a woman were to survive childhood, her average life expectancy was between twenty-five and forty years. Under ten percent appear to have lived to age sixty. There is also the question of whether social status and rank increased one's odds of a longer life. Chris Gilleard concludes that "old age was reached more often by the early-medieval clergy than by the laity of any status."[2]

Now that we have a better understanding of the life expectancy, we should briefly explore how people structured their places of living. Many factors led to the evolution of settlements and medieval villages: religious influences as seen during the immigration era all the way through the conversion period; political influences as lordship became more popular and the legal ownership of land was granted and passed down through families; and economic influence as markets and trading began to increase. Religious sites and their relationship to the physical landscape play a role in the development of settlements, revealing significant implications for scholars: "The landscape has come to the forefront of the theoretical approaches hinging on the belief that changes in religious or political ideology can result in physical alterations to settlement, land use and division, burial practices, and administrative arrangements."[3] Not only does the archaeological and historical record allow for one to comprehend the importance of religious and sacred sites within settlements, but it also gives a hint to the priorities and psyche of the community.

2 Chris Gilleard, "Old Age in the Dark Ages: the status of old age during the Middle Ages" in *Ageing & Society 29.* (Cambridge: Cambridge University Press, 2009), 1070.

3 Sarah Semple "Sacred Spaces and Places in Pre-Christian and Conversion Period Anglo-Saxon England," *The Oxford Handbook of Anglo-Saxon Archaeology* (Oxford: Oxford University Press, 2011), 744.

## *Evolution into a Medieval World*

> *"The Roman Empire was not murdered and nor did it die a natural death; it accidentally committed suicide."*[4]

Rome was one of the greatest and most vast empires to exist in antiquity, spanning over two million square miles at its peak. Reminders of its magnitude can be found all across Europe, now crumbling ruins for tourists to photograph. What brought this powerful organization to its knees? Well, just as Rome wasn't built in a day, it also wasn't torn down in one. In this section, we will discuss a few factors of Rome's decline and the impact it had on the writers during this transitional age.

By 285 CE the Roman Empire had grown too large to rule from a single location and as such was split into two governing regions. The Western Roman Empire ruled from Milan in Italy, and the Eastern Roman Empire, also called the Byzantine Empire, ruled from Constantinople (in present-day Turkey). The two factions appeared to progress relatively equally for about a century. During this time the ruling of the two factions worked like a revolving door, sometimes with co-emperors and others with a single ruler. For examples, Diocletian and Maximian ruled as co-emperors in 285 CE; however, less than a hundred years later Constantine ruled both factions alone in 323 CE. This pattern continued until the rule of Theodosius I, hailed as the last ruler over both halves of the empire. The Roman Empire began to show obvious symptoms of its decline with the rule of Theodosius I. To clarify, no one emperor can be blamed for the fall of Rome, nor can a single reason be discerned for its decline. With Theodosius's reign, however, multiple factors became more evident in the deterioration of the Empire.

One such factor was foreign invasion. Various Germanic groups had been tussling with the Romans, slowly chipping away

4 Guy Hassall, *Barbarian Migration and the Roman West, 376-568* (Cambridge University Press, 2008), 283.

at the borders for centuries; however, foreign soldiers and German mercenaries had made up a significant portion of Rome's auxiliary military units. While this allowed Rome's army to grow in numbers, it also posed a threat. These foreign soldiers were trained in Roman tactics and could turn around and use this training to support their native tribes in revolting against the empire. An excellent example of this weakness was the German leader Arminius, who used his training and time with the Roman military to lead a confederacy of German tribes in 9 CE to decimate three Roman legions and push Rome out of Germania. Regardless of this weakness, Rome still used foreign soldiers in their army. Theodosius had German advisers educate and guide his sons, but after his death, they were more concerned with their tribe's advancement than the success of their custodial charges. Theodosius's son Honorius was a weak emperor who was strongly influenced by his Vandal general advisor. In 410, during Honorius's reign, the Visigoth chief Alaric sacked Rome, and while it was not the capital at the time, this was a devastating defeat for the Roman people. By the end of the fifth century, the Western Roman Empire had collapsed.

Another factor in Rome's demise was the economy. The imperial economy was coin-based and as such was regulated by precious metals. Roman emperors began to dilute the purity of the silver to meet the state's debts and increase their money supply, thereby lowering the *denarii* value. By 215 CE monetary destabilization had caused economic turmoil. With rampant overspending and inflation, Rome was in a financial crisis. The wealthy residents in cities felt oppressed by the liturgies and exactions regularly assessed by the empire. Liturgies (not to be confused with religious services) required wealthier citizens to give money or provide compulsory service to the empire to ease the financial strain. This practice was often used when an emperor wished to commission monuments or other constructions, fund military campaigns, or put on arena games. Exactions called on the local councilors to make up the difference when a community could not pay its taxes. Forced exaction became extremely burdensome, compounding the regular taxes and liturgies required. Many wealthy citizens began to flee from cities to the countryside to escape such taxes, and the archaeological record shows a growth of large estates during this period. The Church also began to gain more lands because ceding lands to the Church provided a tax break for the wealthy. Agricultural production also declined during this time, further abetting the empire's financial crisis.

Instability within religious practice, more specifically the growth of Christianity, has also been cited as a factor for the collapse of Rome. Of course, as stated before no one factor can be blamed for the fall of Rome, and more specifically an ideology cannot be blamed. However, religions can be used as tools to help push forward a political agenda. In 313 CE Constantine established the Edict of Milan, providing religious tolerance and freedom of worship for the citizens of Rome, particularly the Christians. While Constantine did not outlaw polytheistic religion, he did restrict public sacrifices and prohibited new temple construction. By the end of his reign, non-Christian temples were looted and torn down, and after his death, new laws and policies were put in place to persecute non-Christian worship in the empire.

The Church also had internal struggles during this time. No longer under persecution, Christianity was able to spread and flourish. Emperors began to incentivize participation in the Church by providing tax breaks for the creation of religious communities or entering into the religious service. Land and wealth were taken from the looted Roman temples and given to the Church as well as parcels of land from wealthy individuals looking for a break from the taxes abounding from foreign wars. Many joined religious life but were not adequately trained or taught outside the traditional doctrine, causing dissent within the faith by developing beliefs deemed heretical by the Church, such as Donatism and Arianism.

In 325, Constantine convened the first Council of Nicaea to establish unity within the Church. While religious conflict may have been a contributing factor to the fall of Rome, the Church would go on to be one of the few remaining social institutions from the empire, with the pope acting as its head, God's appointed presiding in the holy city of antiquity.

Out of all this turmoil and chaos emerged the early medieval world. The Germanic tribes had carved up the empire, each taking a piece of the pie. By 500 CE the Western Roman Empire no longer existed, though Roman society and administration remained relatively unaffected under the Ostrogoths in Italy. The Vandals had taken control of northern Africa, establishing a powerful kingdom with a significant naval fleet. The Frankish kingdom was established and covered parts of modern-day France, Belgium, Netherlands, and Germany. The Visigoth kingdom stretched from modern-day Spain into France. In the British Isles the Angles, Saxons, Britons, Scots, and Picts battled for land. As these Germanic kingdoms began to form and expand, we can see the predecessors to the modern countries and their borders today. In order to establish themselves, many of these new kingdoms attempted to mimic Rome in several facets. Historians can observe that there is a syncretic nature to the beliefs, laws, and practices throughout the Germanic kingdoms: a beautiful combination of past beliefs and traditions merging with that of Christian Rome. Christmas, All Hallows Eve/All Hallows Day/All Saints Day (more commonly known as Halloween), St. Valentine's Day, and even Easter have traditions acquired from non-Christian cultures. In fact, many of the modern holidays celebrated today are a result of pre-Christian beliefs and celebrations taken by the Church and altered to encourage Christian practice.

The process of Christianizing the Germanic peoples was eased by the use of Rome's existing infrastructure. The roads built to connect the outermost regions of the empire allowed missionaries to travel easily to spread their faith. Many of the Germanic tribes that had migrated into Roman territories, like the Goths and Vandals, had converted to Arianism but were later reconverted by Catholic missionaries, aligning the Germanic kingdoms with the pope in Rome. Most often the missionaries would convert the elite, who would establish a place of worship—often re-using previous sacred sites—or simply add the Christian religion to their own in a syncretic manner. We must also consider that leaders converted not necessarily for purely religious intent, but rather as a political alliance. An excellent example is the East Anglia King, Rædwald. Towards the end of the sixth century, Pope Gregory the Great commissioned a Christian mission, headed by Augustine of Canterbury, to convert the Anglo-Saxons of Britain. King Rædwald converted to Christianity but appeared not to have been fully committed, as he established a Christian altar inside the existing temple and was probably buried with grave goods,[5] a non-Christian practice. Some have interpreted this as Rædwald simply adding the Christian god to the pantheon of existing deities, while others see this move as a way of keeping his popularity with his people, who did not wish to convert. The Church was a powerful organization that had accumulated land and prestige. If you had the backing of the Church, you had the wealth and strength of Rome behind you.

There is ample evidence of syncretic culture between the Germanic-Romano people. However, as Christianity flourished, a sense of unity gradually developed in Europe: burial practices changed, the historical landscape altered as sacred places and spaces were regulated by churches and monastic settlements, laws were changed to fall in line with the Church's teachings, even individuals' status within the society was altered. Christianity and political policies forged in Rome began to shape medieval Europe into the world of knights, castles, and battles.

5 Objects meaningfully deposited in a grave with a deceased individual.

*Society of the "Dark Age Barbarians"*

> *"Celtic is a magic bag, into which anything may be put, and out of which almost anything may come."*[6]

The world outside of ancient Rome's borders was filled with Germanic tribes who were labeled as Celts (*Keltoi)* by the classical historians. This label was applied to a wide range of groups in various geographical areas who identified ethnically and culturally as similar, as seen in the La Tène[7] styled artifacts uncovered throughout continental Europe and the British Isles. Sir Barry Cunliffe defines the Celtic people as the following: "To the Graeco-Roman world, then, the mobile, warlike peoples of western and central Europe were an ethnic group – the Celts – who could be characterized and caricatured as the barbarians from without."[8] There was a migration of these people groups around 400 BCE as they spread into the south from the Alps, west into modern-day Spain, and east into Anatolia or modern-day Turkey. In fact, when Paul wrote his letter to the Galatians, he wrote to the descendants of this La Tène group that had invaded and settled in the third century BCE.

In the transitional world of the early Middle Ages, these groups had evolved into separate identities and cultures. The Goths engaged the Romans in a long series of battles known as the Gothic Wars, spanning from the third to sixth century CE. Goth was an overarching term used to identify a people group of similar culture, of which there were two factions, the Visigoths and the Ostrogoths. It was the Visigoth king Alaric who successfully invaded Rome in 410 CE. In the early Medieval Era, the Visigoths established their own kingdom in the western portion of Gaul (modern-day France)

6 J.R.R. Tolkien, "English and Welsh." Lecture. O'Donnell Lectures in Celtic Studies, University of Oxford, October 21, 1955.

7 The name given to the homogenous Iron Age culture, most recognizable by its art form.

8 Barry W. Cunliffe, *The Celts: A Very Short Introduction* (Oxford: Oxford University Press, 2003), 141.

and well into the Iberian Peninsula. By the sixth century CE, the Visigoth kingdom no longer had Gaul within its borders but had conquered the rest of Hispania, ruling over modern-day Spain and Portugal. Visigothic law provides scholars with an excellent example of syncretic processes at work. Part of an oral tradition, the laws of the kingdom, also known as the Visigothic Code, were written down in the fifth century. In it, there are traces of Roman customs, Celtic or Germanic tribal customs, as well as Christian law. The Visigoths were a powerful early kingdom until they were defeated by the Arabs in 712 CE. The Ostrogoths were the other faction, who established a kingdom in Italy in the late fifth century. They were not as powerful as their Visigoth cousins, and by the end of the sixth century, the Ostrogothic kingdom was weakened by the Eastern Roman Emperor Justinian's forces. They would later merge themselves with the Lombards who set out to conquer Italy. The Lombards occupied Italy from the mid-sixth century to the late eighth century when they were defeated by the Frankish king, Charlemagne.

The kingdom of Francia was briefly mentioned earlier in this chapter in regards to Charles Martel, the institution of feudalism, and a brief introduction to the Carolingian dynasty. Perhaps one of the most famous of the Carolingian rulers was his grandson, Charlemagne, who would expand the nation's boundaries to engulf Gaul, Germania, and northern Italy. Alongside the military incursions by Charlemagne, Frankish missionaries, along with Irish and Anglo-Saxon British missionaries, penetrated into Saxon Germania on a mission to convert the non-Christians. As he continued conquering, Charlemagne wished to Christianize all of the Saxons under his command and thus established several bishoprics,[9] or medieval mayorships of sorts. It should be noted that these bishops were not merely religious figures there to guide a wayward flock

9 An administrative move placing bishops in charge of ecclesiastical districts.

but worked more like feudal lords and warriors.[10] Charlemagne solidified ties with the Church and with Rome as a vassal to the pope, promising military protection in exchange for Papal support. In 800 CE Pope Leo III crowned Charlemagne as Emperor of Rome, sparking outcry from the Byzantine Empire, which had maintained rulers with the title of Roman emperor since the fall of the west. Some scholars claim this moment for the origin of the Holy Roman Empire.

Many more groups interacted with Rome during late antiquity and the early medieval era. However, in order not to overload you with information, we have only discussed a few of the groups which had a larger impact on the creation of the medieval world.

*The Medieval Middle East*

We have focused on the west and its evolution into the known medieval world. Now we ought to dedicate some time to the Middle East. In the seventh century a man named Muhammad from Mecca on the Arabian Peninsula revealed that he had received a series of revelations from God and began to recite these revelations to a scribe; these writings would become the holy book of the new religion of Islam, the *Qu'ran* or *Koran*. Muhammed also preached, imploring the Arab people to convert from their polytheistic beliefs. With any major change, political or religious, the ruling class became uncomfortable, fearing loss of power and control, and attempted to squash any precursors to rebellion or meaningful change. Thus the first converts to Islam were persecuted and driven out of Mecca as the elite felt this new religion destabilized the social status quo. Similar to the earliest converts of Christianity, many of Islam's first converts were the poor or slaves. The converts settled in Medina and established a community known as Ummah, ruled by Muhammad. The community consisted of several Arab tribes,

10 Of course, this did not apply to *all* bishops. See Craig M. Nakashian's *Warrior Churchmen of Medieval England: 1000-1200* if this particular topic interests you.

and eventually by Muhammad's death the majority of Arabic tribes were united under a single religious and cultural identity.

The eighth century begins a period in the Middle East that has often been referred to as the Golden Age of Islam. Under the second Caliphate,[11] the Arab empire expanded and created a homogeneous ethnic and religious identity. The empire united the Middle East, including northern Africa, and spread as far west as the Iberian Peninsula (present-day Spain and Portugal). During the High Middle Ages, Islamic culture blossomed and was expressed through beautiful displays of architecture, art, advances in science, medicine, and technology. Similar to the Christian church, various traditions began to form. There was a split between their religious organization, resulting in two branches of the Islamic faith, Sunni and Shia. Like the Christian monastics we discuss in the next section, Muslim ascetics renounced bodily desires to avoid sin, and their contemplative practices evolved into Sufism, Islamic mysticism. Along with the Irish in the west, the Muslims can be credited for "saving civilisation."[12] Both groups were able to preserve written works, providing the resources necessary for advancement in many fields. Many of the primary sources we are able to enjoy today are a result of the Muslims' fascination with knowledge and education, saving and spreading advanced concepts in medicine, arithmetic, astronomy, ethics, chemistry, and geography, among others. Eventually all this information would flood back to Western Europe, assisting in the Renaissance and Scientific Revolution.

Remember, the Roman Empire had been split, and the Eastern Roman or Byzantine Empire was ruled from Constantinople. Unlike its counterpart in the West, the Byzantine Empire aligned itself more with Greek culture than with Roman.[13] Under Emperor Justinian I, emperor in 527 CE, the Byzantine Empire

11 An Islamic kingdom ruled by a political-religious head known as the caliph.

12 A reference to the book by Thomas Cahill, *How the Irish Saved Civilization* (1995).

13 That is, utilizing Greek rather than Latin

was extremely powerful and successful, claiming back part of Italy including Rome, conquering the Vandals in Africa, and expanding their borders to most of the Mediterranean. By the eighth century however, the empire had lost most of its territory to Arab invasions. The empire continued on and eventually recovered its wealth, influence, and some territory under the Macedonian emperors.

Perhaps one of the more impactful events during this time was not military expanse or wealth gained, but a religious confrontation known as the Great Schism. The Great Schism established the split between the Roman Catholic Church and the Eastern Orthodox Church. This was a result of centuries of poor communication as well as differences in political, cultural, and theological ideologies. It was like a bad relationship with neither party on the same page, with the break-up happening around 1054 CE. The two church organizations mutually agreed to go their separate ways; however, an intense rivalry was instilled in their followers.

Shortly after the Great Schism, the Catholic Church sanctioned a series of religious wars referred to as the Crusades. There was a total of nine crusades called for by the Church, all with the overall goal of pushing back the Muslim kingdom. The first was commissioned by Pope Urban II in 1095 CE as a quest to recapture the Holy Land (Anatolia and the Levant) from the Muslim Seljuq Empire. This campaign lasted for four years and resulted in the successful creation of "crusader states."[14] Nearly fifty years later, the second crusade was a reaction to the fall of one of these crusader states. This campaign was a disaster for the Church, resulting in the fall of Jerusalem and many crusader states. Forty years later another campaign was launched, reclaiming many of the lands conquered by the Muslim leader Saladin; however, the campaign was unable to reclaim Jerusalem.

The fourth crusade was historically important as it solidified

14 Feudal states created by the crusaders as a result of defeating the occupying Muslim or other non-Christian powers.

the schism between the Catholic and Orthodox Churches. Called for by Pope Innocent III in 1202 CE, this campaign had the ultimate goal of recapturing Jerusalem. However, once dispatched, the Crusader leadership decided to divert to Constantinople and assist the Byzantine prince Alexios Angelos to restore his father to power in exchange for financial support. Back in Rome, the pope excommunicated the soldiers for their rogue actions, but the leaders kept this information from the rank and file because they feared they would lose their men without the illusion of papal support. They succeeded in establishing Alexios as a co-emperor in Constantinople and began to move on toward Jerusalem, but Alexios failed to fulfill his promise of financial reward. In response, the crusaders returned and sacked Constantinople in 1204 CE, plundering its wealth, deepening the rivalry between the two Churches, and further weakening the vulnerable Byzantine Empire. The following crusades ultimately were unsuccessful as well, resulting overwhelmingly in Muslim victories. The final crusade for the Holy Land ended unsuccessfully in 1272 CE, with the last Christian foothold lost in 1303 CE. While these wars were deemed religious, over time any truly religious motivations were outweighed by the desire for increased political power, wealth, territory, and sphere of influence.

### *Monasticism*

The earliest Christian monastics were hermits in the deserts of northern Africa and the Middle East. The word "hermit" comes from the Greek word *eremites*, meaning "living in the desert." Students will recall reading some writings from these "desert fathers and mothers" in The World of Caesar and Christ, as they are known to have existed as early as the second century A.D. These devout Christians sought a life of bodily self-denial, contemplation, prayer, and spiritual warfare in response to Jesus's admonition to "go, sell all you have…" and after the example that Jesus himself set when he fasted in the wilderness for forty days and triumphed over the temptations of Satan. By the end of the fourth century, several thousand of these Christian monastics were living in the desert outskirts of Alexandria in Egypt.[15] However, during the period studied in The World of Christendom and Islam, monasticism evolved into something very different: a communal institution rather than a solitary pursuit, and one that came to play an important role not only in the church but in the development of western civilization. Monasticism, as it flowered in the medieval period, was a primary platform for the continuation of the Great Conversation.

When the Roman Emperor Constantine issued the Edict of Milan in A.D. 313 instituting religious freedom and establishing religious toleration, notably the toleration of Christians, the law of the land, the effects were not as entirely positive as one might assume. Because Constantine had publicly credited Christianity for his military success and had even established some new churches himself, many considered him a Christian convert (though the reality of his conversion has long been a matter of debate among historians). The fact that the emperor either was a Christian or at least openly supported Christianity, combined with the fact that Christianity was legally permitted, made the marginalized and often persecuted minority religion more socially acceptable and even advantageous to the higher classes. The more people began openly practicing Christianity, and the more socially prominent the converts were, the more attractive the faith became for reasons other than sincere spiritual conviction—political access, social prestige, economic ambition, and even simple popularity. What had been a dangerous or at least disadvantageous faith to profess became, in a word, fashionable. And when the Emperor Theodosius established Christianity as the one official state religion of the Roman Empire in A.D. 380, what had become fashionable was

15 Logan, F. Donald, *A History of the Church in the Middle Ages* (London: Routledge Taylor & Francis Group, 2002), 11.

now in effect mandatory for anyone who wanted to be part of the mainstream society.

Though they were surely grateful for gaining legal status, financial support, and rapidly growing membership, some older communities of Christians nevertheless suffered a kind of identity crisis: the faith had been born in persecution and had survived in spite of it, so a kind of outsider or even outcast identity was a crucial part of what it meant to be a follower of Christ. Public persecution was the cross that early believers took up to follow Jesus, who was himself the ultimate sufferer of undeserved persecution. So how could this religion with persecution at its core maintain its integrity and sincerity now that it carried social currency and was all the rage among prominent citizens of the Empire?

Some fervent Christians responded to this challenge with a reformist zeal. As you may remember from the previous chapter of this book, around the year A.D. 314 (not long after the Edict of Milan), a man named Pachomius, a Coptic (Egyptian) Christian who had served in Constantine's north African army, struck out alone into the desert not far from his hometown of Thebes in Egypt to devote himself to solitary asceticism and contemplation. (The original solitary connotations of monastic life are preserved in the very word "monastic," which derives from the Greek word *monos*, meaning "one.") He then joined with other ascetic Christians to establish the first formally organized cenobitic (from the Latin *coena*, for "common meal") or communal group of monastics (as opposed to eremitic or individual hermit monastics) living together in an enclosed space under an established order or rule of life. Pachomius is credited with establishing that rule and serving as the community's leader. His model of monasticism worked, and before his death he had established eleven such monasteries that housed over 7,000 nuns and monks in the eastern desert regions of the Roman Empire.

Monasticism was not limited to the desert. In the early fourth century, St. Basil founded the Cappadocian order in what is now Turkey. Early in the sixth century, a man known as Benedict of Nursia (A.D. c. 480-c. 550) left his cave hermitage to found a communal monastery and eventually became the most influential cenobitic monk in western history. After establishing a number of small, communal monasteries in the Italian countryside, he eventually settled on Monte Cassino (near Naples) and established what fairly quickly became the most famous monastery in Europe. Known as the Order of St. Benedict, or the Benedictines, the order he founded still exists today (and the famous monastery itself stood for fourteen centuries, until it was destroyed by the Allied Forces during World War II). Benedict's written rules for every aspect of life in the monastery came to be known as the "Rule of St. Benedict." Largely collected from similar sets of rules from earlier monastics, the Rule formed the basis of most Christian monastic orders (not just the Benedictines) in the medieval period and beyond. To contemporary ears, the word "rule" connotes strictures and legalism, but "rule" comes from the same Latin root as "regular" and "right"; therefore, Benedict's Rule is not only a set of rules in the restrictive sense, but also a description of the regularity, righteousness, and not so much deprivation as *moderation* of monastic life. Medieval church historian F. Donald Logan describes it as "a life of dedication, yet a life of moderation, avoiding extremes of laxity and severity. The Rule strikes the modern reader as sensible, discreet, practical and, in a word, livable."[16] Largely because of the lasting influence of his Rule, Benedict came to be considered the "father" of western monasticism even though he clearly was not its founder.[17]

There were eremitic and cenobitic monks in Western Europe, too, as early as the fourth century. Martin of Tours founded the first monastery in what is now France. Augustine of Hippo (the Augus-

16 Logan, 20.

17 Logan, 19.

tine of *Confessions*) founded the *Servei Dei* (Servants of God) order in A.D. 388, which was re-established in the thirteenth century as the Order of St. Augustine. The first monasteries in Britain were established in the fifth century in Wales and the western areas of England. Near the end of the sixth century, a Benedictine monk was sent by Pope Gregory on a mission to the south of England; he founded the first monastery in that region, became the first archbishop there, and eventually became known as St. Augustine of Canterbury (not to be confused with Augustine of Hippo).[18] Augustine's seat at Canterbury Cathedral is the destination of the pilgrims in Chaucer's *The Canterbury Tales*.

Other prominent monastic orders established during the medieval period include the Franciscans, founded in Italy by St. Francis of Assisi, and the Dominicans, founded in Spain by St. Dominic (who had been a member of the Order of St. Augustine). Both of these influential orders were founded in the thirteenth century and were inspired by a desire on the part of devout Christians (Francis was a layperson; Dominic was an ordained priest) to live a simpler life of faith based on the imitation of Christ. They followed the words of Jesus in Luke 10: "Go on your way. See, I am sending you out like lambs into the midst of wolves. Carry no purse, no bag, no sandals; and greet no one on the road [...]. Remain in the same house, eating and drinking whatever they provide, for the laborer deserves to be paid."[19] True to the scripture, both were mendicant orders, meaning that their members (who are known as friars, not monks) travelled about (often literally "without sandals," that is,

18 The English have traditionally credited Augustine of Canterbury with bringing the faith to their country, though that is not true since we know that Christianity had been well established in Roman Britain by the fourth century (Logan 11), and the region continued to struggle with religious battles between Christianity and other religious traditions that accompanied political battles between the Britons (Celtic and largely Christian peoples) and the Anglo-Saxons (Germanic and largely non-Christian peoples) for decades after Augustine's mission.

19 Holy Bible, New Revised Standard Version, Luke 10: 4-6, 8.

barefoot) preaching and ministering directly to lay people, rather than living in enclosed monasteries. The mendicant orders particularly emphasized the vow of poverty, as they did not at first live in stationary communities that provided them with shelter, clothing, and food, but rather depended on the charity of those they encountered as they went about preaching. However, in time the widespread success of these orders meant that they inevitably had to compromise some purity of principle by organizing themselves on a large scale, which necessitated some ownership of property on the part of the orders, if not by the individual friars.

The rapid growth in numbers and influence of these orders provides evidence of just how much reform spirit existed within the Catholic Church in the centuries before the Protestant Reformation. Like other monastic movements, they arose from a desire for greater purity and less privilege and corruption. Unlike the hermits and cenobitic communities, however, the mendicant orders were started as ways to escape from the complex, privileged, and "set apart" nature of the organized church itself (rather than the secular world of the Roman Empire) and embrace a Christ-like life. Whereas it had once been the world that monastics sought to escape, the mendicants sought to escape the complexity of the organized church by taking the gospel literally to the streets—in their bare feet. Their history and mission are important for under standing the deeper historical roots of the Protestant Reformation.

A large proportion of medieval monastics were women, some of whom made important contributions to Christianity in the period. Two of the most famous of these, and the two most often studied in The World of Christendom and Islam, are Hildegard of Bingen (1098-1179) and Julian of Norwich (1342- sometime after 1416). Like Hildegard, Julian of Norwich was a visionary, but unlike Hildegard she was an anchorite rather than a cenobitic nun. Other influential female monastics in the medieval period include St. Clare of Assisi, who was the first member of the order that St.

Francis founded for women; the order is officially known as the Order of St. Clare but has always been called the "Poor Clares." St. Catherine of Siena (Italy), like Julian, experienced visions and became an anchorite for a time.[20]

By the end of the medieval period, then, Christian monasticism was multiform, widespread, and well-established across the Western world in three main types: the eremitic or solitary hermits, also known as anchorites; the cenobites, who lived in monasteries, convents, or abbeys; and the mendicants or traveling friars.

### *Scholasticism*

As historian Edward Grant puts it, "If reason and rationality had a home during the late Middle Ages, it was surely in the university."[21] To take the point a step further, Jan A. Aertsen echoes many other scholars in asserting that the development of universities "was perhaps the most important contribution of the Middle Ages to Western culture."[22] While the classical academy of Plato was a distant ancestor of the university, the immediate precursors to the medieval university were both monasteries (in the sense that many of them were centers of learning) and the cathedral schools, which were loosely organized centers of learning based in cathedral churches. Because each cathedral was the headquarters of a church bishop, each cathedral was also the workplace of other highly educated clergymen. That concentration of highly educated people

20 Burton, Janet E., and Karen Stöber. *Women in the Medieval Monastic World.* Medieval Monastic Studies, v. 1. (Turnhout, Belgium: Brepols, 2015); Christopher Abbott, *Julian of Norwich: Autobiography and Theology*, Studies in Medieval Mysticism (Woodbridge, Suffolk: Boydell & Brewer, 1999); Fiona Maddocks. *Hildegard of Bingen: The Woman of Her Age* (New York: Image Books/Doubleday, 2003).

21 Edward Grant, *God and Reason in the Middle Ages* (Cambridge: Cambridge University Press, 2001), 98.

22 Jan A. Aertsen, "Aquinas's Philosophy in Its Historical Setting," in *The Cambridge Companion to Aquinas* (Cambridge: Cambridge University Press, 1993), 12. [12-37]

made the cathedrals a natural place for people to seek learning, regardless of whether they had any interest in joining a monastic order or becoming ordained ministers. During the eleventh and twelfth centuries, some cathedral schools became more officially organized as corporations, not unlike trade guilds. All kinds of corporations were called *universitas*, and those that were devoted to education were called *universitas scholarium* (university of students) or *universitas magisterium* (university of masters), or both.[23] By the year 1200, such universities had been established in Bologna, Italy; Paris, France; and Oxford, England, and these three remained the most prestigious and influential institutions of learning throughout the period. (By the end of the medieval period, there were about sixty such institutions in Europe.)[24] These institutions were typically divided into four schools or colleges: theology, arts, law, and medicine.

Of the four schools, arts and medicine from the thirteenth century forward formed their curricula around relatively recent Latin translations of classical Greek texts (those of Plato and more so those by Aristotle), Roman classics (such as Seneca, Pliny the Elder, and Boethius), Latin translations of Arabic texts, and written commentaries on all of those older texts; schools of theology and law depended on separate bodies of scriptures, church teachings, and accumulated legal codes. The works of Aristotle were by far the most extensively studied sources of knowledge in the medieval arts curriculum.

All students were required to complete the bachelor of arts curriculum, which consisted of the seven liberal arts—grammar, rhetoric, and logic (grouped together as the *trivium*) and then arithmetic, geometry, music, and astronomy (the *quadrivium*)—before becoming eligible to study in the schools of law, medicine, or theology and attain a master's degree and the right to become

23 Ibid., 100.

24 Ibid.

teachers or "masters" themselves. Until the mid-twentieth century, colleges and universities in the Western world largely maintained this same basic structure, with undergraduate or bachelor's studies consisting mainly of languages, argumentation, critical thinking, and mathematics, with more specific "arts" such as music, literature, history, and sciences such as biology, chemistry, and physics. Studies in law, medicine, and theology were reserved for masters and doctoral degrees.[25]

The style of learning that occurred in medieval universities is known as scholasticism, the meaning of which was encapsulated by St. Anselm of Canterbury (1033-1109 CE) in the Latin motto *fides quaerens intellectum* or "faith seeking understanding."[26] Scholasticism "in a nutshell," according to medieval scholar Thomas Madden, was an attempt to "bring ancient Greek philosophy, in particular Aristotelian philosophy, ideas about logic [...] and reason together with the Christian faith. What they attempted to do is better understand the faith through reason [...] and this marrying together of faith and reason [...] is what those universities were all about at the beginning."[27] The bread and butter of medieval university education was the *lectio*, or reading and exposition of an authoritative text indicated by the curriculum.[28] While lectio was the default activity of class meetings and individual study, the masters also held *disputatio* or disputation, periodically throughout each academic year. The "dispute" would occur on a scheduled day when the master would pose a question that demanded a yes or no answer to the students. Either the master or some of the students would then offer some preliminary arguments to support both the

25 Grant, *God and Reason in the Middle Ages*, chapter 3, "Reason Takes Hold: Aristotle and the Medieval University," 83-114.

26 Sandra Visser and Thomas Williams, *Anselm* (Oxford: Oxford University Press, 2009), 6-7.

27 Thomas Madden, "Chapter 6: Monasticism" (lecture), Odyssey of the West, Vol. III: The Medieval World,

28 Aertsen, 15.

affirmative and the negative responses to the question, and then a student would be assigned to respond to all of those arguments as a kind summary and advancement of them. The *determinatio* or resolution would take place the next day, when the master would present a carefully weighed assessment of the arguments for and against the disputed question, leading up to a systematic answer. When written down, the proceedings of a *disputatio* and *determinatio* form a genre of philosophical discourse known as *questiones disputatae* or, in plain English, the disputation. Though they may no longer use the same terminology or appear in exactly the same format, variations on the medieval disputation have remained a staple of academic and legal discourse to the present day, perhaps most visibly in formal debates and court proceedings—not to mention honors classes in which spontaneous debates arise in response to a discussion leader's question, whether or not anyone in the room is conscious of participating in a hallowed academic tradition that dates back to the very first universities.

### *Thomas Aquinas: The Great Philosophical Theologian of Christendom*

The greatest of all the scholastic thinkers, one of the greatest products of medieval Western civilization, and one of the greatest Christian thinkers of all time, was Thomas Aquinas. His career and works are the apotheosis of scholastic thinking, the apex of medieval European intellectual achievement. Born sometime between 1224 and 1226 in a small town near Naples, Italy, from which he was sent as a child for early schooling to the Benedictine Abbey of Monte Cassino (the monastery that St. Benedict founded), Thomas went from there at age fourteen to study the liberal arts at the recently established University of Naples. After a stint in Cologne to study directly under Albertus Magnus, who was the most well-regarded scholar in Europe at that time, Thomas *eventually* began his master's study in theology at the University of Paris.

Why the emphasis on *eventually*? Well, Thomas was more than just an ambitious young intellectual. Like many Supper Honors students we have known, he was equally devoted to leading a sincere life of faith. During his undergraduate study at the University of Naples, Thomas was introduced to and eventually joined the fairly new mendicant monastic Order of Friar Preachers, a.k.a. the Dominicans, at age nineteen. Because of the order's newness and lack of prestige, and perhaps even more because of its radical dedication to piety and poverty, Thomas's aristocratic family vehemently disapproved of his decision and went so far as to have him abducted on his way to Paris and then forcibly held in the family castle for more than a year.[29] There are stories (some true, some exaggerated, and some probably false) about his parents bringing attractive young women and even prostitutes to the castle to try to tempt Thomas away from a life of poverty as a wandering radical preacher. Imagine the parental pleadings: "For goodness' sake, Thomas! If you must have a religious career, why can't you join a respectable order like the Benedictines, which could launch you into a prestigious career as an abbot or a bishop or maybe even the pope!" But Thomas held firm, and after one heck of a "gap year," his family accepted his decision.[30]

Like his scholastic peers and their predecessors, Thomas relied heavily on the philosophical insight and even more so on the philosophical system of Aristotle. It makes a certain kind of sense to see scholastic thought as a direct application of Aristotle's logical method to Christian theology, but Aquinas's thought is more complex than that. It is best understood when considered as an intricate layering of philosophy (a logical system of analysis of observed reality) and theology (a system based on revealed truth in scripture, not on logical deductions from observation). Thomas's layering of the two depends on his understanding of the mind of God: if, as

29 Eleonore Stump, *Aquinas* (New York: Routledge, 2003), 3.

30 Ralph McInerny, *Aquinas* (Cambridge: Polity Press, 2004), 11-12.

the Bible tells us, God spoke the universe into being, then all of creation is an expression of the mind of God, and even the world's fallenness reveals truths about the nature of God and human beings. This revealed truth predates and precedes any human philosophical system, and in that sense Thomas applied Christianity to Aristotle at least as much as he applied Aristotle to Christianity; again, it was a kind of layering process that attempts to intertwine two different paths to truth into a unified whole. There should be no ultimate contradiction between what we can learn by observing the world (the collective phenomena known as general revelation) and drawing philosophical conclusions from those observations, and what we can learn directly from God's revelation in scripture (special revelation). Both sources of truth are expressions of the mind of God, and each informs and strengthens the other.

That is not to say that Aquinas and other scholastics believed that philosophy was necessary for salvation or that the revelations of scripture were insufficient sources of Truth for those who believed them. Aquinas clearly believed that scripture is not only sufficient but a more extensive source of Truth than philosophy because some special theological truths are only revealed in scripture and not in the world. (Otherwise there would be no need for God to have specially revealed himself.) Rather, the scholastics viewed the value of seeking truth through nature and philosophy rather than simply relying on scripture as fundamentally evangelical in nature because it was a means for convincing people who did not already accept the Bible as God's revealed truth—non-Christians and unorthodox Christians of any stripe, including those who accepted only part of the Bible as God's truth (Jews and some "Christian" heretics), or who did not accept it as God's *only* revealed truth (Muslims)—of the nature of God and his relation to his creation and particularly to human beings. An advantage of this view for the great scholastic thinkers like Aquinas was that it rendered Jewish and Muslim scholars colleagues in the pursuit of truth via general revelation (the world expounded through logical system), whereas they would come to an impasse rather quickly if discussion were limited to what each religion considered to be divinely revealed scriptures. Scholasticism therefore allowed for and valued the study of Jewish and Islamic philosophers not only for the sake of understanding what non-Christian believers believed but also in the larger pursuit of general truth. As a result, Thomas's works follow the principle that we often recite today, that "All truth is God's truth,"[31] and were significantly influenced by the Greek Aristotle, the Jewish philosopher Moses Maimonides, and the Islamic scholars Ibn Sina (Avicenna) and Ibn Rushd (Averroes).

Thomas attained the status of master of theology in 1256, when he was in his early thirties. His numerous works are meticulous in method and broad in scope. They include early commentaries on some of Boethius's theological treatises; short but influential treatises such as *On Being and Essence*; commentaries on the works of Aristotle; and finally his four major theological syntheses: *Scriptum* (a massive Biblical commentary); *Summa Contra Gentiles* (directed against the various teachings and misunderstandings of all who were not Catholic Christians); *Compendium Theologiae* (as the name says, a compendium of theology, but one left unfinished at his death); and *Summa Theologiae* (widely considered his best and most characteristic work, already very long but nevertheless unfinished at his death).

Clearly, his family's fears that he would live an obscure life of poverty and insignificance seem ridiculous in hindsight. While Thomas never became a bishop or a pope, he was both canonized (officially designated as a saint by the Catholic Church) and also named a Doctor of the Church. There have been a whopping 266 popes (as of 2019) but only thirty-six designated "Doctors" in the entire history of the Catholic Church, which means that Thomas

31 R.C. Sproul, *Consequences of Ideas* (discussing Augustine). This saying is also a paraphrase of a point made in a famous letter written by John Calvin to his mentor Martin Bucer in 1549 (Calvin, *Tracts and Letters*, V: 212-213).

became a member of a club more exclusive than that of the popes. Surely his parents are proud of him now!

*Dante: Poet Laureate of Christendom*

Dante is widely regarded as the greatest literary writer of the medieval west, and the greatness of his epic masterpiece, *The Divine Comedy,* or simply the *Commedia*, is so firmly rooted in the theology of the scholastic tradition and of Aquinas in particular that it is nearly impossible to understand and fully appreciate the former without at least a crash course in the latter. Medieval scholar Timothy Schutt puts it this way:

> The vision of Aquinas finds, in a sense, its richest and fullest and most persuasive expression in the *Divine Comedy* of Dante Alighieri, which, for my money, is the greatest single literary work ever composed. You can argue that the works of Shakespeare as a whole are greater, and that may well be so, but as one work, for me anyway, the *Commedia* takes the cake.[32]

The correspondence between Thomas's theology and Dante's epic applies on many levels, including the very structure of the cosmos. Take the opening stanza of *Paradiso*, the third book (or canticle) of the *Commedia* : "The glory of the One Who moves all things / penetrates all the universe, reflecting / in one part more and in another less" (ll. 1-3).[33] This opening statement is characteristically Aristotelian in that it refers to a prime mover or first cause that put the universe into motion and keeps it moving, and characteristically Thomistic both in its Aristotelianism and in its theistic assertion that the prime mover is a person (a "Who"), God,

32 Timothy Schutt, "Dante: Vita Nuova and Inferno" [lecture], *Odyssey of the West, Vol. III: The Medieval World*, ch. 10.

33 Dante Alighieri, *The Divine Comedy: Paradise. The Portable Dante*, ed. Mark Musa (New York: Penguin, 2004), 391.

whose power and glory pervade the universe that He created. A bit later in the first canto of *Paradiso*, Beatrice reasserts this God-centered understanding of the cosmos, explaining that "Among all things, however disparate, / there reigns an order, and this gives the form/ that makes the universe resemble God / …therein God's higher creatures see/ the imprint of Eternal Excellence— / that goal for which the system is created" (ll. 103-108). So, God is both the creator and the *telos* or goal of the universe, its Alpha and Omega, and He is omnipresent in it. But despite its overarching spirituality, the *Commedia* is not only a theological and devotional allegory; it is also highly autobiographical and personal, and it is almost as heavily invested in the political strife of Dante's own time and place as in the eternal truths of Christianity.

Dante was born in 1265 to a family of the lower ranks of the aristocratic class in the Italian city-state of Florence, and most of what we know of his education is more by implication (from what his works imply about his knowledge and intellect) than from direct evidence. He indicates in *Inferno* that he studied rhetoric under the scholar Brunetto Latini (XV, l. 85)[34] and in his other great poem *Vita Nuova* that he taught himself how to write poetry.[35] His parents died when he was young, and at the age of twelve he was betrothed to Gemma Donati, whom he eventually married and had four children with, but not once in any of his literary works does Dante ever mention his wife.[36] On the contrary, he writes a great deal in both of his most famous poems about another woman, Beatrice Portinari, a girl from one of the wealthiest and most powerful banking families in Florence, with whom he fell

34 Dante Alighieri, *The Divine Comedy. The Portable Dante*, ed. Mark Musa (New York: Penguin, 2004), 82.

35 Dante Alighieri, *Vita Nuova. The Portable Dante*, ed. Mark Musa (New York: Penguin, 2004), 591-92. It is clear from his poems that Dante emulated Virgil in particular, but also Ovid, as well as the Italian troubadour poets who were his more immediate predecessors and contemporaries.

36 Mark Musa, Introduction. *The Portable Dante*, x.

instantly and permanently in love when he first laid eyes on her at a party when they were both all of nine years old.[37] Certainly Dante was deeply infatuated, but there is no evidence that Beatrice was ever more than flattered by his admiration.[38] Beatrice grew up and married a man of her own social station and died at the age of twenty-five. Around that same time, Dante recorded that he began to apply himself seriously to the study of philosophy, particularly Christian philosophy, probably at least partly in an effort to distract himself from grief but also to make sense of his feelings. One of the philosophers he read was Boethius, whose most famous work *The Consolation of Philosophy* features the character Lady Philosophy, who reminds the condemned Boethius that eternal truth transcends temporal suffering and injustice. Clearly Dante benefited from the example of Boethius as he also personifies philosophy as a woman in his work *Convivio*. Describing his newfound love of philosophy, Dante writes that he became "so keenly aware of her [Philosophy's] sweetness that the love of her drove away and destroyed every other thought."[39] Besides Boethius, Dante read deeply in the works of Albertus Magnus, Augustine, and of course, Aquinas.[40]

Dante had become the most celebrated poet in Florence before he turned thirty, but he was also active in civic and political life. Two political parties, the Guelfs and Ghibellines, had fought bitterly for control of Florence throughout the thirteenth century. The Guelfs believed that the pope should have ultimate authority over not only the Church but over all political bodies as well, even kings and emperors and military forces. The Ghibellines believed

37 Dante records this experience and others regarding his feelings for Beatrice in section II of *Vita Nuova* and in his unfinished work *Convivio*, and there are some third-party accounts, including one by the poet Boccaccio, that corroborate certain details of the story (Musa, Introduction, *The Portable Dante*, New York: Penguin, 2003, xi-xii.

38 Timothy Schutt, "Dante: Vita Nuova and Inferno" [lecture], *Odyssey of the West, Vol. III: The Medieval World*, ch. 10.

39 Dante Alighieri, *Convivio* II.2.7.

40 Musa, Introduction, xii.

that the leader of the Church should not have that kind of earthly political and military power, but rather that the Holy Roman Emperor should have political control over Christian countries (that is, Christendom) while the pope governed the realm of the church and spiritual matters. The Guelfs won out, but then they split into two parties: the Black Guelfs (who were staunchly conservative in their view of expansive papal power), and the White Guelfs (who effectively abandoned their previous pro-papal stance in order to resist the efforts of Pope Boniface VIII to put Florence and the entire region of Tuscany under the direct control of the papacy). Dante personally believed that unchecked papal power would corrupt the church, and that in fact it already had.[41] He was one of the Whites, and for years he steadily rose up the ranks of Florentine politics as the two factions competed for power. He served on some important political committees in the government of Florence and eventually became one of its six priors (that is, magistrates or city councilmen). In 1301, when Dante was thirty-six, Boniface mustered an army to take over Florence from the Whites who resisted his power. In a last-ditch effort to convince the pope to change his position, Dante and two other men were sent to represent the Whites on a diplomatic mission to Rome. While they were away, the pro-papal forces took over the city, and Dante's political enemies perniciously accused him of corruption. Dante insisted on his innocence, and because he refused to answer the charges or pay a fine, he was sentenced to exile with the stipulation that should he ever set foot in Florence, he would be seized and burned alive. He never returned to Florence again.[42]

In the years following his devastating exile, this talented man, who had enjoyed a great deal of celebrity as an artist and respect as a public figure at such a young age, found himself in something

41 Musa, p. xiii.

42 Richard H. Lansing and Teodolinda Barolini, eds. *The Dante Encyclopedia.* (New York: Garland, 2000).

resembling what we would call a depression or a serious mid-life crisis. Hence the opening lines of *Inferno*: "Midway along the journey of our life / I woke to find myself in a dark wood, / for I had wandered off the straight path" (Canto I, ll. 1-3). The Dante who is the main character and first-person speaker of the poem begins to find his way out of confusion and despair by allowing himself to be guided by reason in the form of the great epic poet of the Roman Empire, Virgil. Along his guided tour of Hell and Purgatory, Virgil guides Dante from level to level as he encounters the souls of the damned and the penitent. As a non-Christian, however, Virgil is not allowed to enter Paradise. When Virgil leaves Dante with Beatrice to lead him through heaven, Dante is being handed from a guide for his mind to a guide for his soul. Reason can take him from despair to clear-headed understanding, but it cannot save his soul. On this level, the *Divine Comedy* is an allegory of reason and faith: a poetic expression of the relationship between reason and faith that Aquinas and the other scholastics had expressed philosophically.

*Language, Literacy, and Literature in the Medieval West*

Because of the legacy of the Roman Empire, the official language of church, state, and education throughout the medieval period was Latin. Of course, people throughout Europe spoke their own local, native languages, and the vast majority of people only knew the Latin that they had memorized to get them through the parts of church services that required their vocal participation. Augustine and Boethius wrote in Latin when it was still a spoken language, but centuries later the scholastic philosophers who followed—those monks who produced manuscript copies of the scriptures, commentaries, and whatever philosophical, theological, and literary texts they could get their hands on—wrote them in Latin, regardless of the language they had grown up speaking and still used in everyday interactions. In the beginning of his career, Dante wrote poetry in Latin, but even Dante could not resist going with the flow of a linguistic tide that had been slowly rising in Europe for a couple of centuries. Literary historians often refer to this phenomenon as the "turn to the vernacular" or the "rise of vernacular literature."[43]

Though the word comes from the Latin *verna* for "household slave" and once referred to any non-Latin language spoken by people living in the Roman Empire, in medieval Europe a vernacular was simply a language that was actually spoken by a group of people; it was some group's native language. Medieval people everywhere had their own artistic traditions that included poems, stories, and songs in their native languages, but because most of them were illiterate, much of this medieval "literature" was performed and transmitted orally rather than being written down and then read. Technically, the term *literature* refers to verbal compositions that are written down so that they may be read anytime by anyone who has access to the text. By this definition, an epic poem like *Beowulf* was not really literature during the era in which it originated (as a composition that was memorized and performed orally), but it later became literature when someone wrote it down and others read it. And that's exactly what began to happen in Europe more and more often around the eleventh and twelfth centuries.

Closely related to the rise of vernacular literature is the phenomenon of troubadour poets and singers that arose among the people of Celtic descent in southern France during the eleventh and twelfth centuries. These traveling professional performers took storytelling and songwriting to a new level of performance, combining instrumental and vocal music with narrative poetry in *Langue d'oc*

43 As a general topic, the rise of vernacular literatures in Europe is discussed in most major literary reference works that include the medieval and Renaissance periods, including Laura Ashe, *The Oxford English Literary History*, vol. 1 (1000-1350) (New York: Oxford University Press, 2017). Some more specific treatments of this topic include Walter Cohen, "The Rise of the Written Vernacular: Europe and Eurasia," *PMLA* 126, no. 3 (2011): 719-29 and June Hall McCash, "The Role of Women in the Rise of the Vernacular," *Comparative Literature* 60, no. 1 (2008): 45-57.

(the vernacular language of the Provence region) to entertain small groups gathered in towns (similar to street performers today) as well as large crowds gathered in cities for holiday celebrations and public events. As this form of entertainment proliferated throughout Europe, educated, literate people began to write down their own versions of existing tales—translating them from written Latin originals into a vernacular language, or writing down vernacular works that had previously only been orally performed, or simply writing their own original works in their native languages. Some of the most famous examples of early vernacular literature include the anonymous *Song of Roland*, written in the *Langue d'oc* by an unknown poet; the lays and fables of Marie de France, written in Anglo-Norman and in some cases translated from Latin; and the tales of Chretien de Troyes, a Frenchman who is credited for writing down the Arthurian legends of Britain.[44]

This body of poems and tales represents not only a turn to vernacular language but a turn from a view of literature as the serious exposition of large-scale history and universal truth to literature as the expression of the emotional, personal, interior world of characters. It is here that we get a first glimpse of a kind of humanistic focus on emotional life in this world that would become a characteristic feature of Renaissance culture and become even more dominant in the eras that followed.[45] The plots of these

44 Robert T. Lambdin and Laura C. Lambdin, *Encyclopedia of Medieval Literature*. (Westport, Conn.: Greenwood Press, 2012).

45 An important factor in this shift to the personal and emotional was the development of courtly love during the centuries of the Crusades. Monica Potkoy explains that because so many men of the noble classes became soldiers not only for their kings and countries but for Christendom itself during the centuries of the Crusades, a culture of honor or chivalry developed as a way to keep these soldiers honest and virtuous when they were not fighting battles. As the Crusades wound down, moreover, people began to memorialize and romanticize them in stories and songs that glorified the most honorable Christian soldiers for their courage and their courtly behavior, especially towards the women they loved ("The Troubadours and the Lays of Marie de France" [lecture], Odyssey of the West Vol. III: The Medieval World, chapter 8.

stories often revolve around adulterous love affairs; the protagonist is caught between maintaining self-control and going for the emotional gusto, so to speak. When the protagonist is a man, the conflict is often between loyal service to his king and the woman of his dreams, who is frequently the wife of his king or one of his fellow soldiers. When the main character is a woman, the conflict is often between remaining true to her husband (who is often much older, a person her father arranged for her to marry when she was very young) and pursuing an affair with her true love, who is often a relative or a feudal vassal of her husband. Much of the content of these works consists of describing the emotional state of the main character, which can vary from the raptures of romantic love to the torturous pangs of a guilty conscience to actual dishonor and ruin.

Does any of that sound familiar? Of course it does, because that basic plot structure only became more and more popular as time went on, and many of the more modern works that we have read or seen at a theater or on television still use it. But does it remind you of anything else in this chapter? Yes, it sounds a little bit like Dante's situation—arranged marriages kill any hope that a hot young poet might have had to consummate his passionate love for the beautiful and virtuous Beatrice. In fact, the love-story aspect of the *Divine Comedy* owes a great deal to the courtly love tradition, and Dante wrote it in his native vernacular Italian.

Another classic text we read in The World of Christendom and Islam is Geoffrey Chaucer's *Canterbury Tales*, which owes more to the storytelling tradition of its place and time (fourteenth-century England) than the *Commedia* does. Dante may have written in vernacular Italian, but he still aspired to be like Virgil: a serious, philosophical poet who could write the ultimate unified epic of Christendom. Chaucer, on the other hand, was deliberately earthy and eclectic, celebrating in Middle English verse a wild cross-section of English society representing some of its best but far more of its mediocre and worst elements. And that brings this discussion to the last author on the syllabus, Francis Petrarch, who was younger than Dante and older than Chaucer. Like Dante, his most memorable poetry was inspired by his impossible love for a woman he could not have (Laura), and like Dante he suffered both from not having her and from feelings of wretchedness over his own vanity and sin. In that respect, they are not very different from the Augustine of *Confessions*. In fact, in his epistolary essay "Ascent to Mt. Ventoux," Petrarch attempts to climb a mountain but finds himself confused and getting nowhere until he takes out the copy of *Confessions* that he carries in his pocket. As Virgil had brought Dante back to his senses, so Augustine reorients Petrarch, providing him with the trustworthy direction he needs.

All these vernacular expressions exhibit an intense interest in the interior lives of human beings, the inner emotional landscape, rather than a preoccupation with spiritual matters, and thus represent a step in the direction of a more humanistic aesthetic. Influential politicians and poets such as Dante and Petrarch lent literary and intellectual respectability to what had been more of a private, social form of aesthetic expression among aristocratic and royal circles, and Chaucer, on the other hand, raised aspects of some very low-brow forms of entertainment to the level of poetry while lowering more aristocratic forms to the level of low-brow comedy. Dante's impulse was to arrange all of humanity into a great hierarchy of spiritual virtues and vices that reflects the perfect order and justice of the great *divine* comedy, but Chaucer's tendency was to bring all human beings to a similar level as characters in one great *human* comedy.

Augustine might have loved the *Commedia* for its ultimately salvific message that drowns out the notes of courtly love and worldliness of *Inferno,* and certainly Aquinas would have. But it is difficult to imagine either theologian allowing himself to read *The Canterbury Tales* or the kind of love poetry that Petrarch dedicated to Laura. No, something clearly changes when we compare the last two writers on the syllabus to everything that comes before. What Chaucer and Petrarch have in common is an exploration of human emotions and psychology—with a Christian framework, yes, but less focused on salvation than their predecessors—that would come to be known as humanism.

## The World of Christendom and Islam Textual Glosses

### St. Augustine

St. Augustine of Hippo was a Romano-African bishop who lived from the mid-fourth century to the mid-fifth century, making him an excellent example of a "bridge character" between antiquity and the early medieval period. Augustine was raised in a split household that was a corresponding representation of the religious atmosphere in the Roman Empire at the time; his mother was a Christian while his father was not. Augustine converted to Christianity later in his adult life and went on to write numerous works, becoming a prolific early Christian philosopher and theologian. His biographical work concerning his life and conversion to Christianity, *Confessions,* was discussed previously as the final reading in The World of Caesar and Christ.

*On Christian Doctrine (397 CE [Books 1-3], 426 CE [Book 4])*

St. Augustine was appointed a bishop in 395 CE and began writing two of his more famous works, *Confessions* and *On Christian Doctrine.* Through the latter work, Augustine addressed a dire need within the Christian community of his day. Consider for a moment the status of the Bible during the early fourth century: most ecclesiastical communities just had pieces of the Bible, as copying texts was tedious and time-consuming. The biblical texts were translated into only a few languages, so if you were not educated in those languages you could not understand the sources as well; this is why Augustine spends so much time on the question of translation. He also provides his point of view, somewhat framed as an argument, for the proper procedure for interpreting the scripture.

*The City of God Against the Pagans (426 CE)*

As mentioned earlier, the Western Roman Empire was in the process of collapse. Religious struggle ensued between the polytheistic religion of Roman deities and the monotheistic religion of Christianity. Both sides argued that the other was to blame for the deterioration of the empire and the fall of Rome to Alaric. Polytheistic politicians argued that Christianity had enticed Rome to abandon its gods, causing them to be displeased and allowing the Germanic tribes to have victory. The religion of old had emphasized civic rather than individual salvation, and those who had not converted to Christianity felt that being asked to serve a single deity rather than serving the state resulted in a weakened empire. The Christian politicians retorted that it was the polytheistic religion of old that had deprived the realm of moral virtue, resulting in its decline. In this age of contention, and on this particular discourse, St. Augustine wrote his work entitled *The City of God Against the Pagans* to address the claims of the non-Christians. In his discourse, Augustine refutes the claims against Christianity, stating that the empire had seen tragedies before the Christian God was worshiped and therefore any failures of the state could not be blamed on the new religion. Not only does he tackle these accusations but also how Christians should respond in a crisis and reassures that God is still with them. From there the work becomes a long and detailed theology explaining the basic doctrines of Christianity within an overarching theme of the relationship between this world, the kingdom of earth, and the kingdom of heaven, or city of God.

## Boethius[46]

Born in the late fifth century, Boethius was a Roman senator during the reign of the Ostrogoth Theodoric, who had deposed Odoacer as King of Italy. Entering Theodoric's service at a young age, Boethius excelled at public service. By 522 CE, Boethius was appointed to one of the highest administrative roles in the government, and his two sons were made consuls. However, a mere two years later he would be executed for treason. The text discussed below was written while Boethius was incarcerated, awaiting trial.

### *The Consolation of Philosophy (524 CE)*

Written as a dialogue between Boethius and Lady Philosophy, *The Consolation of Philosophy* is one of the more influential pieces written during the early medieval period addressing that age-old question: why do bad things happen to good people? It also explores common themes discussed throughout the honors program such as free will, human nature, and the nature of virtue and justice. Boethius was heavily influenced by Plato and St. Augustine as seen through his discourse with Lady Philosophy.

## Anglo-Saxon Poetry

We have discussed the Anglo-Saxon migration to Britain; however, we only briefly touched on the topic of settlement and society. The Angles, Saxons, and Jutes were the Germanic tribes that invaded Britain from modern-day Denmark and Northern Germany. They were separate tribes with differing cultures, but they shared a form of kinship through their mutual Germanic roots. After migration and settlement, we can see an evolution and assimilation from tribal distinctions to the unity of cultures and shared beliefs, creating a

46 For an interesting experience check out the University of Cambridge's performance of medieval melodies concerning Boethius's work, a breakthrough discovery in 2016.

new entity in the form of petty kingdoms. Christian Anglo-Saxon society carefully planned settlements around prehistoric or previously sacred sites. There are many interesting theories about the motives behind this movement. Some include the idea that perhaps the population believed that by appropriating ancestral sites into their Christian worship they were able to "convert" the ancestors. Another theory is that it could be the "means of legitimizing and underlining the new power of the Church by placing it in a superior position to the surrounding landscape."[47] What we can conclude from this is that the Anglo-Saxon people valued land and the use thereof.

These people were not uncivilized, and while written records are scarce in the early medieval period, an oral tradition was enacted to relay stories through the form of poetry. In Old English poetry, sound repetition occurs in the middle of the line, through alliteration. There is a break in the middle of the line, and the second half of a line works as an appositive or another version of the first half. This poetry is also characterized by metaphors of composite nouns (take two words and put them together), which is called *kenning*[48] and *litotes*, which is a form of understatement.

Poetry can provide the scholar with insights into the cultural and social identity of the society in question. The intended audience of the poetry is its contemporaries, not later scholars, but it provides historians with information about places of importance and political climates. The poet was often the purveyor of propaganda for his patron ruler, or in the case of monastic poets, propaganda for the Church. While some of the poetry presented cannot be taken fully as historical truth, the poem provides scholars with insights into the ideology behind the British Heroic Age and elite warrior cultural identity.

---

47 H., Hamerow, D. A. Hinton and S. Crawford, Eds. *The Oxford Handbook of Anglo-Saxon Archaeology* (Oxford: Oxford University Press, 2011), 752.

48 An example is "swan's road," describing the sea..

### *Beowulf*

*Beowulf* is an excellent example of old English epic poetry. While the story itself can date back to the eighth century, the surviving manuscript found in the Nowell Codex has been dated to the late tenth or early eleventh century. It describes the journey of a Scandinavian hero, named Beowulf, and the obstacles he faces to gain power and prestige; Beowulf is a Germanic Hercules, if you will. While the story is riveting in itself, some of the greatest fascination comes from the revelations regarding Anglo-Saxon culture. Through some of the passages, we can discern the role and value of the poet in the Anglo-Saxon/Germanic society. The presence of an official *scop*, an Anglo-Saxon poet, in an elite's court reveals their importance.[49] As stated before, the poet's job was to recount tales and create poems that solidified and represented the elite ruler's strength and influence, reinforcing his right to rule. Preceded by the likes of the *Iliad, Odyssey, and Aeneid*, we can also see this work as akin to medieval tales of knights on quests to slay the terrorizing beasts. We learn a bit about societal hierarchy practices as Hygelac is referred to as the "ring-giver." In the early medieval society in Britain, lords would commonly gift arm-rings, neck-rings, or brooches to their vassals as an outward sign of loyalty, similar to how a wedding band functions in today's society, excluding the romantic affiliation.

We also see how the utilization of the landscape played a role in the world of the Anglo-Saxon. The great hall that is held by the ruling elite generally appears in the archaeological record as the main structure in settlements. It was not only the elite's residence but a place where the law was conducted, important gatherings took place, and was a safe harbor in times of crisis. A prime example of this settlement structure is the excavated site at Yeavering, which has prehistoric roots as well as Anglo-Saxon settlements. There are

49 Daniel Donoghue, and Seamus Heaney. *Beowulf: A Verse Translation: Authoritative Text, and Contexts, Criticism* (New York: W.W. Norton & Company, 2002), xv.

signs of a square shrine over the western ring ditch (Bede describes a non-Christian temple with altars and idols in an enclosed space),[50] a post in the eastern ring ditch (a possible Bronze Age burial), as well as a structure that is assumed to be a Christian church.[51] This layering of uses on a single site illustrates how the church would appropriate previously sacred spaces as locations for ecclesiastical structures or settlements, to better encourage conversion.

At the end of the tale when Beowulf (spoiler alert) dies, he is given a grand warrior's burial. Burial mounds filled with grave goods are very specifically a non-Christian burial tradition. These burials would have stood out in the landscape, sometimes marking boundary lines for kingdoms. A fascinating example of this is the boat burials of Sutton Hoo,[52] which appear to have artifacts relating to Christianity, suggesting a syncretic culture and discussed earlier in this chapter. It also should be mentioned that the written manuscript most likely is not a direct retelling of the story as the monk inscribing the document would have viewed the tale through his "outsider" lens of Christianity, where the story takes place in un-Christianized Scandinavia.

### *The Dream of the Rood*

Dating this particular piece can be tricky as well. This old English poem is preserved in the Vercelli Book which dates to the tenth century. However, an excerpt from the poem can be found in runes on the Ruthwell Cross, which dates to the eighth century. This makes some scholars consider the *Dream of the Rood* the oldest

50 Bede, *The Ecclesiastical History of the English People.* Translated by Leo-Shirley-Price (London: Penguin, 1991), 1.30.

51 Sarah Semple "Sacred Spaces and Places in Pre-Christian and Conversion Period Anglo-Saxon England" *The Oxford Handbook of Anglo-Saxon Archaeology* (Oxford: Oxford University Press, 2011), 755.

52 A sixth-seventh century Anglo-Saxon burial site containing an undisturbed ship burial which provided archaeologists and historians with artifacts and data of great significance. Located in Suffolk, England.

example of old English literature. The poem is also an example of the genre of dream poetry, in which the narrator or poet has a dream or vision experience. The title of the poem is derived from the old English *rode*, meaning pole or loosely translated, crucifix. The poem details the passion of Christ from the perspective of the cross itself; the narrator serves as a listener and re-teller of the cross's story. The role of the Ruthwell Cross adds interest to this poem's preservation. Containing reliefs of Christian iconography, Latin text, as well as runic inscriptions, it is theorized that the Ruthwell Cross acted as a conversion tool for the Anglo-Saxons. It is debated whether the original structure was a cross or a pillar, as well as whether the portions pertaining to the *Dreamer of the Rood* were a later addition to the carving.

### *The Wanderer*

*The Wanderer* is preserved in part of the Exeter book, which was compiled in the tenth century. The date of the poem is impossible to determine, but we can assume sometime between the eighth and tenth centuries, when scholars see similar examples of literature. The poem follows the wandering warrior in exile, reminiscing on the happiness he once had in serving his lord with his comrades. The tone the poet is trying to express is one of longing for the protection of a good king and fulfillment through service, an example of the role of the vassal. It creates a statement about human history and the loss of life through wars; it also draws on the Christian concept that God is the only form of stability in this earthly life. This beautiful piece also echoes Augustine's discussion of the journey home to God.

## ***Quran***

The Quran is the religious text held sacred by those who practice the Muslim faith. Based on a collection of revelations experienced by the prophet Muhammad in the early seventh century, its complete form did not exist until the tenth century. Just as Christians view the Bible as teaching directly from God, Muslims consider the Quran as teachings from Allah to be used as a means of instruction and edification.

The Quran consists of 114 chapters, or surahs, in order from longest to shortest, excluding the Exordium. The titles are derived from a characteristic word in the text. For example the second surah is called "The Cow", derived from the Arabic word Al-Barqarah, a reference to the golden calf created by the Israelites while wandering the desert. Usually written in prose, the individual surahs were initially preserved in a chaotic format, recorded in an unorganized fashion. They were eventually compiled, a task proving quite tricky, similar to the compiling of the Christian biblical canon. Arabic, the language of the Quran, is quite complex, and many say that it is impossible to accurately translate the book into any other language.

The Islamic faith is one of the Abrahamic religions, alongside Judaism and Christianity, so how similar is this book of faith to the Christian Bible? The Quran does say that Allah is a just, merciful, and loving deity but does not contain any mentions of a personal relationship between believer and God. In reference to the divinity of Jesus, Islam believes that Jesus was, in fact, a prophet but was not actually crucified or resurrected because he was taken up to Heaven beforehand, similar to Elijah. As for human nature, the Quran indicates that there is no belief that the nature of man is sinful; a man is sinless as long as he follows the Quran.

There are many contradictions between the Torah, the Gospel, and the Quran. While there are truths from the Bible within the Quran, those truths have become altered. There are many passages within the Quran that say that the Christian Bible and the Quran point to the same God. However, there are also other passages which state that there is only one way to God: the Quran. There is also a significant degree of contradiction within the Quran, at least partly explaining why there has been so much dissension between Muslim sects as long as there has been a Quran.

*Avicenna, Treatise on Love*

Born in the tenth century, Avicenna was a Renaissance man long before the Renaissance existed. Avicenna was born 980 in a part of the Persian Empire in present-day Uzbekistan. He wrote copiously on a broad range of topics from logic and philosophy to astronomy and medicine. Only half of Avicenna's works survive today, most of which are on philosophy. In contrast to the later scholar Averroes, Avicenna's penchant for Neoplatonism is evident in his works (perhaps due to his famous struggle with Aristotle's *Metaphysics).* As a man of science and medicine, he wished to prove the existence of God through a logical scientific process alongside reason—Islamic humanism if you will.[53]

**Averroes**

Averroes was a twelfth-century Muslim philosopher, lawyer, and physician. He was born in Andalusia, or Muslim-ruled Spain, in 1126. While he served under the Almohad caliphate, his career is most noted by his scholarly works rather than his public service. He wrote extensive commentaries on Aristotle's work.[54] Averroes had a fascination with these works, and his Aristotelian views can be seen through his discussion on philosophy and theology. The Quran encourages contemplation of creation, and Averroes takes this to heart as he returns to natural theology and the physics of matter and motion. Aristotle is important to Averroes because Averroes is writing to sects of Islamic subgroups who have different ideas of creation and God. His works were not just known and respected

53 Lenn Evan Goodman. *Islamic Humanism* (Oxford University Press, 20013), 8–9.

54 He also wrote a commentary on Plato's *Republic.*

by Muslim scholars but by Christian and Jewish philosophers as well. It became a common practice in the thirteenth century to supplement the study of Aristotle with Averroes's commentary.

*Faith and Reason in Islam*

Some have interpreted this work to be a response to Avicenna, but many see it as his address to the disagreeing sects. He claims that none of them have conformed in their interpretation to the intent of the prophet Muhammad. He uses this piece to address propositions and refute previous claims about God. He tackles some of the biggest philosophical questions, similar to those asked in Christianity, such as proof of God's existence, the nature of God and his attributes, God's knowledge, how to discern true prophets and messengers of God, predestination, justice versus injustice, and the resurrection.

**Rumi**

Jalal ad-Din Muhammed Rumi, known as Mawlana or Maulana in the Islamic world and in the Western world simply as Rumi, is one of the best-selling poets of our own time, even in America. To understand the near-universal appeal of his poetry is to see a beautiful side of Islam that is usually invisible to contempo rary Christians.

Rumi was born in 1207 into a Sufi Muslim family in the Persian region of present-day Afghanistan. During his youth the Mongols invaded that region, and Rumi's family fled west, stopping for periods of time in many of the cities of the Muslim world, including Baghdad and Damascus. They finally settled in present-day Turkey, almost all of which had been controlled by Muslims for about 150 years by that time. When his father died, the twenty-five year-old Rumi inherited his position as head of a madrassa, an Islamic religious school, while also continuing his own advanced studies. He eventually became a jurist of shariah, or Islamic law, and also preached in local mosques. He was highly respected and influential in his region when, during a trip to Damascus in 1244, he met a Sufi dervish[55] named Shams-e Tabrizi who would influence him to embrace mysticism and, after Shams died four years later, become a poet.

### Hildegard of Bingen, *Scivias*

Born in 1098 in Bingen (a town on the Rhine River in what is now Germany), Hildegard was dedicated to God by her parents at age eight and was raised in a local monastery for the next six years, until she took vows and joined another Benedictine monastery, St. Disibod. There she eventually rose to the position of *magistera* or mistress of nuns. She had experienced visions since her childhood and at age forty-three began openly speaking of her visions and the revelations she had received. Though she knew that anyone, especially a woman, who made claims about having insight or knowledge of spiritual truth from sources other than the established church risked being deemed heretical, insane, or even satanic, Hildegard managed to avoid those outcomes because of the many years of respectable monastic life that she had led before she began sharing her visions, and because she always insisted on her own position of humility as a messenger of God.[56] She became widely known and respected as a monastic leader, a teacher, and even a preacher, writing three books that combine her visions with theological interpretations, the most famous of which is *Scivias* (from the Latin phrase *scito vias domini*, "know the ways of the Lord"). She also composed over seventy pieces of sacred music,

55 Dervishes are a kind of Sufi Islamic monastic whose tradition dates to the twelfth century. Dervishes practice mysticism and asceticism, aspiring to abandon ego and worldly pleasures in the pursuit of love and service.

56 Chad Meister and J.B. Stump, *Christian Thought: A Historical Introduction*, 2010, 271-74.

most of which survived and are still performed today,[57] and she made significant contributions to medieval medicine and botany. As historians Chad Meister and J.B. Stump put it, "Hildegard's place in the history of Christian thought comes not from carefully argued treatises, but from the originality with which she used metaphors from the organic world to interpret the Christian story and from the influence she exercised on her contemporaries."[58]

### Julian of Norwich, *Revelations of Divine Love*

*Revelations of Divine Love,* also known as the *Showings* (or *Shewings*) *of Julian of Norwich*, is the earliest known book written in English by a woman.[59] Though there is ample evidence of Julian's existence, her visions, and her fame and influence during her lifetime, we do not know when she became an anchorite and we know almost nothing about her life before that, not even the identity of her parents or her original name. We do know that she lived as an anchorite in a closed cell attached to a church in Norwich, England, which still exists and holds regular services as St. Julian's Church. Anchorites lived as hermits, but not in the wilderness like their desert predecessors. Their cells were small rooms connected to the outside world only by windows or other small openings through which other people could pass food and water and remove waste, and through which the anchorites could receive communion and pastoral guidance from priests and also counsel those laypeople who came to them for spiritual direction. Thus, anchorites were separate from the world but attached to the church, cut off from the temptations of the world, but connected to the people who needed their guidance and prayers. In *Revelations of Divine Love*,

57 Hildegard and Barbara Newman, ed. *Symphonia: A Critical Edition of the Symphonia Armonie Celestium Revelationum.* Ithaca, Cornell University Press, 1988, 7-12.

58 Meister and Stump, 274.

59 Baker, Denise M., "Introduction," *The Showings of Julian of Norwich, ed. Baker* (New York: W.W. Norton, 2005), x.

Julian explains that she had a series of sixteen visions at age thirty during an illness so serious that she was receiving the last rites. She eventually recovered from the illness and wrote down the visions, expressing the tremendous comfort that they brought her—not only relieving her bodily suffering but assuring her of her own salvation and of the infinite love that Jesus has for his people, a love that she compares to the love of a mother for her children. The theological core of the revelations is the idea that sin is necessary, for it shows the sinner her own nature, thus revealing her need for God's love and forgiveness and motivating her to flee to Jesus. The most famous lines, variations of which Julian repeats often throughout the work, are "and all shall be well, and all shall be well, and all manners of things shall be well."

### Thomas Aquinas, *Selected Philosophical Writings*

To put it bluntly, the philosophy of Aquinas is hard to understand. It's no harder to understand than most of Aristotle's philosophy, particularly his *Metaphysics*, compared to which his *Nicomachean Ethics* is blissfully easy to follow. Struggling through Aristotle's *Metaphysics* is great preparation for reading anything by Aquinas. But since the only writing of Aristotle that many honors students read is his *Ethics*, they may be mystified by the dense technicality of most of Aquinas's writings. However, Aquinas's questions and conclusions are typically much easier to understand than the arguments in between, so we recommend that students read the introduction and conclusion (the "Hence") of any given section of Aquinas first, then go back and read the entire section through, without getting too bogged down by any particular step in the argument. The confusing parts in the middle often make excellent points for classroom discussion. What follows here are three general principles that might, at most, keep students from grossly misunderstanding the fundamentals of Thomistic philosophy and theology.

*Essence and Existence*

Perhaps the hardest of the hard in Aquinas is his discussion of essence and existence, or forms and things, or substances and matter. Aquinas follows Aristotle (and both diverge from Plato) in thinking that Plato's idea of forms as actually existing in the universe is wrong, and that forms in Plato's sense (which are more often referred to as "universals" in medieval philosophy) only "exist" in the mind as thought-constructs and not as realities. While human beings are a kind of composite thing consisting of both an organizing substance (the soul) and matter (the body), there is not one perfect Platonic form of a human being that exists somewhere to which all actual human beings to some degree conform; rather, in Aquinas's theistic view, each individual human soul is created by God and is the organizing substance of each individual human being. Thus, human beings are not imperfect instances of a perfect human, but rather imperfect (fallen) versions of their own individually created selves.

*"There Exists a God"*

Aquinas's five arguments or proofs of the existence of God are among the all-time most influential statements on the subject, (Others include the ontological argument of the earlier scholastic St. Anselm and the argument of Rene Descartes, which you will read in The World of Reason and Revolt.) This particular essay takes the form of a disputation and is from *Summa Theologiae*, but Aquinas discusses the same arguments in greater detail in *Summa Contra Gentiles*. The five arguments are (i) the argument from motion or change: there must have been some initial motion that caused all other motions; that first mover is God; (ii) the argument from efficient cause: everything in the world is brought about or caused by some other thing, so there must have been some first cause that started the entire web of cause and effect; that first cause is God; (iii) the argument from contingency: everything in the world arises at some time, before which it did not exist, meaning that there must have been a time when nothing existed—but if that were true, then nothing would exist now, which is absurd; therefore, something must exist which is not contingent on other things for its existence, and that is God; (iv) the argument from degree: all comparisons of things describe their degrees of nearness to some superlative exemplar, so there must be a thing that is the absolute most excellent of all things and that causes excellence in all other things; that source is God; (v) the argument from goals: everything in nature has tendencies toward particular goals (for example, acorns tend toward growing into oak trees), but a thing that is unthinking cannot tend to a goal unless directed by someone with understanding; as Brian Davies puts it, "Goal-directed behavior in nature would seem to imply the activity of a director beyond nature,"[60] and that director is God.

### *"Eternity and Time"*

In this chapter of his *Summa Theologiae*, Aquinas uses arguments of both Aristotle and Boethius to formulate his own definitions of time and eternity that differ from theirs. Aquinas's distinction between time and eternity hinges on the differences between the things that each measures. Eternity is the measure of existence itself, whereas time is the measure of things that exist but change. Thus, time measures perishable things by marking the progress of their successive appearance and their perishing, and time is included in eternity. Eternity measures non-perishable things and is simultaneous and whole; eternity is not a process or a collection of moments, but a whole thing in and of itself that has no beginning and no end and never changes. This distinction is fundamental to his later conclusions about the nature of God, creation, and the paradox of free will and determinism.

60 Davies, Brian. *Aquinas* (New York: Continuum, 2002), 53.

*"Free Will" and "Providence: Chance and Freedom"*

These two sections, the first of which is from Aquinas's "Disputed Questions on the Nature of Evil" and the second from his commentary on Aristotle's *Physics* (specifically Aristotle's philosophy of motion), both come to a similar conclusion but on slightly different grounds. The common conclusion is that people do have free will, even though God is omnipotent and omniscient. God uses his power as he chooses, and He chooses not to force people into performing certain actions or wanting certain things. Rather, He chooses to transform their wills from desiring the wrong things to desiring the one right thing, which is to draw nearer to God by conforming to His will. The role of the human will in the process is that while often willing the wrong things because we are fallen, we can at the same time learn from scripture or from other people that God loves us and that we can find fulfillment and eternal life in Him; we can begin to wish or pray that we did truly desire communion with God. If God answers that wish, it is by transforming our wills. In this way, there is a kind of give and take involved in which the more we want God, the more God transforms our wills, and the more we desire Him in return. The argument of the first essay here relies on a discussion of how human will and God's will interact in light of God's omnipotence, and the second essay relies on how God in his omniscience knows exactly how we will in fact use our free will—what choices we will make and what desires we will pursue—because in his eternity he sees all of time from beginning to end at once. The fact that God knows what we will do, according to Aquinas, does not mean that he is controlling our actions or that free will is an illusion.

## Dante Alighieri, *The Divine Comedy*

*The Divine Comedy*, abbreviated the *Commedia*, is structured into three books called canticles exploring the three regions of the afterlife: *Inferno*, *Purgatorio*, and *Paradiso* (Hell, Purgatory, and Heaven). *Inferno* is shaped like an inverted cone, situated directly underneath Jerusalem and growing narrower and narrower until finally coming to a point at the center of Earth where Satan lies confined in a sea of ice. Just beneath this lowest point the mirror image of the cone begins to widen in ever-widening layers of Purgatory, leading to the opposite side of Earth and culminating in the Earthly Paradise, which is the Garden of Eden from which the original humans originally fell into the broken world and sinful state that we have lived in ever since. Students should study some of the many graphic representations of the geographical structure of the *Commedia* to fully grasp the idea here: over the course of the poem, Dante the Pilgrim will traverse the entire diameter of the planet, entering below Jerusalem and emerging in the Garden of Eden, then rise through the successive "spheres" of heaven until he finally comes to the dwelling place of God himself. In other words, he will travel through the entire cosmos as best minds of the medieval world understood it. The structure of the epic is, then, identical to the structure of the cosmos; therefore the structure of Dante's artistic creation reflects the structure of God's creation.

Besides its geographical and cosmological symbolism, the *Commedia* also features extensive numerical symbolism. Each canticle is a series of cantos; *Inferno* has thirty-four cantos, while the other two each have thirty-three. The very first canto serves as a kind of prologue to the entire epic in which Dante the character, traditionally referred to in discussions of the work as Dante the Pilgrim to distinguish him from Dante the poet, wakes up to find himself lost in a dark wood and meets the spirit of Virgil, who offers to lead him out of the woods "through an eternal place."[61] The two figures

61 *Inferno* I.115, *The Portable Dante*, ed. Musa, (New York: Penguin, 2004), 7.

enter the path that leads to Hell in Canto II. From this point, each area of the afterlife is explored through thirty-three cantos. Since three is the perfect number of the divine Trinity, multiples of three symbolize the infinitely expansive glory of God. The total number of cantos, one hundred, is also loaded because ten and multiples of ten were also considered spiritually significant; consider the ten plagues in Egypt and the ten commandments revealed to Moses. By structuring his masterpiece using these "perfect" numbers, Dante mimics the artistry of God and lends his poem a kind of inherent perfection that renders it a worthy reflection of spiritual truth.

Another aspect of the *Commedia* that involves numbers and theology is its incorporation of the seven deadly sins (lust, gluttony, sloth, greed, envy, wrath, and pride), the four cardinal virtues (courage, temperance, prudence, and justice) and the three theological virtues (faith, hope, and love). The various levels of Hell reflect the seven deadly sins, which are further divided into the sins of the flesh, which result from lapses in judgment and self-control in the face of temptation (lust, gluttony, sloth, and wrath) and mortal sins, which are deliberate misuses of human reason to bring harm to others or to rebel against God (envy, violence, and pride). Students may recognize that the seven sins resemble Aristotle's discussions of virtues and vices in *Nicomachean Ethics* and that the first four virtues are the same ones that Plato describes in *The Republic*. Likewise, as Dante the Pilgrim and Virgil ascend through the terraces of Purgatory, Aristotle's discussions of the deficiencies and excesses of these four virtues are further expounded and reflected. By contrast, the three theological virtues, of course, are biblical, originating in the apostle Paul's famous description of love in I Corinthians 13. By incorporating both classical and Christian teachings into his depiction of the afterlife, Dante affirms the truth, albeit limited truth, of pre-Christian ethics without grace, while asserting the transformed, transcendent Truth of Christ.

The *Commedia* is both an epic poem and an extended allegory, and as such it operates on multiple levels.[62] First there is the more literal, surface-level story: a character named Dante wakes up in the woods, and a dead poet named Virgil takes him on a tour of the spiritual realms of the cosmos. Then there is the sense in which the whole poem is the spiritual autobiography of a thirteenth-century Italian poet named Dante Alighieri; on this level waking up in a dark wood allegorically represents the real Dante's betrayal and exile from Florence, and the journey through the afterlife represents how that real man found his way back, with lots of spiritual assistance, from despair to the hope of eternal life in Christ. Closely related to the spiritual autobiography is the story of the creation, fall, and redemption of the human race through the resurrection of Christ; every major part of the biblical metanarrative is represented in the *Commedia*, either in its geography or in its cast of characters. Similarly, the *Commedia* serves as an evangelical purpose as a declaration of the good news of Christ; just as Dante finds his way through a revelation of grace, so that revelation extends to all who hear the gospel and believe it, repenting and embracing new life in Christ. Finally, that revelation extends to us as readers. As we read, we trace the steps of Dante from despair into hope, and thus the *Commedia* influences us to believe in and accept God's gifts of love and grace.

### Geoffrey Chaucer, *The Canterbury Tales*

Chaucer was born around 1342 and probably in London, though the exact circumstances are not known. His middle-class parents had connections to industry, government bureaucracy, and they had distant ties to aristocracy; young Geoffrey had some formal schooling before becoming a page in the house of a countess. A page was a kind of intern who did the humble work of a servant

62 Though our number of levels differs from his, we are indebted to Timothy Schutt's discussion of the levels of allegory in the *Commedia* for our discussion in this paragraph (Schutt, "Dante: Inferno" [lecture 9], *Odyssey of the West, Vol. III: The Medieval World.*)

but was from a higher class than other kinds of servants.[63] One purpose of becoming a page was to develop the manners needed for interactions with the upper classes, and another was to make connections among the upper classes that might prove beneficial in one's adult career. As a page, Chaucer waited on the Duke of Lancaster and John of Gaunt.

Chaucer might have started composing poetry as a result of some time he spent as an English soldier fighting in France (during the Hundred Years' War) and as a prisoner of war there for some months. Scholars speculate that he might have become well acquainted with troubadour-style poetry and the conventions of the courtly love tradition during that time. In any case, soon after his return to England, he began writing a translation of the French Romance of the Rose, which Neville Coghill calls "the gospel" of courtly love.[64] By 1367 he had attained a position as valet to the king and married one of John of Gaunt's sisters-in-law. Over the next twenty years he composed most of his long narrative poems, including *The Parliament of Fowls* and his first work that came to be considered a masterpiece, the quintessentially courtly tragic story of *Troilus and Criseyde*. By the late 1380s he was working on *The Canterbury Tales*, with plans to have each pilgrim character tell two stories on the way to Canterbury and two on the way back to London. With at most one story by any character, the work was largely unfinished when he died in 1400—but still long enough to make up a full volume that would become a world literary classic.

If it's so incomplete, then how did it become so important? Part of the answer lies in its variety: among the tales we find serious theology as in the Parson's Tale, secular romance and jealousy plots as in the Miller's and Reeve's tales, a standard (if somewhat over the top) courtly love story (the Knight's tale), as well as parodies of

63 This tradition survives to this day in the United Kingdom and even in our American tradition of Congressional pages.

64 Coghill, Neville. Introduction to *The Canterbury Tales* (New York: Penguin, 2003), xii.

courtly love that cast a skeptical light on the entire courtly tradition (such as the Wife of Bath's tale). That range of treatments of human experience provides something for every reader's taste, which translates into broad popularity. More importantly, though, that very range results from the work's status as culturally transitional: while the frame story of the *Tales* is a Christian pilgrimage to the shrine of St. Thomas Becket in Canterbury, and the framing tales of the Knight and the Parson convey serious messages about both faith and romantic love, the individual stories in between those serious bookends are anything but serious or religious—at least not in any straightforward sense. On one hand, the pilgrims clearly inhabit a world saturated with the assumptions of medieval Christendom, but with the exceptions of the Knight and the Parson their tone, or at least Chaucer the pilgrim's tone toward them, is more earthy and secular than anything else we read in the course.

## Francis Petrarch

While Dante and Chaucer are seen as transitional figures between the medieval and Renaissance eras, Petrarch is generally regarded as the first Christian humanist of the Renaissance.[65] Petrarch's father was a native of Florence, who had been exiled from his home city for political reasons on the very same day as Dante. Petrarch was born in 1304 in Arezzo, Italy, but when he was a young boy his father moved the family to Avignon, France, in hopes of finding work in the recently relocated court of Pope Clement V. Petrarch was educated mostly in the rarefied cultural atmosphere of the papal court in France but also studied law at the University of Bologna in Italy. In time, both Italy and France would claim him as poet laureate. What distinguishes his work from Dante's is its intense, sustained focus on the lights and shades of his own emotions, his thoughts on his inner

65 This labelling may seem odd given that Chaucer was seventy-five years younger than Dante and nearly forty years younger than Petrarch, but the Renaissance started earlier in Italy than in England.

life in relation to his public life of activity and celebrity. His most famous writings are his *Canzoniere* or *Sonnets* addressed to Laura, the object of his courtly devotion. In this course, we typically read two short prose works that circle all the way back to the end of The World of Caesar and Christ and Augustine's *Confessions* while at the same time capturing Petrarch's spirit of humanism.

Both "Ascent to Mount Ventoux" and "To Posterity" are, in effect, essays in the form of letters, and both are included in Petrarch's collection, *Familiar Letters*. The latter is a partial autobiography that enumerates his many accomplishments and showcases a level of unapologetic confidence not previously encountered in this course. The former is addressed to his former priest and confessor Dionisio da Borgo San Sepolcro, but scholars believe that Petrarch did not write the letter until several years after Dionisio had died. Hence this "letter," like most in the collection, is more accurately a meditative reflection on a spiritual journey, rather than an objective account. Like the mountain of Purgatory that Dante must climb to reach Paradise, Mount Ventoux represents a spiritual struggle for Petrarch, who wastes time and energy vainly searching for an easier path to the top before finally applying himself to the climb. However, that's as far as the comparison to Dante's journey goes, for what we expect to be a sublime, transcendent "mountaintop experience" turns out to be only the starting point of the journey into the self. After finally reaching the summit and admiring the view, he takes time to read from his handy copy of Augustine's *Confessions*: "People go off to marvel at the height of mountains and the great wave of the sea and the broad courses of rivers, and the flow of the ocean, and the circuits of the stars: but they neglect themselves" (X.8.15).[66] In Petrarch's hands this passage becomes inspiration to stop looking outward but rather to turn to self-contemplation as a path to truth; he then proceeds down the mountain as into the valley of his own inner being.

---

66 Augustine, *Confessions*. Edited and translated by Carolyn J.-B. Hammond (Boston: Harvard University Press, 2014), 93.

# CHAPTER FOUR

# THE WORLD OF HUMANISM AND REFORM

ELIZABETH STICE

*Humanism and Reform*

The greatest stumbling block to understanding a time period is mistakenly thinking we understand it already. Instead, we should remember the saying, "the past is a foreign country." In the case of the Renaissance and the Reformations, it is especially true. "Italy" was the heart of the Renaissance and "Germany" was the birthplace of the Protestant Reformation, but neither country existed yet as a nation state. Italy was a peninsula of warring states built around cities with varied forms of government, from the Republic of Venice to the Kingdom of Naples to the Papal States, where the pope exercised temporal political power. Powerful families such as the Medici and the Borgias sought to dominate these states and sometimes even control ecclesiastical government. This was the world of brutal competition for power, reflected in Machiavelli's treatise of advice for a young ruler, *The Prince*. It was also the world of the court culture found in Castiglione's *Book of the Courtier*. Up north, what's now Germany was part of the Holy Roman Empire: a loose confederation of over 1,000 states, some large and powerful like Prussia and Austria, others very small, like the free imperial cities. The ruler who protected Martin Luther, Frederick III of Saxony, was a lifelong Catholic with a renowned collection of relics. This unfamiliar political landscape was the context of the Renaissance and the Reformations. To understand it in its complexity we must go beyond the familiar narratives and be prepared for what may seem foreign.

*The Renaissance*

The Renaissance began in Italy in the fourteenth century and spread throughout Europe, lasting until the end of the seventeenth century, though the term itself dates to the nineteenth century. Historians consider it a cohesive time period because of the widespread movement to create a break with the past and return to the classical virtues of Greece and Rome. It began with people like the Italian writer Petrarch (1304-1374) and his love of Cicero. Petrarch "conceived of himself as reviving the glories of ancient Latin after a period of medieval 'darkness' had obscured the light of classical eloquence."[1] Petrarch and fellow writer Giovanni Boccaccio (1313-1375) disdained their immediate forebears in favor of ancestors long gone, creating the Renaissance *and* the idea of the "Dark Ages." The catchphrase of the Renaissance was *Ad Fontes*, which means "back to the sources." The works of Cicero and even Augustine had been neglected for some time among Europeans, but now they were reexamined and elevated.

When we think of the Renaissance today we often begin with art, but humanism was the foundation of the Renaissance, including its art. Humanism was then defined primarily as a style of learning. It included "the fields of grammar, rhetoric, poetry, his-

1 Zachary Schiffman, ed., in *Humanism and the Renaissance* (New York: Houghton Mifflin, 2002), 1.

tory, and the study of the Greek and Latin authors."[2] Humanists were those well-versed in the classical disciplines and familiar with classical texts, like Petrarch or the Dutch author Desiderius Erasmus (1466-1536). Revisiting classical texts also led to a rebirth of classical philosophy, as people adopted and adapted thinkers like Plato and Aristotle for themselves, creating Renaissance Neoplatonism. Though not everyone became a Neoplatonist, it is reflective of a shift in the intellectual world of Europe. Many medieval thinkers were cautious about embracing philosophers associated with paganism, but many Renaissance thinkers found ways to assimilate key aspects of classical thought. Some even attempted allegorical or redemptive readings of thinkers like Plato while acknowledging their view of the divine was limited.

Rhetoric and the other humanities disciplines led Renaissance thinkers to "deep consideration of philosophical and theological matters, of how men might best live in the real world as creatures made in the image of God."[3] Society valued rhetorical eloquence, but classical education was also meant to "equip a man to lead a good life."[4] It has even been argued that man became a "spiritual individual," aware of his uniqueness during the Renaissance.[5] This humanist style of learning led naturally to a second understanding of humanism, as a way of viewing human potential and significance. It can be seen in Giovanni Pico della Mirandola's *Oration on the Dignity of Man* (1496), a classic Renaissance text.

2 Paul Oskar Kristeller, "Humanism and Scholasticism in the Italian Renaissance," in *Humanism and the Renaissance*, ed. Zachary Schiffman (New York: Houghton Mifflin, 2002), 61.

3 Zachary Schiffman, ed., *Humanism and the Renaissance*, ed. Zachary Schiffman (New York: Houghton Mifflin, 2002), 57.

4 Hanna H. Gray, "Renaissance Humanism: The Pursuit of Eloquence," in *Humanism and the Renaissance*, ed. Zachary Schiffman (New York: Houghton Mifflin, 2002),74.

5 Jacob Burckhardt, "The Civilization of the Renaissance in Italy," *Humanism and the Renaissance*, ed. Zachary Schiffman (New York: Houghton Mifflin, 2002), 21.

It demonstrates rhetorical eloquence in disputation and also asserts that man is a remarkable being at the center of creation, able to ascend or descend among other forms of life—capable of reaching the heights of angels or of becoming as spiritually and intellectually inanimate as tree bark.[6] This type of humanism, which centers on understanding humans and their potential and achievements, is more familiar to us and is deeply connected to how we understand and appreciate the Renaissance.

This new excitement about humanity was especially notable in the world of art. Renaissance art was a dramatic and significant departure from medieval art. Medieval artists were often anonymous, but some Renaissance artists became celebrities. Many of their names are still familiar, including Brunelleschi, Leonardo Da Vinci, Donatello, Ghiberti, and Masaccio and their northern counterparts such as Hieronymus Bosch, Albrecht Dürer, and Jan van Eyck. Michelangelo was even called "the divine one." Our appreciation of Renaissance art is in keeping with a greater appreciation of human endeavors. The names of Renaissance artists continue to be memorialized, known even by those unfamiliar with their art but at least familiar with the Teenage Mutant Ninja Turtles.

Renaissance artists were exciting because they transformed the art of their time. Though not as stylized as Byzantine art, Medieval art was more stylized than realist. It was also often two-dimensional, with little regard for depth of field, and limited perspective and limited shading. Nearly all the subjects were religious. During the Renaissance, paintings and sculptures became more realistic and less stylized. Artists used math, especially ratios, to make breakthroughs in perspective and shading. The vanishing point began to be widely used. The scientific study of bodies was also used to make depictions of people more anatomically accurate. Artists like Leon Battista Alberti created new standards for their work. As in

---

6 Giovanni Pico della Mirandola, *Oration on the Dignity of Man* (Washington, D.C.: Regnery Publishing, 2015), 7-9.

literature, artists also turned to the past for guidance, reviving the old arts. In 1450, Donatello created the first full-scale equestrian statue since classical times with his *Gattamelata* (1453), which commemorated a mercenary soldier. It was an enormous bronze statue, an impossible feat for the previous hundreds of years. In Florence, Brunelleschi shocked the world when he completed a dome for the Cathedral of Santa Maria del Fiore. It was the world's largest masonry dome, on a building too tall for external scaffolding, which Brunelleschi designed with engineering genius and insights he had from studying classical Roman architecture. In both Italy and northern Europe, oil painting was rediscovered independently and spread everywhere, adding a vibrancy to paint which had long been absent. The art of the Renaissance inspired wonder even in its own time.

When we think of Renaissance art, we picture large canvases and brilliant colors, with inspiring images. Representative works include the Sistine Chapel, painted by Michelangelo, which tells the story of man's creation. Michelangelo represents the "Renaissance man." Not only is the ceiling dramatic and moving, but Michelangelo himself designed the scaffolding needed for the project and considered himself more of a sculptor than a painter. His *David* is a seventeen-foot marble statue which is the centerpiece of Florence's tremendous collection of Renaissance art. Florence was, in many ways, the heart of the Renaissance. Raphael of Urbino was known chiefly for his paintings and their vivid use of color and shading. While he frequently painted religious art, his most famous work may be *The School of Athens.* It is a textbook example of the use of the vanishing point and shows advancements in use of color, shading, and perspective. *The School of Athens* is a fresco which depicts all of Greek philosophy, but it resides in the Vatican. In the arts we can see the extent to which Renaissance thinkers appropriated the classical era. Some artists attempted to use classical imagery to relate Christian themes. Botticelli's famous painting

*The Birth of Venus* depicted a classical, pagan story and featured a prominent female nude but many suggested that the story could provoke contemplation of divine love, even meditation on God. This should remind us that even with the use of classical images and ideas, those images and ideas were adapted and transformed in the Renaissance.

Though people often speak of "secular humanism" and its opposition to Christianity, humanism during the Renaissance was not always opposed to Christianity. The broadening appreciation of human ability was in the context of a theistic universe, and the remarkable abilities of humans were considered God-given. There was even something called "Christian humanism." This humanism also engaged early texts and the past, but focused on early Christianity. For example, after extensively reading and researching the earliest biblical documents available, Erasmus published a new Greek New Testament in 1516. It was closer to the original texts and an improvement upon the Vulgate, the Latin Bible then in use which was removed from the original texts by translation. The humanist quest to go back to the original sources extended to Christian writings. It also affected church history. It was a fifteenth century Italian priest, Lorenzo Valla, who used his skills in philology to prove that the "Donation of Constantine" was a forgery. The Donation was an alleged imperial decree by Constantine giving territory and authority to the pope, which had been used by later generations to support the authority of the pope. Thinkers like Erasmus and Valla looked to early church documents to help the Church along the way, putting the skills of humanism into the service of faith.

Italy was the epicenter of the Renaissance, but the northern Renaissance was also very artistically productive. Many of these artists were influenced by southern Europe, but developed their own style. The transition from Gothic to Renaissance style can be seen in the work of Jan van Eyck (c.1390-1441), who was from the Netherlands and known for his distinctive paintings. Van Eyck was skilled in the use of oil paint, which was a new phenomenon in European painting. His paintings were also more realistic than those of his predecessors and he was particularly known for his ability to emulate reality, as seen in his depictions of different surfaces and reflections. Van Eyck's most famous works are religious paintings and altarpieces, such as the Ghent altarpiece. In Germany, Albrecht Dürer (1471-1528) was known for his paintings, engravings, and woodcut prints, which reflected Renaissance techniques and sensibilities and made him a celebrated artist. Though Dürer traveled to Italy and studied art abroad, he had his own style. His *Praying Hands* is still used as decoration in many Christian homes today. His self-portrait of 1500 has been considered especially significant by art historians. Hans Holbein the Younger (1497-1543) was another German artist renowned for his realism in painting and printmaking, who worked in Germany, England, and Switzerland. The artists of the Northern Renaissance demonstrate the connections between the different parts of Europe and the spread of Renaissance ideas from Italy as well as the importance of individual style and creativity in Renaissance artists of all regions.

The art of the Renaissance is inseparable from the economics of the Renaissance. Foreign trade and advancements in banking made Italy a center of wealth. For a time, the coin of Florence, the florin, was the monetary standard for much of Europe. It may be surprising, but the vast majority of Renaissance artwork was commissioned and guided by wealthy patrons rather than inspired by artistic sentiments. Artists often used specified materials and even techniques. Colors reflected metaphorical ideas and the status of patrons. For example, ultramarine blue was the most expensive color of paint at the time, made from ground lapis lazuli, and therefore often reserved for special figures, such as Christ or the Virgin Mary. But dramatic use of blue also reflected the wealth of the patron. Renaissance paintings are, as described by Michael Baxandall, "fossils of economic life."[7] The world of the Renaissance had a strong class hierarchy and the wealthy and titled sought to emphasize their status. Much of the "public" art we see in Renaissance churches was privately financed. Patrons commissioned art for public spaces, such as churches, where it was meant to serve religious devotional purposes but where it also publicly proclaimed their private wealth.

While Renaissance art was a dramatic transition from medieval art, what followed it was a less obvious break. Especially in southern and Catholic Europe, Renaissance art gave way to the baroque. This style began in the seventeenth century and maintained many of the themes and techniques of Renaissance realism but intensified use of color, motion, and feeling. It had a heightened sense of emotion. The sculptor and architect Gian Lorenzo Bernini (1598-1680) was an early figure in baroque art and produced some of the greatest marble sculpture of all time, such as his stunning work *The Rape of Proserpina*. In architecture, baroque style was considerably more ornate and laid the foundation for rococo. In northern Europe and especially where the Protestant Reformation took hold, art became considerably more muted, with less vibrant use of color and less emotion. Lucas Cranach the Elder (1472-1553) was a Renaissance painter who depicted images from mythology and the Christian tradition, but whose later work included realistic and sober portraiture of Martin Luther and other significant figures. Later northern painters like Rembrandt (1606-1669) often depicted realistic figures on dark canvases. The Protestant Reformers were explicitly averse to bright colors and displays of wealth, especially in religious settings.[8] Over time, there was considerably less use of pagan imagery and bold colors where the Protestant Reformation was embraced.

7 Michael Baxandall, *Painting & Experience in Fifteenth-Century Italy*, 2nd ed. (New York: Oxford University Press, 1988), 2.

8 Michel Pastoreau, *Red: The History of a Color*, trans. Jody Gladding (Princeton: Princeton University Press, 2017), 108-112.

Within literature, the love of the classical rose alongside the elevation of vernacular languages. Vernacular languages are the everyday languages of people, such as English, French, German, and Italian, as opposed to a universal language, such as Latin. From the fourteenth century onward, various authors demonstrated the beauty of the vernacular, though it was once thought to be incapable of true artistic expression. In England, Chaucer (1340-1400) broke new ground with the *Canterbury Tales*. In France, Christine de Pizan (1364-1430) wrote a variety of works in French. Even Petrarch and Boccaccio, who helped to begin the Renaissance and promote classical authors, wrote in both Italian and Latin. Petrarch's sonnets became so famous that the style is still called after his name. The other common style of sonnet is named after Shakespeare (1564-1616), another Renaissance figure who wrote in the vernacular. The development of the vernacular began before the printing press (1440) but would accelerate and expand once the printing press made works in the vernacular physically more accessible to people. The value of the vernacular also began to rise in religious settings. Even before the Reformation, figures like Wycliffe and Erasmus encouraged use of the vernacular in church.

Many important transformations which took place over longer periods of time also began during the era of the Renaissance. This was the beginning of the "Age of Exploration." Columbus discovered the Americas in the Quattrocento (fifteenth century), before Martin Luther posted his *95 Theses*. The discovery of new lands and new peoples began new forms of literature and prompted questions about society and human nature even as they generated new trade networks, launched empires, and changed the dynamics of state power inside Europe. This can be seen in works like Thomas More's genre-defining *Utopia* (1516), and in many of the works read in the Reason and Revolt class. Captivating figures like Sir Walter Raleigh and Queen Elizabeth I cannot be understood apart from the expanding world they lived in and the competition for control over global trade. And just as new lands were being discovered, the skies were being re-discovered as figures like Tyco Brahe (1546-1601) and Galileo Galilei (1564-1642) observed the planets and challenged geocentrism, serving as important bridge figures to the Scientific Revolution. Michael Servetus (1511-1553) was burned at the stake in Geneva for his non-trinitarian views during the Reformation, but he was also one of the first people to properly identify the role of the heart in pulmonary circulation.

What has been called the "military revolution" began during the sixteenth century and transformed Europe for the next three hundred years. The revolution included the widespread adoption of firearms and advanced artillery, changes in fortifications, and an increase in the size of armies. At sea, the adoption of firepower changed the nature of ships and of naval battles. While we may not associate these changes with the Renaissance, Venice replaced all the crossbows in its army with guns in 1490 and the new style of fortification was advanced by Italians and known as *trace italienne*.[9] In fact, Ft. McHenry, where the flag in "The Star-Spangled Banner" was waving in 1812, was built in this style. The new and emerging military practices of the Renaissance would be tested in the conflicts generated by the Reformations. Indeed, the time period 1500-1700 saw the most warfare in European history.[10]

Though the Protestant Reformation has a fairly clear beginning, there was no decisive break with the Renaissance. Many people and ideas belong in both the Renaissance and the Reformation. Thomas More is remembered both for *Utopia* and his martyrdom for the Catholic cause in England. Elizabeth I was a Renaissance queen who enjoyed Shakespeare's plays even while she finalized the transition to state Protestantism begun by her father, Henry VIII. Some of Shakespeare's plays, such as *Hamlet*, engage the same

9 Geoffrey Parker, *The Military Revolution: Military innovation and the rise of the West, 1500-1800*, 2nd ed. (Cambridge: Cambridge University Press, 1996), 17.

10 Parker, 1.

theological questions at the heart of Reformation debates. While Milton's 1667 *Paradise Lost* claimed to "justify the ways of God to man" by raising many theological questions, it did so in the form of an epic poem from the classical period. Humanism and Reform were inseparable.

*The Reformations*

From the Middle Ages through the Renaissance, there were many movements and moments of reform within the Catholic Church. Frustrations within Christendom touched on many different themes. One major theme was the perceived lack of piety among the people of Europe. It was not uncommon for wandering friars to travel through towns in the Middle Ages and Renaissance, urging people to lead more righteous lives and cast aside the things of the flesh. In 1497, a Dominican friar in Renaissance Florence named Girolamo Savonarola led a "bonfire of the vanities." People from across the city built a bonfire and threw in anything that might be associated with sin or vanity, including books, paintings, and makeup. In the city most closely associated with the wealth and excess of the Renaissance, people threw priceless paintings into the flames. The desire for more serious faith created several new movements across Europe. On the heretical side, the Cathars sprung up in France, with an emphasis on abstinence and attempting to lead sinless lives. Within orthodoxy, the *devotio moderna* (modern devotion) movement began within the Catholic Church, in northern Europe. It taught a life of simplicity in accord with Christ, emphasizing Scripture reading, close communication with God, and approaching the sacraments in the right manner. This type of devotion animated Thomas à Kempis's *Imitation of Christ* (1418) and the Brethren of the Common Life, a religious community responsible for the education of both Erasmus and Martin Luther.

While many people were concerned about a lack of piety within Christendom broadly, there were also concerns with the governance of the church. In some communities, lay people were unhappy with the behavior or education of local priests. At another level, many priests and monks were unhappy with the governance within orders or the behavior and abuses of bishops and archbishops. Many regions sent tithes to bishops who rarely visited. Much of northern Europe felt it was unfair to send money to Rome when so few popes were from their region. Because of the importance of clerical authority, church hierarchy could also be subject to politics and even Machiavellian behavior. Not all popes seemed chosen for their good character, and many kings wanted more power to appoint bishops in their own countries based on politics rather than piety. A particular crisis in church leadership also gave birth to the conciliar movement, a significant reform effort. The movement began after the Schism of 1378, when there were two popes simultaneously claiming authority. "Conciliar" comes from "council," and the movement looked past the pope to the use of ecumenical church councils to resolve problems. The conciliar movement was a challenge to the authority of the pope that empowered others within the church, such as cardinals and bishops, with regard to authority and theology. Because the pope held so much temporal power in the fifteenth century, secular authorities also supported the conciliar movement to resolve the crisis. Councils also provided an important forum for addressing issues within the Church. The Schism of 1378 was resolved at the Council of Constance (1414-1418), which also closely examined the theology of certain dissenters.

But in 1517, Europe would be set on fire by flames bigger than those at the bonfire of the vanities. The resulting conflagration would ultimately not be resolved by a council. It would not be resolved at all. Instead, the Church would split with the Protestant Reformation, a reform movement which eclipsed others. It was a movement that included concerns about personal piety *and* church governance *and* the relationship between church and state, among other things.

There were several key figures on the road to the Protestant Reformation. One of the first significant figures was John Wycliffe (1330-1384). He was priest and a professor at Oxford who was responsible for the first translation of the Bible into English and put an emphasis on common people reading the Bible. Wycliffe was a would-be church reformer who had doubts about transubstantiation and contributed to debates about the authority of the pope. He "claimed that an unworthy pope did not have to be obeyed."[11] Wycliffe preferred local secular authority to Roman church authority on some matters. Though some of Wycliffe's ideas were very empowering to secular authority, his ideas on the equality of believers and a less hierarchical vision of the church influenced the leaders of the 1381 Peasants' Revolt in England. The Peasants' Revolt failed to secure much for the peasants, and Wycliffe found himself censured. But emerging from the ashes of that revolt was the tradition of the Lollards, who also took inspiration from Wycliffe (though not leadership). The Lollards were from the poorer classes and "criticized the Church's landed wealth and espoused a simpler religion. Led by gentry known as 'Lollard knights,' the Lollards rose up in rebellion in 1414, but were brutally crushed by King Henry V."[12] Though Wycliffe died of natural causes, he and his writings were posthumously condemned at the Council of Constance. His body was dug up and burned, with the ashes scattered to prevent them from becoming relics.

Following in the footsteps of Wycliffe was Jan Hus (1369-1415). He was a Bohemian (Czech) professor and priest. As a young man, he helped pay his way through university by singing but he had a transformative religious experience as a result of close reading

11 John Merriman, *A History of Modern Europe, Vol. 1 From the Renaissance to the Age of Napoleon,* 3rd ed. (New York: W.W. Norton & Company, 2010), 88.

12 Merriman, 88.

of the Bible. As a priest, he preached in the vernacular language, criticized indulgences, and raised questions about the sacraments. He resented the way that indulgences sent local money to Rome. He also disputed the way the Eucharist was administered at the time. Priests took the bread and the wine, but parishioners only the bread. His preaching in Czech put him at odds with the German authorities, who ruled Bohemia, and his questions about the sacraments and indulgences put him at odds with church authorities. In 1414, Hus was promised safe conduct to the Council of Constance, but, once there, he was arrested and put on trial. He was on trial not only for his own ideas, but for holding to the teachings of Wycliffe. Hus refused to recant, and he was condemned as a heretic. He was burned at the stake by the Holy Roman Emperor in 1415 and died praying. Both Wycliffe and Hus were considered threatening by authorities for their theological differences and their challenges to authority. The followers of Hus became known as the "Hussites" and were involved in several rebellions after his death. They were the "only major fifteenth-century dissidents" within the Catholic Church and, after fighting off various papal armies, won a "dispensation for the faithful to take communion in both bread and wine."[13]

Between the dissent of Hus and the protest of Martin Luther was Desiderius Erasmus. The saying is that "Erasmus laid the egg that Luther hatched." Erasmus was the illegitimate son of a Dutch priest and became a monk and a famous humanist and author. Best known for his satirical work *Praise of Folly* (1511), Erasmus wrote an improved Greek New Testament and advocated preaching in vernacular languages. Erasmus taught that salvation came from the mercy of God and he encouraged personal devotion and reading of the Scripture. Erasmus wanted to reform the church and Christendom. He criticized clerical abuses, often satirically, but also wrote earnestly, as he did in *The Education of a Christian*

13 Merriman, 89.

*Prince* (1516). In it, Erasmus emphasized the need for a Christian upbringing and continued reliance on faith. According to Erasmus, the prince should be like a father to his people and their welfare was his primary responsibility. *The Education of a Christian Prince* also discussed another topic close to Erasmus's heart: avoiding bloodshed among Christians. Erasmus believed that Christians should be slow to go to war, especially with each other. And in a Europe that was riven by conflict and periodic face-offs against the Ottoman Turks, he even believed that the Turks would best be converted by love. But Erasmus was uninterested in becoming a martyr like Hus and unwilling to abandon his vows like Luther. As one who was firmly against wars within Christendom, he was also unwilling to endorse change which could lead to violence within Europe. Like Wycliffe and Hus, he wanted reform but he did not start, and later would not join, the Protestant Reformation.

In 1517, Erasmus was the most published living author in Europe. In 1518, Luther surpassed him.[14] Who was this Martin Luther and what happened? In Protestant churches, Martin Luther is often seen as a David against a Goliath, a lone, free-thinking, and pious individual against a corrupt and callous institution willing to sell salvation. The reality is more human and more complex. In 1505, Luther was a law student who vowed to become a monk after a near-death experience in a lightning storm. Soon after, he was in a monastery. By 1507, he was a priest—one with many persistent and personal questions about man's sinfulness in relation to God's righteousness. His deep thinking was taken as a sign of vocation, and he was sent back to school to study theology and become a professor. By 1512, he was a professor at the University of Wittenberg, where he lectured on Psalms, Romans, and Galatians. Over time, as he read the Bible more closely, he began to reevaluate some of the teachings and practices of the Catholic Church.

In 1517, Luther went from obscurity to the world stage when

14 Andrew Pettegree, *Brand Luther* (New York: Penguin Books, 2015), 227-228.

he publicly criticized the practice of selling indulgences. His *95 Theses* was originally published in Latin, but was soon translated into German and then read widely thanks to the printing press. What prompted Luther to post his theses on the church door at Wittenberg, asking for a public debate on the topic of indulgences? Indulgences were intended to be a remittance of the penalties of sin for the breaking of canon (church) law; essentially, the pope had the power to forgive sins against church law. An indulgence would lessen one's time in purgatory because it would be a sin forgiven. Indulgences could be granted for particularly noble actions, like fighting in the Crusades. Indulgences still exist today, though they are no longer sold. However, in Luther's time, indulgences were often sold and often abused. The money from the sale of indulgences went to bishops or to Rome, to fund buildings like St. Peter's Basilica, or to fight Crusades—much of which drained local economies. More significantly, the sellers of indulgences often misled the public, telling people that they could be forgiven of any sin at the right price. Near Luther, Friar Johann Tetzel sold indulgences by "emotionally depicting the wailing of dead parents in Purgatory, pleading with their children to put coins in the box so that they could be released from their suffering."[15] This behavior upset Luther. He wanted the public to be aware of the true nature of indulgences, and he wanted the Church to be aware of what sellers, like Tetzel, were telling the public. Luther's 27th thesis was a direct response to Tetzel: "There is no divine authority for preaching that the soul flies out of purgatory immediately the money clinks in the bottom of the chest."[16] In his other theses, he reminded the public that the pope could only forgive sins against canon law, that canon law had no claim over the dead and that "any Christian whatsoever, who is truly repentant, enjoys plenary

15 Merriman, 80.

16 Martin Luther, *95 Theses* in *Martin Luther: Selections From His Writings*, ed. John Dillenberger (New York: Anchor Books, 1962), 493.

remission from penalty and guilt, and this is given him without letters of indulgence."[17] In 1517, Luther had no intention to split from the Catholic Church. He still believed that indulgences could be granted to forgive sins committed against canon law but thought that sellers of indulgences were corrupt and should be reined in by higher church authorities. But his burgeoning fame drew him into direct confrontation with the church.

In his attack on the sale of indulgences, Luther antagonized local and distant church authorities. While some of the theses seemed to just remind the public of the fine print about indulgences—that they were only good for canon law—other theses seemed to question the role of the Church in salvation. He separated repentance from the church practice of penance. Luther's insistence that death freed one from the bonds of the Church also seemed to lessen church authority. Though not intended as a Reformation tract, the *95 Theses* contained elements of Luther's developing theology and his insistence on the personal relationship between the individual and God and the role of personal faith and repentance, outside the practices of the Church. At the same time, Luther was clearly not yet leading a schism. His seventh thesis asserted that "God never remits guilt to anyone without, at the same time, making him humbly submissive to the priest, His representative."[18] Luther had hoped for a debate among scholars, but he found himself under a papal ban. When he learned of the ban, Luther "proclaimed that the papacy had no ultimate power with respect to a man's relation to God."[19]

Luther's confrontation with the Catholic Church radicalized rather than modified his positions. While Luther initially believed that the pope and other leaders in the church were not to blame for the abuses he saw around him, he became convinced that the

17 Martin Luther, *95 Theses*, 491, 494.

18 Martin Luther, *95 Theses*, 491.

19 John Dillenberger, "Introduction," in *Martin Luther: Selections From His Writings*, ed. John Dillenberger (New York: Anchor Books, 1962), xxi.

church was corrupt from top to bottom. He was outspoken like Jan Hus, whose ideas he largely came to embrace. Unlike Hus, however, Luther had the favor and protection of Frederick the Wise, ruler of Saxony. In 1519, Luther defended his ideas in a public debate against Johann Eck in Leipzig. In 1520, all of Luther's writings were condemned by a papal bull, and he was given sixty days to recant. But Luther wrote at a frenetic pace during his dispute with the church, including the works "Two Kinds of Righteousness" (1519), "The Freedom of a Christian" (1520), and "An Appeal to the Ruling Class" (1520). The first two outlined his views in an attempt to find common ground with Rome while the "Appeal" asked for German nobles to circumvent church hierarchy and reform the divine institution themselves. Erasmus had always avoided calling people out by name, hoping to "teach and warn rather than bite."[20] Luther was willing to bite. In "An Appeal to the Ruling Class," he described the pope as "a barefaced liar letting the Evil One dominate him."[21] These and other works did little to build a bridge to Rome and, in 1521, Luther was excommunicated from the church.

Men had been excommunicated from the Catholic Church before, but Luther's protest became the Protestant Reformation. Like-minded individuals and communities across Europe began to separate themselves from the Catholic Church. In some churches it was a simple matter of saying Mass in a vernacular language or a new emphasis on grace. In some places peasants stormed churches and destroyed the Eucharistic elements or ran priests out of town. In 1522, Huldrych Zwingli declared himself for the Reformation by publicly eating sausage during Lent.[22] Across Europe, Prot-

20 Erasmus, *In Praise of Folly*, trans. John Dolan, in *The Essential Erasmus* (New York: Penguin Books, 1983), 100.

21 Martin Luther, "An Appeal to the Ruling Class," ed. John Dillenberger, *Martin Luther: Selections From His Writings* (New York: Random House, 1962), 429.

22 Or simply being among those publicly eating sausage during Lent; there are different accounts.

estantism spread most quickly in the north, taking off in urban centers and more decentralized states. This was a movement that Luther began, but not one that he controlled. It was geographically dispersed, with various leaders and, very soon, various streams of theology.

What were the theological distinctions of the Protestants? They had three catchphrases: *Sola Fide*, *Sola Gratia* and *Sola Scriptura.* Martin Luther had spent much of his adult life concerned with how sinful man could be justified in the presence of a righteous God. His conclusion was that Christians are justified by faith (*fide*) and saved by grace (*gratia*). But the understanding of faith was not as simple as salvation by faith versus works. Catholics and Protestants both believed in faith *and* works. Martin Luther's "Two Kinds of Righteousness" were "alien righteousness," imputed by Christ, and "proper righteousness," which came from good works. The debate was about the relationship between faith and works. And the "works" in question were often the sacraments. The Catholic Church has seven sacraments, viewed as the external signs of God's grace and the path to Heaven. Protestants began to question the significance of the sacraments, downgrading all but two: baptism and the Eucharist. With regard to those sacraments, Protestants kept the tradition of infant baptism, but largely abandoned belief in transubstantiation.[23] Reducing and changing the sacraments reflected Protestant beliefs that the church was less instrumental in salvation. The sacraments had been the path to salvation, and were only available through the Church. In contrast, Luther taught that faith was more personal, a matter between an individual and God. The external practices that had traditionally accompanied faith were not seen as necessary steps, and the Church's role in guiding an individual to salvation was less significant. The faith and grace needed for a right relationship with God could exist outside of the structure of the Catholic Church.

23 Luther tried to maintain a middle ground with consubstantiation.

The other catchphrase of the Protestant Reformation was *sola scriptura*, "by Scripture alone." While the Catholic Church had long valued church tradition and Christian teachings outside the Bible for wisdom, Protestants began to question many traditions and texts, testing everything by the Scripture. Protestants abandoned some teachings that were not found in the Bible, such as purgatory. Church teachings and tradition were considered less significant than the original texts of the Bible and, in some cases, not very significant at all. Protestants also separated the Apocrypha within the Bible and eventually excised it. While Catholics viewed the Church as a divinely guided institution, Protestants were like humanists seeking the earliest texts and disregarding more recent teaching. Leaders such as Luther and Calvin saw themselves returning to the ways of the early church.

Though they distinguished themselves from the Catholic Church, the Protestant Reformers did not abandon the concept of church at all. However, it took some time for the different streams of Protestant thought to emerge. The Lutheran Church did not have a comprehensive overview of its theology until the 1530 Augsburg Confession. The Lutheran tradition was one branch of Protestantism. Meanwhile in Switzerland, Huldrych Zwingli (1484-1531) in Zurich and John Calvin (1509-1564) in Geneva became the founders of what is called the Reformed tradition in Protestantism. The Reformed branch of the Reformation is so closely associated with Calvin that it is more commonly called Calvinism. Though originally a lawyer from France, John Calvin became a prominent theologian and a city leader in Geneva. Calvin wrote many texts but his ideas are best displayed in his monumental work, *The Institutes of Christian Religion* (1536). The core ideas of Calvinism are often summarized in the acronym TULIP: total depravity, unconditional election, limited atonement, irresistible grace, and perseverance of the saints. Though it is a very simplified version of Reformed theology, it reflects a strong belief in humanity's sinfulness, the need for God's grace, and predestination. Calvinism became associated with the kind of industrious and sober living that later became connected to the so-called "Protestant Work Ethic."[24]

In 1525, the Radical Reformation began when the Anabaptists emerged—radicals who believed in adult rather than infant baptism.[25] They were soon persecuted by Protestants and Catholics alike. Anabaptists put a fresh emphasis on the Holy Spirit, reminding believers that God is not silent and teaching people to read Scripture *and* listen for the Holy Spirit. Anabaptists were also committed to transforming society to be more Christlike. Lutherans and Calvinists, sometimes called "magisterial reformers," had questioned the Catholic Church but maintained faith in secular authority. Radical reformers wanted to reform secular authority, too. From 1524-1525, German peasants rebelled against their masters in the Peasants' War, demanding an end to serfdom, more humane and Christlike treatment and taxes, and church reform, such as the ability to choose their own pastors.[26] Some Anabaptists, such as Thomas Müntzer (1489-1525), joined with the peasants. Both sides of the war looked to the ideas of Luther. Luther pleased neither; he told the peasants to respect authority in "Against the Murderous, Thieving Hordes of Peasants" but suggested more kindness toward the peasants in "An Admonition to Peace." Müntzer lost his life alongside perhaps 100,000 peasants in the failed cause. Though some early Anabaptists participated in violent movements like the Peasants' War and the Münster Rebellion (1534-1535), the fruit of the Radical Reformation was ultimately non-violent. The form of Anabaptism which emerged from the sixteenth century was largely pacifist and best understood through the life and ideas

24 See Max Weber's *The Protestant Ethic and the Spirit of Capitalism* (1905).

25 The denominations called "Baptist" today emerged later.

26 Like Luther, they published their grievances in numbered articles, such as the "Twelve Articles of the Swabian Peasants," the "Forty-six Frankfurt Articles," and the "Articles of the Black Forest Peasants."

of a figure like Menno Simons (1496-1561), a Dutch Anabaptist for whom the Mennonites are named.

Despite the emergence of Protestantism, many believers chose to remain in the Catholic Church, which underwent its own transformations. In a 1539 letter to the people of Geneva, Cardinal Jacopo Sadoleto wrote to remind them that the Catholic Church had stood the test of time, and so true Christians "proceed in humility and in obedience, and the things delivered to us, and fixed by the authority of our ancestors (men of the greatest wisdom and holiness), we receive with all faith, as truly dictated and enjoined by the Holy Spirit."[27] Many people believed that the Catholic Church was divinely instituted and that the Protestant Reformation went against biblical commands for unity in the church. During this time period, the Catholic Church had its own reformation, known as the Catholic or Counter Reformation. There were seven popes between 1521 and 1555, and they moved in both positive and negative directions. During this time the Inquisition actively persecuted non-Catholics in Catholic territories. Pope Paul IV invented the ghetto; Jewish people were required to live in a segregated part of town and wear distinctive clothing. But various popes curbed the excesses of the clergy, reformed religious orders, and improved the education of priests. The Council of Trent (1545-1563) delivered the official Catholic theological response to the Protestant Reformation. The rise in personal devotion in the Protestant Reformation was mirrored within the Catholic Church as well, and certain parts of the Church were revitalized. In 1522, a Basque nobleman and soldier named Ignatius of Loyola (died in 1556) gave his cloak to a poor man and began a journey of asceticism and devotion that would lead him to become an ordained priest, author of *The Spiritual Exercises* (1548), and founder of the Society of Jesus—the Jesuits. Ignatius's work continues to have an impact on the world

27 Jacopo Sadoleto, "A Letter to the Genevans," *A Reformation Debate*, ed. John C. Olin (Grand Rapids, Michigan: Baker Book House, 1976), 37.

today. *The Spiritual Exercises* are still used as a guide for "preparing and disposing the soul to rid itself of all inordinate attachments, and, after their removal, of seeking and finding the will of God in the disposition of our life and for the salvation of our soul."[28] The Jesuits carried the Gospel to the ends of the earth and became one of the boldest missionary organizations in history.[29] They also became important in the world of education, as the founders of institutions like Georgetown University.

The Protestant Reformation started with theology and religious authority, but it transformed the world of secular authority as well. Protestant defiance of the church strengthened the power of secular authority in many places as rulers no longer yielded to church authority. Some took church authority for themselves. In England, Henry VIII split with the Catholic Church in the 1530s and became the head of the new Protestant Church of England, the Anglican Church. In Germany, Frederick's protection of Luther was in defiance of the Holy Roman Emperor, highlighting the weakness of that empire and the power struggles within it. Luther himself had a complicated understanding of secular authority. He believed a Christian was a "perfectly free lord of all, subject to none" and did not need secular laws because a Christian was filled with the Spirit, but he also believed that a good Christian was a "perfectly dutiful servant of all, subject to all," who would submit to (or serve in) secular authority solely for the benefit of others.[30] Luther believed that the state existed to punish the wicked and protect the good, hopefully turning the wicked to repentance before it was too late. Calvin took a more extreme view, believing that Christians and non-Christians were both naturally subject to secular author-

28 Ignatius of Loyola, *The Spiritual Exercises of St. Ignatius*, translated by Louis J. Puhl (New York: Vintage Books, 2000), 5.

29 Two excellent movies about Jesuit missionaries are *The Mission* (1986) and *Silence* (2016).

30 Martin Luther, "Freedom of a Christian," *Martin Luther: Selections From His Writings*, ed. John Dillenberger (New York: Anchor Books, 1962), 53.

ity, which existed to punish the wicked but also to promote true worship. In his view, even wicked rulers reflected the will of God and should be obeyed, with the only exception being in matters of personal belief and worship. Anabaptists rejected secular authority, which they considered out of line with the teaching of the Scripture; they were not interested in promoting secular authority, generally even where it was not abusive. Even today, many Anabaptist groups, such as the Amish and Mennonites, maintain a distance from the state, which they see as a rival for the affections and loyalties of believers.

In many ways, the Protestant Reformation can be compared to Pandora's box. Luther's defiance of authority and resistance to indulgences split the Catholic Church, and the splitting continued from there. Like Latin, the Roman Catholic Church had long served as a universal, but in 1521, it lost its universality in Europe. Like the vernacular languages, religious devotion became more personal. Sadly, that increased personal devotion was accompanied by a rise in religious persecution and warring kingdoms. Christendom divided into warring camps, ostensibly over religion. Though the Reformations emphasized the importance of personal belief and following one's conscience, religious liberty was rare. In 1555, the Peace of Augsburg guaranteed that in the Holy Roman Empire princes would determine the religion of their subjects. Across Europe, rulers persecuted their subjects who did not align with their beliefs, Catholic or Protestant. From 1562-1598, France was destabilized by the "French wars of religion." These were conflicts between nobles seeking to seize power from the throne, divided along religious lines; the power vacuum that resulted led to widespread religious-based violence on the community level. From 1618-1648, central Europe was depopulated by the Thirty Years War, a dynastic struggle first sparked by religious conflict in the Holy Roman Empire. Wars like these remade the map of Europe and created alliances that would shape the following century.

English history provides a good window into the intersection of religion and politics during this time period. In 1534, Henry VIII became the head of the Church of England. He used his position as head of the church and state to ban Catholic worship, seize Catholic monasteries, and sell off their lands. His first successor, Edward VI in 1547, continued to maintain Protestantism in England, but when Mary I came to power in 1553 she brought back Catholicism. Mary widely persecuted Protestants, earning the nickname "Bloody Mary." In 1558, however, Mary I died without an heir; her sister, Elizabeth I, took the throne. Elizabeth was Protestant and re-established the Church of England, initiating a wave of persecution against Catholics and requiring religious services to use the Book of Common Prayer. Protestantism became the norm within England, but even then, religious conflict was entangled with political tensions. The English Civil War (1642-1651) was a struggle between the King and Parliament, but it was also a war of Anglicans against Puritans (Calvinists). Not only were the two religious traditions associated with different political leanings, Puritans considered the Anglican Church to be too Catholic in its practices. This conflict was the context for John Milton as he wrote *Paradise Lost* and imagined the struggle between God and the fallen angels. Religion and politics were never far apart. One of the reasons for the Glorious Revolution of 1688, which put William and Mary on the throne and helped cement the power of Parliament, was Protestantism. In fact, no Catholic could inherit the English throne from 1701-2013. English history demonstrates the ways in which religious fault lines could be exploited for political divisions and power.

### *Conclusion*

The Renaissance and Reformations may seem like two very distinct movements. There is a great contrast between the stunning domes and painted ceilings of Renaissance churches and the simple steeples and plainer interiors of Reformed churches. But both the plainer paintings of Protestant Rembrandt and the more colorful paintings of Catholic Rubens display realism and depth. The Renaissance and Reformations overlap more than just chronologically. Renaissance humanists sought to return to origins and revive classical texts. The Renaissance injunction *Ad Fontes* ("back to the sources") nurtured the Reformation zeal for the Scripture. In the same way, like Renaissance artists, reformers from Calvin to Müntzer rejected their immediate forebears and wanted to return to the perceived purity of the early church. The Renaissance celebrated the individual and put new confidence in the abilities of humans. Despite belief in sinful human nature, Martin Luther would proclaim that every believer could interpret the Scripture for himself. Shakespeare was repeating a common Renaissance saying when he wrote that "all the world's a stage." In the Reformations, prominent individuals took to the stage, challenging the authority of the church and of tradition. These challenges fractured Christendom and began its transition into Europe, creating the context for the events and ideas explored in the time period of Reason and Revolt.

## The World of Humanism and Reform Textual Glosses

### Petrarch, *Secretum* (c.1347-1353)

Petrarch's *Secret* was originally written in Latin and subtitled "The Soul's Conflict with Passion." It is an imagined conversation between Petrarch and Augustine in three dialogues. In it, Augustine guides Petrarch to a fuller awareness of his sinful nature and what Petrarch must do to overcome it. Petrarch's imagined Augustine is full of "tough love." Augustine begins by reminding Petrarch that "there can be no doubt that to recollect one's misery and to practice meditation on death is the surest aid in scorning the seductions of this world."[31] He encourages Petrarch to focus his attention on the Creator, but also integrates the wisdom of the Stoics when it comes to method, such as meditating on death and adjusting to one's circumstances. The dialogues draw on specific words and ideas of Augustine but also invent some, an unfamiliar writing convention for many of us today, but one we will see in other religious books of the era.

Petrarch was one of the founding fathers of the Renaissance. His *Secret* integrates his close reading of Augustine and his appreciation of the Stoics and other classical thinkers. As such, it helps us see the role of humanism as a style of learning and the ways Renaissance thinkers borrowed from non-Christian authors. Petrarch's *Secret* is also very much a book of religious devotion, which in the medieval way encourages a constant meditation on death and emphasizes the sinfulness of man. This book is a bridge between the worldviews of the medieval and the Renaissance eras.

### Thomas à Kempis, *The Imitation of Christ* (c.1418-1427)

*The Imitation of Christ* is one of the most popular devotional works of all time and influenced most of the religious thinkers whose works you will read in the Humanism and Reform class as well as many religious authors up until the present. It was written by Thomas à Kempis, a German monk who worked as a copyist at the monastery of Mount St. Agnes in the Netherlands for most of his life. It is one of the best examples of *devotio moderna*, or "new devotion," a trend within the church which put an emphasis on personal devotion and encouraged people to push past the mere external observance of religion to experience the true effects of faith and internal change. *Imitation of Christ* tells readers that Christ should be "interiorly experienced."[32] Thomas was a member of

---

31 Petrarch, *Petrarch's Secret, or The Soul's Conflict With Passion*, trans. William S. Draper (CreateSpace Independent Publishing Platform, 2015), 4.

32 Thomas à Kempis, *The Imitation of Christ,* trans. Joseph N. Tylenda (New

the Brethren of the Common Life, a religious community which emphasized new devotion and would also be responsible for the education of Erasmus and Martin Luther.

*The Imitation of Christ* contains four books, each of which speaks to man's relationship with God. Everywhere in it we see the influence of the Bible. In addition to writing devotional books, Thomas copied the Bible at least four times, and its ideas and words permeate the text of *Imitation of Christ*, though the modern reader will likely need footnotes to catch all of the references because citation was different in that time. Book III includes an imagined dialogue between the disciple and Christ, similar to Petrarch's conversation with Augustine. This dialogue relies extensively on the Bible for its content, but may still be surprising for those unaccustomed to the genre.

The book was intended to be a guide for young/new members of a religious community, and it offers guidance for monks seeking to deepen their relationship with Christ and learning to live in community and in submission to authority. Much of the advice given will seem counter-cultural in the twenty-first century. In John 3:30, John the Baptist says of Christ, "He must increase, but I must decrease." This is very much the spirit of the devotional. *The Imitation of Christ* is an excellent book for examining the heart behind much of monastic living and those who passionately pursued religious orders in this time period. Book IV, which is about the Eucharist, provides insight into how people understand the importance of the sacraments. It is a good place to begin understanding religious devotion within the Catholic Church.

---

York: Vintage Books, 1998), 47.

### **Giovanni Pico della Mirandola, *Oration on the Dignity of Man* (1486)**

If Psalm 8:4 asks, "What is man, that thou art mindful of him?" Pico imagines God's reply to be "a creature neither of heaven nor of earth, neither mortal nor immortal, in order that you may, as the free and proud shaper of your own being, fashion yourself in the form you may prefer."[33] Pico was an exceptional twenty-four-year-old scholar when he penned this oration, a marvel of Renaissance rhetoric and thought. The work is a good example of the product of Renaissance learning by someone who attempted to read nearly everything and attempted to combine all forms of learning in one coherent structure. In particular, Mirandola sought out very old and sometimes obscure texts, including works on magic and early Jewish mystical writings. He was deeply influenced by Greek thought, especially Plato. Like St. Augustine, he found many of Plato's ideas consistent with his understanding of Christianity. But many of his ideas were too syncretistic for the Catholic Church, and his *900 Theses* was considered heretical. Like many other Renaissance luminaries, he spent time in Florence, where he had the support of Lorenzo de Medici. Lorenzo's support was of great assistance to Mirandola when the church was displeased with his unorthodox views.

The ideas in *Oration on the Dignity of Man* have been viewed by later scholars as the best summation of the Renaissance understanding of humanity. Essentially, Pico argues that man is a special being, capable of ascending or descending the Great Chain of Being.[34] Because of free will, people can choose whether to become more like the angels or to become more like the animals. Pico elaborates

33 Giovanni Pico della Mirandola, *Oration on the Dignity of Man*, trans. Robert Caponigri (Washington, D.C: Gateway Editions, 1984), 7.

34 The "Great Chain of Being" is a concept from ancient times, even referenced by Lucretius, which sees all created beings linked together like a hierarchical ladder, starting from the smallest and least significant and ascending all the way to the gods.

the paths for either direction. Those who would improve their lot will pursue the liberal arts and philosophy, which will lead them naturally to theology. Those who will descend will neglect learning and their reason, failing to pursue justice and knowledge (of the arts and of God). Though we may think of Renaissance humanism as creating such a glorified image of man that God is crowded out of the picture, Pico's work still clearly demonstrates that though humans can become like angels, God still reigns supreme.

### Niccolò Machiavelli, *The Prince* (1513/1532)

*The Prince* is one of the most widely read books of all time and is still considered a leadership text in the realms of politics, business, and elsewhere. The simplest summary of *The Prince* is that it is a book of advice for a new, young ruler, neatly organized into short chapters and chiefly about the exercise and maintenance of power. Machiavelli was a former diplomat of Florence who had lost his position and was sent into exile in the countryside when the Medici family took over Florence. Machiavelli dedicated *The Prince* to Lorenzo de Medici, the new ruler, hoping to find favor and possibly employment. *The Prince* speaks to the fractious and competitive environment of the Italian city-states. Machiavelli would likely not have written it if the Republic of Florence had not been taken over by one of its own citizens, who imposed less than republican rule. The book itself is full of insights into the political world of the Italian Renaissance, with its mercenary armies, French invasions, and power struggles among wealthy elites. It describes many different types of states and their strengths and weaknesses. The book also shows Renaissance learning with Machiavelli's examples drawn from history and classical thought.

*The Prince* is considered significant for several reasons. In it, Machiavelli disregards religious and ethical considerations, and his *virtú* is about effectiveness. *The Prince* is very much associated with the idea of *Realpolitik*, a style of diplomacy that centers on practicality and not ethics, demonstrated in the actions of figures like Otto von Bismarck and Henry Kissinger. Machiavelli does not recommend that rulers be generous or kind, but rather be known for their tough reputations. When he asks his most famous question, "Is it better to be feared or loved?" he responds that, if forced to choose, fear is preferable to love. The extent to which Machiavelli favored the type of ruler he described is unclear, but the book provides insight into the "man of action" for the time period and understandings of human nature.

### Desiderius Erasmus, *In Praise of Folly* (1509)

Desiderius Erasmus was the illegitimate son of a priest. Erasmus himself took religious orders as an adult, and, despite his inauspicious beginnings, became the foremost humanist of the northern Renaissance. At one point, he was the most published author of his time, renowned for his learning and intelligence. Though a monk from Rotterdam, Erasmus spent time studying and teaching in Paris, living in England, and traveling as a secretary for a bishop. He was very close friends with Thomas More and was friend, by correspondence, to many of the great thinkers of his time.

Erasmus was a reform-minded thinker who took the Renaissance emphasis on human potential and connected it with an emphasis on faith, which he believed should be personal and heartfelt. He urged individual piety, through sermons like "Concerning the Immense Mercy of God" and through his encouragement of preaching in the vernacular languages. He wrote a Greek translation of the New Testament which was an improvement on the Vulgate and a great aid to religious thinkers (including Luther). Among his serious works was *The Education of a Christian Prince*, a handbook for rulers very different from Machiavelli's.

Despite his serious writings and strongly held religious convictions, Erasmus is often best known today as a satirical writer. His most famous work, by far, is the satire *Praise of Folly*. In 1515,

Erasmus wrote to a friend, "I almost regret myself that I published *Folly*," because it overshadowed his other work.[35] In the book, Folly critiques society, from the everyday people and practices to the clergy and secular authorities, revealing some of Erasmus's true ideas, but mixing in definite ambiguities and considerable silliness. In his dedication of the book to Thomas More, Erasmus wondered if it would be considered "too frivolous for a theologian" or thought to have "a sarcastic bite which ill becomes Christian decorum."[36] But he hoped that his sarcastic castigation of society would teasingly warn people away from true folly while avoiding the wrath he would provoke if he called people out by name. He wrote to More, "anyone who protests that he is injured betrays his own guilty conscience, or at any rate his apprehensions."[37]

Though very reform-minded, Erasmus avoided direct provocation and hoped to turn people to better ways through persuasion and warning. He was not interested in creating conflict or making himself a martyr. Despite many similarities, he did not join with the Protestant Reformers. But neither would he go as far as the Catholic Church wanted in order to rally opposition to them. His exchange with Martin Luther on free will is also very useful for understanding some of the distinctions between reform-minded Catholics and Protestants. In 1524, Erasmus published "On Free Will," which publicly took on some of Luther's ideas. In 1525, Luther replied with "On the Bondage of the Will." Both were originally published in Latin, but translated and read more widely.

---

35 Desiderius Erasmus, "Letter to Dorp," *Praise of Folly*, trans. Betty Radice (New York: Penguin Books, 1993), 138.

36 Erasmus, *Praise of Folly*, 4.

37 Erasmus, *Praise of Folly*, 7.

**Thomas More, *Utopia* (1516)**

Thomas More was a fascinating figure. He was best friends with Erasmus and a devout Catholic who observed many of the disciplines of monks, though he was married with children. At times he even wore a hair shirt. More was also a high-profile civil servant, even serving as Lord Chancellor for Henry VIII. When the Protestant Reformation broke out, More wrote strongly against it and famously became chief antagonist to the Bible translator William Tyndale. But when Henry VIII left the Catholic Church, More's opposition to Protestantism led to his destruction. More refused to take the Oath of Supremacy that recognized Henry VIII as the head of the church. Despite years of loyal service, he was convicted of treason and beheaded in 1535. Today he is considered a saint by the Catholic Church.

More's *Utopia* is altogether different from his life in England and has been intriguing readers ever since it was written. It can be a hard book to place because it began an entire genre—utopian literature. Like all utopian literature since, at its heart is the organization of the society it describes. In a utopia or dystopia, the good life is closely connected to the organization of society. *Utopia* was also a satire. It is not always easy to determine what in the book is meant to be taken seriously and what is meant to be taken humorously. *Utopia* also overlaps with the genre of travel literature. It was written during the "Age of Exploration," when Europeans seemed to be discovering new lands all the time. Though "utopia" literally means "no place," it opens in such a way that it appears to be describing a real place; some of the earliest readers thought it was real.

*Utopia* describes an ideal, foreign land shown in contrast with England. In Book I, the character Raphael Hythloday, a learned traveler, discourses on England, offering very real criticism of the English commonwealth and asking many philosophical questions about the nature of the state. In Book II, Hythloday goes on to describe Utopia, an ideal commonwealth, with a well-ordered society where people live in harmony and devote themselves primarily to productive tasks. This is where the satirical side of *Utopia* becomes tricky; it is not always clear which aspects of this foreign land More thinks would be well-adopted back in England and which are meant to be absurd. There is no death penalty for theft as there is in England, but there is also very limited private property. In Utopia, no one needs to lock their doors, but they also rotate houses every ten years. Not all of the recounted characteristics of *Utopia* seem to be serious suggestions for the improvement of England, but neither is it entirely a joke. This makes *Utopia* an excellent place to begin discussing the ways in which society is organized and what would be the most moral and rational ways to organize a commonwealth.

**Martin Luther, "On the Freedom of a Christian" (1520)**

The philosopher Isaiah Berlin once characterized thinkers as being of two types: hedgehog and fox. He took the idea from the Greek thinker Archilochus, whom he paraphrased, saying that "the fox knows many things, but the hedgehog knows one big thing."[38] The fox has many varied insights; the hedgehog is a more systematic thinker with one idea that organizes the others. The next two authors fit this description. In many ways, Martin Luther is a fox and John Calvin is a hedgehog.

Luther became a monk to fulfill a vow he made to St. Anne while fearful for his life. Many of his writings would be more motivated by circumstances and the world around him than by a comprehensive vision of theology. But, despite some definite missteps, Luther's writings are full of insights and compelling phrases and arguments.[39] In 1517, he made his *95 Theses* public. Those arguments were chiefly against the sale and abuse of indulgences.

---

38 Isaiah Berlin, *Russian Thinkers* (New York: Penguin Books, 1978), 22.

39 Luther was certainly not above name-calling in his writing, and he also penned some anti-Semitic works.

But as the church hierarchy responded to Luther, he became engaged in more dramatic and consequential arguments and began to write on more and more aspects of faith. Erasmus wanted to avoid conflict, but conflict energized Luther. His most important writings were created before he was excommunicated and while he was in conflict with the Church. In 1519, he wrote "Two Kinds of Righteousness"; in 1520, "The Freedom of a Christian"; and, also in 1520, "An Appeal to the Ruling Class."

Today, Luther is best known for his assertion that salvation is by faith and not by works. This message comes through very clearly in "Two Kinds of Righteousness," which asserts that we are granted salvation because of "alien righteousness"—the righteousness of Christ is imputed to us. But there is also "proper righteousness," the righteousness of good works, which follows alien righteousness and is impossible without it. In this sermon, Luther outlines what he sees as a basic understanding of salvation. In 1520, Luther went farther, with "The Freedom of a Christian," which Luther thought contained the whole of the Christian life in a simplified form. "Freedom" contained one of Luther's most interesting and controversial phrases: a Christian is a "perfectly free lord of all, subject to none" and also a "perfectly dutiful servant of all, subject to all."[40] According to Luther, followers of Christ did not need external authorities; Christians were made perfectly free and completely liberated from sin by Christ. But Christians would also submit to laws and authorities for the benefit of others, specifically the unsaved. Christ's love prompts us to serve one another. This applied to the use of the state as well. Luther thought that believers should use the power of the state to punish wrongdoing for the benefit of the wrongdoer only, not for self. He believed that religious and secular authority were in place to benefit others.

Chronology reveals the circumstances of Luther's writings and

40 Martin Luther, "Freedom of a Christian," *Martin Luther: Selections From His Writings*, ed. John Dillenberger (New York: Anchor Books, 1962), 53.

the evolution of his views. In 1517, Luther believed the problem with indulgences was a local one. In 1520, Luther dedicated "Freedom of a Christian" to Pope Leo as "most blessed father," but also referred to him as "Daniel in Babylon" as he described the sins of Rome.[41] But in "An Appeal to the Ruling Class," Luther described the pope as "a barefaced liar letting the Evil One dominate him."[42] "An Appeal to the Ruling Class" is a longer treatise to German nobles, in which Luther attacks "three walls" propping up church authority. He first suggests that the distinctions between clergy and regular people are not based on superiority of any type, but on vocation. Luther takes this idea of the "priesthood of all believers" further in the second part, where he suggests that the pope and the church have no special ability or authority to interpret Scripture. In the third part, Luther urges the nobility to call a council—circumventing church authority—for the reform of the church, and he outlines the matters to be discussed by a council. This appeal was an attempt to use conciliar practices for church reform—not rupture—but it was doomed to failure. It alienated Luther from Church authorities while suggesting increased power for secular authorities. Reading Luther's works in order allows one to see both the central ideas of the Protestant Reformation and the process of the division of the Church. Together with their dedications, Luther's early treatises show the Protestant Reformation in real time.

### John Calvin, *The Institutes of Christian Religion* (1536)

Before he was John Calvin, as we call him today, he was Jean Cauvin, a Frenchman from Picardy. As a young man, he was interested in theology, but he turned to the study of law at his father's

41 Martin Luther, "Freedom of a Christian," *Martin Luther: Selections From His Writings*, ed. John Dillenberger (New York: Anchor Books, 1962), 43, 44.

42 Martin Luther, "An Appeal to the Ruling Class," *Martin Luther: Selections From His Writings*, ed. John Dillenberger, (New York: Random House, 1962), 429.

request. The influence of his legal training can be seen in the clear argumentation of his writings and in his precision with words. When his father died, Calvin turned from law to literature and, like so many other humanists, developed a love of Seneca.[43] But after an intense conversion experience, Calvin became a participant in the Protestant movement. French Protestants, known as Huguenots, were persecuted at the time and, after making some waves in Paris in 1533, Calvin fled to Basel, Switzerland. Coincidentally, this was where Erasmus was living the final years of his life. Calvin became permanently associated with Geneva, where he went first in 1536 and then again more permanently in 1541. Calvin was a leader in the second generation of Protestants. He became one of the founders of the Reformed tradition and transformed the city of Geneva, which enacted his "ecclesiastical ordinances" to govern life there.

In contrast to Luther's flashes of brilliance spread out across many disparate works, Calvin is known for one monumental work, *The Institutes of Christian Religion*. At over eight hundred pages, it demonstrates Calvin's methodical approach. After the first 1536 edition, he continued revising it until 1559. *The Institutes* is the most recognized and comprehensive summary of Reformed theology, which touches on everything from justification by faith, to the sacraments, to civil government, and the Christian life. Though it is certainly not the only work by Calvin, it is considered the most definitive summary of his ideas.[44] *The Institutes* was also a massively popular book in its time, with editions in various languages.

Calvin intended *The Institutes* to help readers understand the Bible. It begins with knowledge of self and knowledge of God. Calvin believed that humans are "totally depraved," meaning their nature has been completely warped by sin. Though we may

43 His first book was an edition of Seneca's *On Clemency*.

44 Calvin was a very productive author, also known for numerous biblical commentaries, tracts and treatises, sermons and letters.

manage human accomplishments, our nature prevents us from any accomplishment on God's plane. Our need for God's grace is total. According to Timothy George, Calvin was "haunted by the specter of the apparently haphazard and meaningless course of existence"; he was "keenly aware of the precarious and utterly contingent character of human life."[45] As a result, much of Calvin's work focuses on God's providence; he believed that all events were essentially directed by God. In keeping with providence, Calvin believed in predestination. This was a concept which, he thought, demonstrated both that salvation was not achieved by works (even self-directed faith) and that God was a guiding presence in human lives, which then could not be meaningless or random. *The Institutes* also addresses the practices of the church, such as the sacraments and Christian life in society. Calvin believed that the Catholic Church had added to the teaching of Scripture and drifted away from its purpose. He considered Protestant theology not to be new, but to be a return to the old. In a letter to Francis I defending Protestants, Calvin wrote, "[I]n calling our teaching new, they do great wrong to God, whose holy word does not deserve the charge of novelty."[46] For Calvin, Protestantism was meant to clear away years of accretions and return to the original, early church. Though he differed from Luther on some points, his theology was consistent with the spirit of the first generation of Protestants and their touchstones: *sola gratia*, *sola fide*, *sola scriptura*.

### Shakespeare, *Hamlet* (c.1599-1602)

Shakespeare is perhaps the most famous author in the English language. It would be difficult to graduate high school in the United States without some exposure to his plays. But how does Shake-

45 Timothy George, *Theology of the Reformers*, 3rd ed. (Nashville, TN: B&H Publishing Group, 2013), 212.

46 John Calvin, "Prefatory Letter to Francis I," *Institutes of Christian Religion*, trans.Robert White (Carlisle, PA: Banner of Truth Trust, 2014), xxiii.

speare fit into the Renaissance or the Reformation? Shakespeare fits very well within the Renaissance tradition. He was a prolific author in the vernacular, which he helped to elevate and expand. Though many of his plays deal with English history, he also very much engaged the classical tradition, and his plays demonstrate an awareness of classical learning. The basic plots of *Romeo and Juliet* and *Titus Andronicus* were borrowed from Ovid's *Metamorphoses*. A theme of the Renaissance was that "all the world's a stage"—a phrase that Shakespeare borrowed—and like the rest of the Renaissance, his works tended to center on human activity and potential. Shakespeare's plays showcase both sides of humanism, the appreciation of the classical past *and* the appreciation of human potential.

A play like *Hamlet* demonstrates the ways in which Shakespeare was interacting with the Reformation context. His own views are notoriously tricky to pin down, but Shakespeare used *Hamlet* to raise many theological questions even if he didn't always provide answers. The play begins with Hamlet, who has been away at Wittenberg—the birthplace of the Protestant Reformation—being visited by his father, from Purgatory. Is the presence of the ghost and the concept of Purgatory real? In Act III, Hamlet refuses to kill Claudius after his prayer, for fear that a freshly penitent Claudius will go straight to heaven. And in the final act, Hamlet and Laertes make certain to exchange forgiveness in preparation for their own deaths. *Hamlet* is not a theological treatise and it does not make clear which theological traditions Shakespeare was partial to, but it raises questions about forgiveness, grace, the nature of salvation, and what people can expect after death. As such, it presents many of the questions at the heart of the Reformation.

### John Milton, *Paradise Lost* (1667)

Homer is celebrated as the blind poet and the bard credited with *The Iliad* and *The Odyssey*. Like Homer, John Milton was a blind poet when he composed his epic poem *Paradise Lost,* a blank verse masterpiece that mimics the conventions of classical epic poetry and was considered an instant classic. Milton is one of the most celebrated English authors of all time and an excellent bridge figure to the World of Reason and Revolt. He lived and wrote in the seventeenth century, and the religious and political conflicts within England were the backdrop for his many writings. In particular, the English Civil War and its divisions were the context for *Paradise Lost.* Milton himself was associated with the Puritan and republican cause and even worked as a civil servant.

The goal of *Paradise Lost* is to justify the ways of God to man. In it, Milton expands upon biblical sources in providing a narrative for the fall of Satan and the fall of man. In fact, Milton's account of Satan and the arrival of sin into the world were so convincing that many people today still reference passages in *Paradise Lost* without realizing that they are not in the Bible. Milton's masterpiece raises many questions about knowledge, man's sinful nature, and the relationship between God and man. Milton explores the reasons behind Satan's rebellion against God and man's rebellion in the Garden, while around him England was handling the consequences of rebellion against its own monarch. Interestingly, Satan is arguably the main and most sympathetic character in *Paradise Lost.* Though Milton supported the English Civil War, he was a supporter of God's case against man and the devil, which leads to certain ambiguities within the text. Like Calvin and the Puritans, Milton was a believer in God's providence, and *Paradise Lost* seeks to show the ways in which God's plan for redemption was in play from the very beginning. Milton's God, like Calvin's, is beyond the ken of human beings. Borrowing from the Renaissance with its resemblance to earlier epic poetry, *Paradise Lost* is consistent with the Reformation in its focus on rebellion and redemption.

## CHAPTER FIVE

# THE WORLD OF REASON AND REVOLT

Samuel Joeckel

*Rules and Exceptions*

Historians love and hate generalizations. Generalizations organize history into tidy periods, which makes teaching the subject coherent, but they simultaneously overlook the many exceptions to the rule, the aberrations that fall through the epochal gaps. Consider, for instance, medievalists. They take umbrage at the phrase "Dark Ages," pointing to such counter-examples as Thomas Aquinas, monastic learning, and Chaucer. Nevertheless, if you happen to use that phrase, they will know what you mean and maybe even concede that it holds *some* truth. (After all, the barbarian hordes who ransacked the Roman Empire and who heralded the dawn of a new era were not exactly bookworms.)

The same is true of the World of Reason and Revolt. Yes, this period witnessed the birth of the Scientific Revolution and the Enlightenment itself, and yet so much that happened during this time was unreasonable or at least testified to the limits of reason. So let's get the exceptions out of the way before we proceed to the rule.

Arguably the most important philosopher of the eighteenth-century was David Hume (1711-1776). One pervasive tenet of his philosophy was that reason is weak and wavering. Consider, for instance, Hume's reflections on personal identity. As a thinker who took empiricism (more on that later) to its logical conclusion, Hume maintained that all knowledge must originally derive from sense impressions. That is, the first cause of all our ideas comes from something we have seen, heard, felt, etc. So do we have a sense impression of our own identity? I can see, feel, and even hear my body, but is my body my identity? Of course not. We might try to locate identity in the mind or soul. But do we have a sense impression of these? Hardly. When I try to peer into my own mind to find the source of identity, all I find is a deluge of sense impressions. I naturally try to organize these sense impressions into ideas and thus into knowledge, but I have no sense impression of the thing doing the organizing. Hume concludes that we are a mere "bundle of perceptions."[1] Our mind is like a movie screen upon which flashes in rapid succession the objects of our sense impressions, but there is no director or even projector operator running the show.

Repeatedly Hume shows how little we can know. Connections between ideas cannot be empirically verified. Thus it is by "custom or habit"—not logical necessity—that we conclude that the movement of one billiard ball will cause a second billiard ball to move when the former strikes the latter.[2] Thus Hume suspends judgement with respect to arguments for the existence of God; the cosmological argument might very well suggest that God exists, but we cannot possibly know anything about God's character from that argument. Hume asserts that the only difference between "fiction and belief" is that belief produces stronger emotions within us.[3] Belief is thus not the result of rigorous reasoning and hard-earned intellectual assent;

1 David Hume, *A Treatise of Human Nature* (New York: Penguin, 1984), 303.

2 David Hume, *An Enquiry Concerning Human Understanding*, in *Modern Philosophy*, eds. Forrest Baird and Walter Kaufmann (New Jersey: Prentice Hall), 351.

3 Ibid., 354.

it is the gravitation toward ideas that produce a lively emotional resonance. Hume is not exactly a poster boy for the scientific method.

Another exception to the Enlightenment rule is the Evangelical revival that took place during the second half of the eighteenth century in England. The standard historical narrative informs us, of course, that the Enlightenment occasioned a gradual process of secularization that would culminate with the "death of God" in the twentieth century. This may be true, but the Evangelical revival, spearheaded most visibly by John Wesley (1703-1791), threw a God-shaped wrench into that process, nearly grinding the secularization juggernaut to a halt.

Wesley was no dispassionately reasoning, deist-leaning, doctrine-denying religionist. He was a Bible-believing Christian on fire with the Holy Spirit. While at Oxford, he and a few friends met regularly to discuss the Bible; they became known as "the Holy Club," "the Godly Club," "Bible Moths," and, by 1732, the Methodists. In 1738, Wesley had his famous "Aldersgate experience," a moment during which his heart was "strangely warmed" by assurance of salvation in Christ.[4] (If ever you are in London, check out the Aldersgate Experience Monument, carved into the shape of flame to symbolize the Holy Spirit, located in front of the Museum of London.) By the time of his death, Wesley had traveled over a quarter of a million miles to preach over 40,000 sermons.[5] During some of his open-air revivals, Wesley stirred his audience with a spiritual fervor that would make the Enlightenment blush with embarrassment. Here is Wesley's own account of one such revival: "I have seldom seen an audience so greatly moved, since the time of my first preaching at Bristol. Men, women, and children wept and groaned, and trembled exceedingly; many could not contain themselves in these bounds, but cried with a loud and bitter cry."[6]

4 John Wesley, *Journal* (London: Epworth, 1967), 51.

5 See Kenneth Collins, *A Real Christian: The Life of John Wesley* (Nashville: Abingdon Press, 1999).

6 Wesley, 158.

Hume and Wesley are just two examples of counter-Enlightenment figures who problematize that standard historical account of their time. Poets like Thomas Gray (1716-1771), William Collins (1721-1759), and Edward Young (1683-1765) explored ranges of emotion and mysticism using poetic forms that lie well outside the comfort zone of Enlightenment norms. Novelist Laurence Sterne (1713-1768) weaved non-linear narratives that made a mockery of the scientifically precise unities of time and space.

By the time we get to the end of our period (the "Revolt" part), these exceptions transform into the rule, exemplifying the truism that intellectual history is reactionary: one generation does things one way; the next comes along and rebels. By 1800, the French Revolution and literary Romanticism created a new paradigm that redefined the definition of genius and re-engaged categories of experience that had been long neglected. As I tell my students, the eighteenth-century could only be emotionally repressed for so long. The *Zeitgeist* rupture that occurred at the end of the eighteenth century was drastic; consider that only seventy-five years separate the preeminently reasonable poetic essays of Alexander Pope (1688-1744) from the emotionally indulgent poetry of John Keats (1795-1821).

We will return to this paradigm at the end of the chapter. But first we must explore the World of Reason, beginning with three theories to explain the origins of the Enlightenment and the Scientific Revolution. These three theories are obviously not exhaustive, but they are a good start in getting a handle on the period.

### *Theory #1: The Continuation of Humanism*

Students make progress when they see continuity between their classes. Well, you are seeing it now. The intellectual renaissance you studied in The World of Humanism and Reform maintains much of its momentum through most of the Enlightenment. This momentum is part of the legacy of influential book lovers like

Pope Nicholas V (1397-1455) and Cosimo de'Medici (1389-1464), who wielded their wealth and power to help create a culture of intellectual curiosity and discovery. A little over one hundred years later, this culture shaped the scientific pursuits of Francis Bacon (1561-1626) and, less than fifty years after him, the creation of London's Royal Society, a scientific organization that secured science unimpeachable intellectual credibility when it was granted a charter (officially made into a legitimate, nationally recognized society) in 1662 by the King of England, Charles II.

The focus on the individual found in humanistic thinking likewise carries over into the Enlightenment. Recall, for instance, Petrarch's intense introspection in the sonnets, his poetic dissection of his own consciousness. Similarly, Rene Descartes (1596-1650), the founder of modern philosophy, begins his colossal epistemological project not by building upon his predecessors but by secluding himself in his study and analyzing his own ideas. He builds a new foundation for philosophy basically from scratch; he has the *chutzpah* to become a sort of philosophical everyman, deeming his own premises and conclusions absolute and universal.

This leads to yet a third commonality between humanism and the Enlightenment: confidence in reason to discover truth and improve humankind's lot on earth. Consummate Renaissance man Leon Battista Alberti (1404-1472) wrote, "Men can do all things if they will."[7] This utterance might serve as an epigraph of Renaissance humanism, registering the immense optimism (hubris?) of human potential.

Compare Alberti's audacity to the opening sentences of Isaac Newton's *Principia* (1687): "In the preceding books I have laid down the principles of philosophy [that is, natural science…] These principles are the laws of certain motions, and powers or forces, which chiefly have respect to philosophy [… ] It remains that from

7 Leon Alberti, qtd. in Jacob Burckhardt, *The Civilization of the Renaissance*, trans. D. Wooten (Indianapolis: Prentice-Hall, 1995), 48.

the same principles I now demonstrate the frame of the System of the World."[8] This display of bravado is the intellectual equivalent of a boxer talking trash before stepping into the ring for a championship fight.

But the thing is, Newton (1642-1727) pulls it off. To continue the analogy, the boxer KO'd his opponent (which I suppose would be ignorance or flawed theories of physics in my analogy). Fifty years after the publication of the *Principia* (which is plenty of time for the scientific dust to settle), Alexander Pope wrote an epitaph for Newton's memorial in Westminster Abbey: "Nature and Nature's laws lay hid in night; / God said, Let Newton be! and all was light."[9] In other words, in an act of beneficence, God created Newton to shed scientific light on everything else God created. Placing Newton in this biblical context, assigning him a role in the Genesis account, Pope gives us some idea how groundbreaking, how monumental Newton's work was. Newton's accomplishment was nothing short of unraveling the mysteries of the universe. Hume said of Newton that he was simply "the greatest and rarest genius that ever rose for the ornament and instruction of the species."[10]

### *Theory #2: Asking Different Questions*

Occasionally paradigm shifts in intellectual history occur not by pursuing existing paths of inquiry as far as they will go but by asking entirely new questions that change the paths of inquiry themselves. Such is the case with the Scientific Revolution. For much of the Middle Ages, the dominant questions were "why" questions. Why do planets move? Why does human suffering occur?

---

8 Isaac Newton, *Principia*, trans. Florian Cajori (Berkeley: University of California Press, 1934), 397.

9 See the Westminster Abbey website for more information: <http://www.westminster-abbey.org/our-history/people/sir-isaac-newton>.

10 David Hume, *History of England* (Philadelphia: Lippincott, 1859), 653.

These questions call for distinctly theological answers, answers, that is, that necessarily focus on the existence and nature of God. "Why" questions generate the sort of theological discourse found in the scholasticism of Thomas Aquinas. Aquinas addressed all the "why" questions—metaphysical questions about being and essence, causes and ends—and pushed them about as far as they could go. Intellectual inquiry had reached a dead end; thinkers became bored and dissatisfied by the same old answers.

So they began to ask new questions: "how" questions. And "how" questions are mostly scientific questions. Consider the two questions I posed earlier, but this time replace the "why" with "how." How do the planets move? This is the question that interested Copernicus (1473-1543), Galileo (1564-1642), and Newton, which in turn generated different sorts of answers in a new field that came to be known as science (after it was called "natural philosophy" for centuries). How does suffering occur? This is the sort of question that interested William Harvey (1515-1559), whose analysis of the human body—what made it function and malfunction—led to his discovery that the heart pumps blood, which is then circulated throughout the body. (Recall for centuries that scholars believed that blood was just one of the four humors inside the body and that all illness resulted from an imbalance among these humors.) Understanding blood circulation in turn helped Harvey and others asking these new questions to develop cures for the body when it did malfunction.[11]

"How" questions produced practical knowledge: knowledge that scientists and doctors—Christian or otherwise—could use to reduce human suffering in this world. This is why Bacon is widely attributed as coining the now-common phrase, "knowledge is power."[12] He was not interested in "why" questions because the

11 See Basil Willey's *The Seventeenth-Century Background* (Columbia: Columbia University Press, 1950).

12 See Francis Bacon's *Meditationes Sacrae* (1597). Bacon wrote this text in

best they could do is generate abstruse metaphysical answers that amounted to little in real life; they became for Bacon a sort of intellectual parlor game that, while full of sound and fury, signified nothing. "How" questions, on the other hand, were the first step in equipping humans with the power to make concrete changes that could quantifiably improve people's day-to-day lives.

Asking new questions furthermore generated a new (or at least revitalized) intellectual orientation: empiricism. As noted before, empiricism maintains that all knowledge is acquired through the senses. It is obvious why "how" questions necessitated strictly empirical analyses. To figure out *how* something works, you must observe, get your empirical hands dirty—looking, touching, and hearing. As the father of the scientific method, Bacon moreover believed that empirical knowledge-acquisition should occur through experimentation: observe nature, collect specimens, analyze and compare data. Experimentation meant reasoning through induction, a type of inference that begins, not from assumed first premises, but from observed particulars. You begin with what you observe, what is tangible and concrete, then you reflect via induction upon those observations, creating hypotheses that are empirically verifiable.

This intellectual orientation creates an interesting schism within the Enlightenment. While Bacon and other scientists used empiricism to acquire knowledge, Descartes and the philosophers who followed in his wake made use of rationalism, which is the intellectual orientation that maintains that knowledge is acquired independently of the senses, through the mind alone. In this sense, empiricism and rationalism are opposites. Descartes mistrusted his senses because they "sometimes played [him] false."[13] That is, sometimes things are not what they appear to be through the senses: think of the illusions of an oasis in the desert or a stick that appears

Latin. "Ipsa Scientia potestas est" might be translated as "Knowledge itself is power."

13 Rene Descartes, *Discourse on Method and the Meditations*, trans. F.E. Sutcliffe (London: Penguin, 1968), 66.

to bend when placed in water. Thus we are in the strange position of identifying the father of the scientific method (Bacon) as an empiricist and the father of modern philosophy (Descartes) as a rationalist.

Later in this chapter, I will show some ways in which they nevertheless share some distinctly Enlightenment characteristics. For now, you will just have to acknowledge this weird fact and concede that intellectual history can sometimes be sloppy.

*Theory #3: Organized Religion, for and against...*

Scholars disagree (naturally) about how Christianity fits into the rise of the Enlightenment and the birth of the Scientific Revolution. I will limit myself to two (among many) theories, two theories that happen to be antithetical.

There are those who maintain that Christianity went hand-in-hand with the Enlightenment and the Scientific Revolution. The thinking goes like this: science observes natural laws; since these laws are intelligible, they imply an intelligent natural-law giver; that intelligent natural-law giver is God. In other words, natural order suggests divine creation. Since we are made in the image of God, we can use our God-given reason to study the order that God has created. Without God, there would not be order—only chance and thus chaos. You of course have not yet studied Darwin, who will purport to show that natural laws—the algorithm that is evolution—necessitates neither God nor chance nor chaos. Nevertheless, for the time being, without God, there would be no natural order; without natural order, there would be no science and thus no Scientific Revolution and no Enlightenment.

Christianity helped to give birth to the Enlightenment in other ways. I will mention one that is circuitous and unexpected. Recall that Martin Luther translated the Bible into German, insisting that people have the right to read Scripture on their own. One predictable result of this insistence was a gradual rise of literacy rates; you cannot understand Scripture on your own if you do not know how to read. The gradual rise in literacy rates created over time a bookish culture, one in which intellectual curiosity blossomed; in other words, more people wanted to know more stuff. We might call this widespread desire to know Luther's inadvertent democratization of knowledge, which is one component of the Enlightenment.

On the other hand, there are those who believe that the failure of organized Christianity gave birth to the Enlightenment. These scholars point to the words of Flemish humanist Justus Lipsius (1547-1606): "Good Lord, what firebrands of sedition hath religion kindled in this fairest part of the world? The chief heads of our Christian commonwealths are at strife among themselves, and many millions of men have been brought to ruin and do daily perish, under a pretext of piety."[14] Lipsius is part of a chorus of voices during the period who came to believe that organized religion could not unite people; it instead usually caused bloodshed. Other voices then explicitly or implicitly began to sound the need for something else that could unite people, something more fundamental, something we all hold in common. That something, they concluded, might be reason. If only we all could equally use the faculty of reason, then perhaps we could agree. The dictates of reason, after all, are irresistible, undeniable to anyone who is reasonable. This chorus of voices include Thomas Hobbes, Baruch Spinoza, John Locke, Voltaire, Alexander Hamilton, and Thomas Jefferson, all of whom are champions in one way or another of the Enlightenment. They all registered in some form the dangers of organized religion and summoned reason as a less fallible guide; in so doing, they were committed to Enlightenment principles.

I turn now to two ways these Enlightenment principles manifested themselves in the seventeenth and eighteenth centuries, one within literature and the other in philosophy.

---

14 Quoted in Eric Wilson, *The Savage Republic* (Leiden: Martinus Nijhoff, 2008), 336.

### *The Enlightenment and Literature*

The Enlightenment's collision with literature follows hard on the heels of an important historical event of the seventeenth century. In 1642, England became embroiled in a civil war. This civil war pitted the royalists—who believed that political power should be reposed in the monarch—against the parliamentarians—whose fear of the abuses of monarchy compelled them to conclude that parliament should keep the monarch in check. What is significant for our purposes is that these parliamentarians tended to be dissenters—that is, people who were not Anglicans, who "dissented" against the Anglican Church. More specifically, they tended to be particular types of dissenters known as Puritans.

In 1649, the parliamentarian forces, under the leadership of Oliver Cromwell, defeated the royalist forces. Charles II, the King of England, was executed. For eleven years—1649-1660—England had no monarch. This period of English history is known as the Interregnum (literally meaning "between reigns"). Puritans by and large ran England. They shut down the immoral theatres and tried to clean up England's act. Within a few years, however, it became increasingly obvious that this new political order and the life it brought were not the utopian dreams many had envisioned. In the eyes of many, Cromwell amassed as much power as any monarch and wielded it just as ineffectively. (At Cromwell's funeral, one attendee noted in his diary, "It was the joyfullest [*sic*] funeral that ever I saw for there was none that cried but dogs, which the soldiers hooted away."[15]) By the end of the decade, the English had had enough, and so the son of Charles I was summoned to return.

In 1660, Charles II assumed the throne. The monarchy had been restored, an event that gives this period of history the first of its three prominent names: the Restoration. Restored to the throne, Charles II was hailed as the second Augustus Caesar, who,

15 Quoted in Richard Valpy French, *Nineteen Centuries of Drink in England* (London: Longman, 1884), 214.

you might remember, brought peace to Rome (the *Pax Romana*) after the turmoil surrounding the assassination of Julius Caesar. This parallel between Augustus Caesar and Charles II gives this period of history the second of its three prominent names: the Augustan Age.

With the chaotic, destructive rise and fall of the Puritan-led Interregnum indelibly ingrained in their collective minds, Augustans (as they came to be called) developed a contempt for all things Puritan; after all, the Puritan political experiment ended in failure. The foremost object of contempt was Puritan enthusiasm, the private and passionate convictions which Puritans claimed to have received from the Holy Spirit. In his *Dictionary of the English Language*, Samuel Johnson defines enthusiasm as a "vain belief of private revelation; a vain confidence of divine favour or communication." These private revelations and communication are attended with what Johnson calls a "heat of imagination"—that is, with emotional flights of fancy, with misplaced passion.[16]

To counter these supposed supernatural, idiosyncratic, private deliverances, Augustans privileged a faculty maintained to be more uniform, more stable, more publicly acceptable. By now, that privileged faculty should be obvious: reason. During the Restoration, the belief in private revelations became an object of suspicion and distrust, as was the emotional fervor that accompanied these revelations. Augustans desired the opposite of enthusiasm and all it connoted; they desired clarity, order, balance, and stability. This desire gives this period of history its third and final name: the neo-classical period. As you might recall, those characteristics I just listed—clarity, order, balance, and stability—defined the aesthetic principles of Greece during its golden age, otherwise known as classicism.

Literature of the late seventeenth and early eighteenth

---

16 Samuel Johnson, *Samuel Johnson's Dictionary*. ed. Jack Lynch (NY: Walker & Company, 2002), 166.

centuries is often referred to as Restoration literature, Augustan literature, and/or neoclassical literature. (I will restrict myself to the term "Augustan literature" because it is the most widely used of the three.) Augustan literature assumed the spirit and traits of the age that produced it. Augustan literature thus championed reason and tended to be distrustful of extreme states of emotion. Augustan literature emphasized clarity, order, balance, and stability.

The most obvious exemplar of these traits and thus Augustan literature is Alexander Pope. His poetry, often referred to as philosophical poetry, structurally and stylistically privileges reason and order. The *Essay on Man*, for instance, is written in heroic couplets. The lines of the poem, each ten syllables, are rhymed in pairs. The fulfillment of a rhyme adds a polemical punch to the completion of a thought. It brings a sense of irrefutable closure to a philosophical claim. One might analogize this polemical punch to dunking on someone in basketball—versus, say, sinking a wide-open jump shot from ten-feet out. The dunk and the jump shot both count as two points, but the dunk is so much more emphatic. When Pope concludes an argument with a heroic couplet, he is metaphorically dunking on those who disagree with him. One must also bear in mind that Pope's poem, which some scholars believe defined an age, is entitled *Essay on Man*. Only in the eighteenth century, the century of philosophical poetry, could a poem be called an "essay."

Another exemplar of Augustan literature is Jonathan Swift. Swift, of course, is known as a satirist. Satire is a literary genre that well-serves the values of Augustan thought, especially its distrust of individual, idiosyncratic thoughts and feelings, like those found in Puritan enthusiasm. While enthusiasm is a private experience, satire is preeminently a public form of literature. Bringing truth to light through the use of ridicule and humor, satire wants to get everything out in the open; nothing is safe from exposure. Moreover, satire, as it descends as a genre from the Roman writer Horace, ridicules extremes and explicitly or implicitly plants norms. That is, if human behavior is spread across a spectrum, then on the edges of the spectrum you would find the moral aberrations and intellectual eccentrics; in the eighteenth century, satire ridicules these monstrous and freakish outliers. In the middle of the spectrum, you would find those who follow moral common sense and, most importantly, reason. (Here you see a nod toward the period's third moniker: neoclassicism; the mechanism of satire looks a lot like Aristotle's argument for the golden mean.)

To conclude this foray into Augustan literature, we might plot the literary priorities of the period on a triangle. Think of the three corners of a triangle as three things that literature can do. In one corner stands didacticism. Literature that wants to teach or instruct gravitates toward this corner; the focus here is on the reader, since literature in this corner seeks to effect a change in the reader. Mimesis resides in the second corner. If a work of literature offers realistic representations of the actual world—in Hamlet's words, if it holds a mirror up to nature (Act 3, scene 2)—then it stakes its claim in this corner; the focus here is on the world. In the final corner you will find self-expressiveness. Literature in this neighborhood reveals the inner emotions of the writer. Love poetry, odes, and lyrical poetry can be found in this corner, where the focus is on the poet or writer.[17]

In the late seventeenth century and for the first half of the eighteenth century, most of the action takes place near the didactic and mimetic sides of the triangle. Poets are trying to teach and edify you. They are also offering authentic representations of how the world operates, even if they tell stories set in Brobdignag or the land of Houynhmys. Augustan literature is public literature. With reason and common sense as its guides, it sets its eyes on universal truths that transcend all particularities; it is wary of experiential idiosyncrasies.

---

17 For more on this literary triangle, see M.H. Abrams's *The Mirror and the Lamp: Romantic Theory and Critical Tradition*, published in 1953.

What makes studying this period so fascinating is that within a matter of decades, with the rise of Romanticism, these literary values will be completely upended and reversed. The triangle will be tilted in the opposite direction, hurtling literary representations toward the self-expressive side of the triangle.

### *The Enlightenment and Philosophy*

The Enlightenment witnessed the birth of modern philosophy; the birth of modern philosophy is inextricably linked to Rene Descartes. In 1637, Descartes helped to codify what we might call the Enlightenment project with the publication of his *Discourse on Method.* Employing mathematical methods and universal doubt, he sought to break down knowledge and experience to indubitable certainties. This rationalist approach was highly optimistic because it held that truth was "out there" and merely needed to be discovered. Descartes wrote, "There is only one truth to each thing, whoever finds it knows as much about the thing as there is to be known."[18] The one truth that Descartes claimed he knew for certain is expressed in the celebrated phrase, "*cogito ergo sum,*" "I think, therefore I am."[19] The search for truth, Descartes maintained, could be built upon this certain and unshakable foundation; the search for truth was furthermore undergirded by the belief that truth was stable and knowable.

Pursuing his project, Descartes implemented two procedural guidelines that I wish to identify as hallmarks of the Enlightenment; although Descartes was a rationalist, these guidelines are then appropriated by eighteenth-century empiricists. First, Descartes established *foundationalism* as the normative blueprint for epistemological structures. Such structures must rise upwardly upon a foundation of propositions deemed to be justified to the point of

18 Rene Descartes, *Discourse on Method and the Meditations*, Trans. F. E. Sutcliffe (New York: Penguin Books, 1968), 43.

19 *Ibid.*, 103.

certainty. Propositions higher up on the structure attain their truth status by virtue of their logical and coherent relationship to propositions lower on the structure, all of which are anchored by the foundational beliefs. Nancey Murphy and James Wm. McClendon define foundationalism this way:

> The foundationalist doctrine, a legacy from Descartes, assumes that it is the philosopher's job to justify the knowledge claims of other disciplines by finding indubitable or incorrigible beliefs upon which they depend. The reasoning behind the search for foundations is this: In the attempt to justify a given belief, the chain of supporting beliefs must not be circular or form an infinite regress. Therefore one must at some point reach a belief that needs no further justification—it must be something that cannot fail to be believed.[20]

For Descartes, that something was not only the existence of self but the existences of God and the external world. These beliefs constituted the foundation of Descartes's epistemological structure.

It must be noted that in the history of modern philosophy (from, say, the early seventeenth century to the late nineteenth century) all epistemologies were by and large foundational in nature.[21] However, within this history, there do exist various forms of foun-

20 Nancey Murphy and James Wm. McClendon, "Distinguising Modern and Postmodern Theologies." *Modern Theology* 5.3 (1989): 192.

21 In the mid twentieth century, postmodern pioneer Willard V. O. Quine eschewed foundationalism when he developed his web theory of belief—a holistic approach to epistemology in which beliefs assume an interdependence within a non-foundational architecture. Beliefs are not built upon indubitable certainties but are rather interlocked in an elaborate pattern of mutual dependence. See Quine's "Two Dogmas of Empiricism," *Philosophical Review* LX (1951); reprinted in T. Olshewsky, ed., *Problems in the Philosophy of Language* (New York: Holt, 1969). In the World of Despair and Hope, you will encounter Friedrich Nietzsche, another pioneer of postmodernism; Nietzsche offers a radical challenge and alternative to the Enlightenment project. That challenge and alternative reach their culmination in Richard Rorty and Michel Foucault, legit postmodernist thinkers.

dationalism. The Enlightenment project, I suggest, espouses *strong* foundationalism—a variation that sets up stringent criteria for justifying truth claims. These stringent criteria become apparent when we look at another procedural guideline adopted by Descartes.

The second procedural guideline concerns Descartes's method for building his epistemological foundation. As stated above, Descartes resolved to doubt everything that he had been taught in order to arrive at certainty, in order to find his foundations. He thus assumes a hyperbolically objective, impartial, and assumedly neutral stance that I call *de-conversion.* If conversion refers to the acceptance of particular beliefs and views, Descartes reverses that process and assumes that he can strip away particular beliefs and views in order to achieve that objective stance. De-conversion involves a self-imposed manipulation of one's own identity whereby the self is supposedly cleansed of all presuppositions in order to apprehend truth impartially. The self thus sheds the incrustations of historical, political, social, religious, and communal contingencies and particularities. Having done so, the self assumes a new identity—one of a neutral inquisitor. Assuming that anyone can undergo this de-conversion experience, Descartes maintained that this neutral inquisitor will render philosophical conclusions with which any reasonable or rational person must agree.

As time passes and as philosophers challenge Descartes, it becomes clear that Descartes's foundations are not as unassailable as he thought; Nietzsche and the postmodern thinkers will show that Descartes's foundationalism is untenable. Nevertheless, it is important to note the optimism of Descartes's philosophy. This optimism defines the intellectual temper of the period. Philosophers and scientists of this time believed that truth was out there and that they would find it.

This optimism, however, was paradoxically built upon skepticism. While Descartes's philosophy might end in optimism, it began with skepticism. Specifically, it began with methodological doubt. That is, Descartes began by doubting everything that he had learned, everything that he had taken for granted as true. Trust no one; doubt everything. The optimism thus had a sort of symbiotic relationship to skepticism. Regardless, methodological doubt is part of Descartes's legacy to philosophy.

This is why some scholars refer to the Enlightenment as the Age of Critique. Following the legacy of Descartes, thinkers of the eighteenth century subjected everything to critique; nothing, including the sacred truths of Christianity, escapes a rigorous—sometimes merciless—intellectual interrogation. Immanuel Kant's essay, "What is Enlightenment?" sounds the Enlightenment call to arms: critique everything with unflinching intellectual integrity. As time passes and the philosophical tides turn, the optimism in Descartes's symbiotic epistemological structure subsides; skepticism begins to consume optimism.

I wish to conclude this section by pointing to an historical event that unfolded alongside these philosophical developments, an historical event that gave momentum to the period's growing skepticism. This historical event is the rise of the public sphere. The scholar who has written most influentially and powerfully on the public sphere is Jürgen Habermas. My overview of this historical event depends heavily on his account.

According to Habermas, the public sphere develops at the turn of the eighteenth century. Habermas traces this development to (among other historical events) the shifting oppositional dynamic between "court and town."[22] During the first half of the seventeenth century in England, the court served as the epicenter for learned discourse; as Habermas puts it, "literature and art served the representation of the king."[23] The age of courtly patronage kept artists and intellectuals beholden to the monarch; after all,

22 Jürgen Habermas, *The Structural Transformation of the Public Sphere: An Inquiry into a Category of Bourgeois Society,* trans. Thomas Burger (Cambridge, Massachusetts: The MIT Press, 1989), 32.

23 Ibid., 32

the monarch (as patron) was keeping the artists clothed and fed. Toward the end of the seventeenth century, however, the town began to eclipse the court in influence, becoming the new cradle of learned culture. The cultural influence of the town gained more and more strength with the advent of novel institutions: the coffee house and the salon. These locales became the birthplace of the public sphere.

Acting as social spaces for public dialogue, literary discourse, intellectual debate, and information exchange, the coffee houses and salons assumed the "social functions" once held by the court.[24] These social spaces also became metaphorical social spaces, not confined to literal coffee houses and salons. The public sphere could metaphorically be found within the pages of periodicals that could be had cheaply in eighteenth-century England—periodicals with names like *The Spectator*, *The Tatler*, and, under Samuel Johnson's editorship, the *Rambler*, the *Idler*, and the *Adventurer*. Figurative or literal, the period witnessed an explosion of social spaces for public dialogue and information exchange, what Habermas calls a "public sphere of a rational-critical debate."[25] A byproduct of the rise of the public sphere is the birth of public opinion, forged by the debates among these various social strata. "The medium of this public confrontation," writes Habermas, "was peculiar and without historical precedent: people's use of their reason."[26] The rise of the public sphere, in fact, helped secure the legacy of the Enlightenment as expressed, and as we have already seen, in the following procedural guideline: reason is the preeminent faculty of humankind; it is the chief source of authority—not faith, not tradition, not religious or political powers.

Fulfilling the pragmatic purpose of finding truth, reason within the public sphere produces arguments that must prove rationally

24 Ibid., 32

25 Ibid., 51.

26 Ibid., 27.

compelling (as suggested above) to an increasingly pluralistic audience with divergent beliefs: religious, irreligious; high church, low church; Anglicans, dissenters; Tories, Whigs, etc. Performing this task necessitates a unification of the diversity, a method of appealing to commonalities lying beyond the differences. The public sphere vouchsafes a critical unifying principle by assuming the existence of uniform experience across the religious, philosophical, political, and socio-economic spectrum. While particularities divide those of conflicting convictions, at the root of all experience there exists a foundational sameness. Thus, despite the increasing heterogeneity of the period, the principle of homogeneity paradoxically becomes the operative principle of the public sphere as well as an assumed pillar in the framework of Enlightenment discourse. Predisposed to favor homogeneity, public discourse acts as a unifying agent, uniting people around what they have in common rather than how they differ. As Alasdair MacIntyre explains, during the Enlightenment, "Rational justification was to appeal to principles undeniable by any rational person and therefore independent of all those social and cultural particularities which the Enlightenment thinkers took to be the mere accidental clothing of reason in particular times and places."[27]

It should be clear by now how the rise of the public sphere worked in harmony with the rise of modern philosophy. As they ascended, the two phenomena shared numerous characteristics. For both, reason is the operative procedural guideline. For both, the goal is to arrive at universal truth, a truth that no one can deny: in the case of philosophy, universal truth serves the aim of foundationalism; in the case of the public sphere, universal truth serves the aim of consensus, of getting a large and diverse group of people to agree with you. Moreover, the public sphere, like modern philosophy, encourages de-conversion. In order to enter the public sphere for the purposes of winning an argument and thus forging a

27 Alasdair MacIntyre, *Whose Justice? Which Rationality?* (Notre Dame: University of Notre Dame Press, 1988), 6.

consensus, one must de-convert. Like Descartes, one must become hyperbolically objective and impartial. Even when, say, you are defending a claim for which you have a clear interest, you must come across as disinterested, unbiased, and neutral.

Nearly all of these guidelines and procedures operated within philosophy and the public sphere during this time: de-conversion; arguing toward universals and essences; basing arguments on absolute truths and indubitable foundations (foundationalism); and appealing to reason above all other faculties. It is difficult for me to restrain myself from pointing you ahead to the World of Despair and Hope in order to show what happened to these guidelines and procedures—the ways in which they were challenged and undermined, in some cases devastatingly so.

It is also hard for me to restrain myself from likewise pointing out how some Christians in the twentieth and twenty-first centuries have been misguided in appropriating these Enlightenment guidelines and procedures—that is, how they mistakenly assume that their insistence on absolute truth is biblical when it is in fact a legacy of the Enlightenment.

It is, however, an easy mistake to make, one that I believe Milton made. In the *Areopagitica*, Milton grounds his argument against censorship in the burgeoning public sphere (though of course he did not call it that). He maintains that *all* opinions—even if they are wrong—should be given vent within the public sphere because, in the end, truth will win out. Milton had faith in the guidelines and procedures of the public sphere; public opinion would eventually side with truth. Must we count the ways since the eighteenth century in which truth definitely did *not* win out in the public sphere?

In hindsight, it seems apparent that the Enlightenment needed a corrective. Besides (and as I commented earlier), the eighteenth century could only be emotionally repressed for so long. Enter the French Revolution and Romanticism.

*Revolt*

The French Revolution was an explosion of contrasting energies: hope and fear, benevolence and violence, optimism and cynicism. It marked a breathtaking reversal of the Augustan ethos, which, as we have seen, privileged order, balance, and stability; revolutionaries perceived these values as a thinly disguised legitimization of oppression. The Great-Chain-of-Being metaphor aptly illustrates these rival perceptions. From one vantage point, the Chain maintains order and stability by allotting everyone and everything its God-ordained and thus rightful place in the Chain's hierarchy; as seen in Alexander Pope's appropriation of the metaphor (in the *Essay on Man*), as long as everyone knows his or her place on the hierarchy, peace and harmony will be maintained. From another vantage point, however, the Chain perpetuates oppression, for the Chain's hierarchy places aristocrats above peasants, the clergy above craftsmen, men above women, white Europeans above Africans, and so on. The animating spirit of the French Revolution is progressive, challenging the conservative values that defend, and depend upon, this traditional way of seeing things. This conservative/progressive split is exemplified in the polemical war between Edmund Burke and Thomas Paine. In his *Reflections on the Revolution in France*, Burke opposes the Revolution from what will become classic conservative principles. In *The Rights of Man*, Paine defends the Revolution from a progressive orientation.

The French Revolution was inspired by the American Revolution. Six years after Great Britain signed the Treaty of Paris, which recognized the independence of the thirteen American colonies, King Louis XVI of France convened his parliament (in 1789). He needed to get France out of debt, a debt fueled in part by—ironically enough—its support of America in its revolt against Britain. The proposed taxes that resulted from this parliament fell heavily upon the middle and lower classes.

These classes decided that they had had enough. They saw the aristocracy and the clergy amass more and more money and power. Peasants struggled to survive while they saw on a daily basis the increasing opulence of the nobility and clergy. As an example of this opulence, consider the Palace of Versailles. It took approximately 36,000 workers twenty years to complete it. When it was finished, it was almost half the size of the city of Paris itself. It was against this sort of opulence that the French revolted; the motivation for the revolution was (and is) age-old: class inequality. The hatred directed toward the beneficiaries of this inequality—again, the aristocracy and the clergy—is illustrated in a statement attributed to Diderot: "Let us strangle the last king with the guts of the last priest."[28]

Two famous moments of the French Revolution took place during its first year, 1789. July witnessed Bastille Day, when thousands of peasants stormed the Bastille, the French state prison but also, more importantly, a symbol of the traditional French political order, the *ancien regime*. In July of that year came the Woman's March on Versailles, when nearly 7,000 working Frenchwomen attacked the palace. It was during this march on Versailles that the French queen, Marie Antoinette, supposedly attempted to appease the protestors by declaring, "Let them eat cake." While she almost certainly never said this, the apocryphal response does point to a historical fact: the aristocracy were out of touch with the very people they ruled.

Also in 1789, revolutionaries formed the National Constituent Assembly, which suspended the power of the king (the monarchy was eventually abolished in 1792) and introduced representative government. It framed a constitution, inspired by the American Constitution, founded on principles of liberty, equality, and fraternity, all of which became known as the "Rights of Man." Since clergy were seen as part of the problem, the French Republic, which was formed in 1792, formally began to sever France's ties to Chris-

---

28 Quoted in Jean-Francois de la Harpe, *Lycee* (Paris: Firmin-Didot Freres, 1840).

tianity in an attempt to reclaim the money and land owned by the Catholic Church. Priests were exiled, and the assets of the Church were appropriated and placed into a national treasury. Reason supplanted faith; the God of the Catholic Church was replaced with the Supreme Being.

Eventually the French Revolution became violent. Castles and abbeys were burned, along with the priests and nuns who inhabited them. Manor houses were torched, along with the aristocratic families (and servants) who lived there. In 1793, Louis XVI and Marie Antoinette were sent to the guillotine. Also that year began the so-called Reign of Terror, during which suspected opponents of the Revolution were likewise beheaded. Over the course of two years, tens of thousands of people were executed by guillotine. Turmoil spread over the next five years until 1799, when Napoleon Bonaparte brought order to France and eventually turned France into an empire.

### *Romanticism*

Romanticism illustrates how intellectual history is reactionary. I can begin defining Romanticism by pointing out that it reacts against pretty much everything I have outlined in this chapter. The Enlightenment champions reason; Romanticism explores emotion. The Enlightenment seeks the universal; Romanticism is interested in the particular. The Enlightenment hero is a philosophical Everyman pursuing absolute truth; the Romantic hero is an individual genius seeking inspired expression. The Enlightenment hero pounds out polemical points in the public sphere; the Romantic hero strolls alongside a river or reclines beneath a tree, communing with nature (or his lover). The Enlightenment produces public poetry; Romanticism produces private, personal poetry. The Enlightenment values poetic balance and symmetry; Romanticism encourages poetic experimentation and exuberance. And returning now to our literary triangle, we have obviously tilted toward self-expression, for whereas Enlightenment poetry is didactic, Romantic poetry searches the soul to lay bare what it finds there.

William Wordsworth and Samuel Taylor Coleridge put British literary Romanticism on the map. They are preceded, however, by various movements as well as explorations in genre that, in retrospect, paved their way. Consider, for instance, the so-called "Pre-Romantics," a designation that literary scholars despise (but use all of the time anyway). Scholars claim to despise it because it implies that there was a bunch of thinkers and poets in the mid-eighteenth century who knew Romanticism was coming and, like some sort of literary John the Baptist, set about preparing the way. I will forgo the obligatory qualifications about how literary history is not telic and about how identifying anyone as "pre-" anything is unjust because it fails to take the individual identified as a "pre-" something or other on his or her own terms. I will just get right to it.

The pre-Romantic roster might start with Edward Young. His essay entitled "Conjectures on Original Composition" (1759) called for innovation in poetry and maintained that, when it achieves genius, poetry produces a beauty that cannot be put into words (in contrast to the Enlightenment, which likes to put everything into words, often in the form of critique). Thanks to his poem "Night-Thoughts" (1742), an extended meditation upon, among other subjects, death, Young is included in what became known as the "Graveyard School," a group of poets who make death and gloom the subjects of their poems. The most famous of these poets is Thomas Grey, whose "Elegy Written in a Country Churchyard" (1751) is the most famous specimen within the Graveyard School. Along with William Collins, Grey is credited with resurrecting the poetic genre known as the ode, a flexible form that allows for intense, occasionally rhapsodic, emotional expression—a far cry from the emotional restraint found in Pope's heroic couplets.

The Gothic novel is often considered a "pre-Romantic" phenomenon. Like the Graveyard School, the Gothic obsesses with death and gloom. Its narrative twists and turns are often generated by the "unspeakable," moments of supernatural intervention or horrific spectacle that defy logic. (And logic, of course, is the very thing that the Enlightenment banked on.) Horace Walpole's *The Castle of Otranto* (1764) was the very first Gothic novel and thus was in many ways an anti-Enlightenment text.

Goethe is an important figure in early German Romanticism. His novel, *The Sorrows of Young Werther* (1774), helped to establish what became known in German as *Sturm und Drang* (in English, "Storm and Stress"). Like British Romanticism, *Sturm und Drang* was a reactionary movement, revolting against established literary conventions to produce something new. *Sturm und Drang* "was characterized by fervor, enthusiasm, restlessness, the portrayal of great passion, and a reliance on emotional experiences and spiritual struggles."[29] Goethe was thus part of the brewing movement that culminated in Wordsworth and Coleridge.

As previously stated, Wordsworth and Coleridge put Romanticism on the British map; in their Preface to the *Lyrical Ballads* (1798), they codified the principles of Romanticism, thus making them, with the help of their prodigious literary output, the most important figures of literary Romanticism anywhere. At the outset, it is important to note that they were inspired by the French Revolution. Wordsworth especially saw great promise in the movement, even traveling in 1790 and 1791 to France, where he, alongside the revolutionaries, championed liberty, imbibing the countercultural spirit, and even falling in love. To understand Romanticism's connection to the French Revolution, perhaps the following analogy will be helpful: Romanticism is to the French Revolution as Rock and Roll in the 1960s is to the Civil Rights Movement, Vietnam War protests, and the burgeoning hippie culture. Those events in

29 Eds. C. Hugh Holman and William Harmon, *A Handbook to Literature* (NY: Macmillan, 1992), 460.

America challenged the status quo and created an entirely new *Zeitgeist*, which in turn encouraged innovation and experimentation in music (as well as in other facets of life). The upheaval and energy of the day opened the floodgates for youth culture to express themselves in ways that their parents' generation definitely did not understand. As the Civil Rights Movement and Vietnam produced Bob Dylan and Jimi Hendrix, so did the French Revolution produce Wordsworth (as well as a second-generation poet like Percy Shelley, who identified poets as the "unacknowledged legislators of the world"[30]).

Wordsworth bears the marks of the Revolution in his poetic tendency to privilege the common man through the use of common language. He often champions peasant folk in his poems while employing rustic diction. In such poems, he gravitates toward the use of ballad stanzas, which have a sing-song quality, like a nursery rhyme or a drinking song. (A ballad is made up of four-line stanzas, the first and third line consisting of eight syllables, the second and fourth line comprised of six syllables.) As the French Revolution aimed to empower the working class, so many of Wordsworth's poems ennobled the common folk. In contrast to the lofty poetic subjects of, say, Milton in the seventeenth century or Pope in the eighteenth, Wordsworth liked to make common incidents important; he poeticized the everyday, thus elevating common life through his art.

Many of Wordsworth's poems offer retreats to nature, a nature uncorrupted by civilization. Rural life is often a sort of salvation. At the very least, nature serves as the backdrop for moral dilemmas that a Wordsworth poem tries to work out. If you have ever been to the Lake District in the northern part of England, where Wordsworth lived for many years, you might understand his love of nature. (Dove Cottage in Grasmere, where Wordsworth resided, is

30 Percy Shelley, "A Defense of Poesy," in *Shelley's Poetry and Prose*, eds. Donald Reiman and Sharon Powers (NY: Norton, 1977), 480.

now a historic home that you can tour.) The idealization of nature, however, might also be a response to the Industrial Revolution, which by the end of the eighteenth century was churning out in cities across England the factories that the poet William Blake called "dark Satanic mills."[31]

More than anything, however, what unifies Romantic poetry is its strong emotional component. In the Preface to the *Lyrical Ballads*, Wordsworth and Coleridge famously called poetry the "spontaneous overflow of powerful emotions."[32] This emphasis on emotion made the human breast sacred. To put it more strongly, it tended to divinize humankind, for from the sacred chambers of the heart proceeded holy truths—holy truths that transcended clear description, holy truths conveyed instead in poetic hints and guesses. In this way, Romanticism enters the river of the Enlightenment as they both slowly erode the truths of Christianity. And while Enlightenment embattles the faith through critique, Romanticism does so by providing alternative structures of meaning that deify human experience. Thus, when Percy Shelley searches the depths of his heart, he does not find faith but rather a love-infused infinite striving that he likens to "the desire of the moth for the star."[33] And thus when Shelley's fellow second-generation Romantic poet John Keats writes of religion and martyrs, he bypasses Christianity and the heroes of the faith and instead proclaims, "Love is my religion."[34]

31 Blake, *Milton* (London: A.H. Bullen, 1907), xix.

32 Wordsworth, *Preface to the Lyrical Ballads* (Copenhagen: Rosenkilde and Bagger, 1957), 64.

33 Shelley, "To ----," *Posthumous Poem of Percy Shelley* (London: John and Henry L. Hunt, 1824), 13.

34 Keats, *Letters of John Keats to Fanny Brawne* (New York: George Broughton and Barclay Dunham, 1901), 41.

*Human Dignity, Human Rights*

Romanticism likewise enters the river of the Enlightenment insofar as both ultimately champion human dignity irrespective of social class and religious beliefs. As we have seen, the French Revolution was an attack on the very notion of social rank and a dismantling of the Church; as such, the Revolution robbed the aristocracy of the two forces it had historically used to keep the common folk in their place: money and religion. After the Revolution, people began to be valued not because of their place in the social or religious hierarchy but simply because they were human. The measure of a person's worth had shifted.

Enlightenment figures like Voltaire and Thomas Paine demonstrate the attempt to effect this shift; critiquing the Church and appealing to reason, they recalibrate a human being's worth. Voltaire saw in the Church systematic oppression of the masses; according to Voltaire, the Church kept most people ignorant and afraid in order to hold them in their place. Like Voltaire, Paine saw the Church as an instrument of oppression. Linked to the State, the Church ran roughshod over the common folk. Paine insisted that all men are born equal and should be treated as such throughout their lives. (Alas, Paine did not publicly proclaim his belief that *women* are equal as well, though he did work alongside feminist pioneer Mary Wollstonecraft, who wrote *A Vindication of the Rights of Women* [1792].)

The recalibration of a person's worth is illustrated through a fascinating linguistic phenomenon. As Peter Berger explains, during the late 1700s and early 1800s, the word "honor" began its steady decline into obsolescence; it falls off the textual grid during this period. Conversely, uses of the word "dignity" begin to multiply. We might say that "dignity" replaced "honor." What does this linguistic phenomenon signify? According to Berger, the "concept of honor implies that identity is essentially, or at least importantly, linked to institutional roles. The modern concept of dignity, by contrast, implies that identity is essentially independent of institutional roles."[35] These institutional roles are dictated by institutions such as the Church, the monarchy, feudalism, the aristocracy, and so on. Thus, the concept of honor depends upon a socially constructed rank along a spectrum of privilege. Those on one side of the spectrum, which would be most people, lack privilege and thus possess no honor. Those on the other side possess varying degrees of privilege and thus varying degrees of honor.

When Enlightenment figures and French revolutionaries rebelled against the very notion of privilege, they brought down that spectrum and the concept of honor along with it. From the wreckage emerged the concept of dignity, which, as Berger explains, "always relates to the intrinsic humanity divested of all socially imposed roles or norms."[36] Take the crown off the monarch and the miter off the bishop, divest them of power and the accoutrements that accompany it, and you have a mere human being, no better and no worse than a blacksmith or tenant farmer. The concept of dignity levels the playing field, so to speak. You are valued—you have dignity—not because you are landed gentry or an archbishop but because you are human. The linguistic shift thus amounted to a restructured understanding of what it means to be a human being.

And it created a ripple effect through history. As Berger also notes, the focus on dignity rather than honor reflects the "classic formulations of human rights," as they are expressed in the Preamble to the Declaration of Independence and in the Universal Declaration of Human Rights of the United Nations.[37] These formulations now seem obvious and quaint to us: that we all have rights regardless of race, color, creed, and by the late twentieth century, sexual orientation. The road to these rights began in the

35 Berger, "On the Obsolescence of the Concept of Honor," in *Revisions: Changing Perspectives in Moral Philosophy*, eds. Hauerwas and MacIntyre (Notred Dame: Notre Dame UP, 1983), 177.

36 Ibid., 176.

37 Ibid., 176.

Enlightenment. And as the French Revolution at the turn of the eighteenth century and the Civil Rights Movement in the twentieth century show, that road has never been smooth.

Nevertheless, in its full maturation, the Enlightenment endorsed both reason and human rights, a two-pronged emphasis that many believed—and still believe today—is humanity's best hope for progress.[38]

## The World of Reason and Revolt Textual Glosses

### Francis Bacon, *Novum Organum Scientiarum* (1620)

Francis Bacon is considered by many to be the father of the scientific method. *Novum Organum Scientiarum* (usually referred to as *Novum Organum* for short) might be translated as "new method (or instrument) of science." This title is adapted from Aristotle's work *Organon* (arranged and collected in 40 BCE), which champions deduction and the syllogism as the preeminent forms of logic. Bacon disagrees, replacing deduction with induction, otherwise known as the Baconian method.

Deduction is a form of reasoning that uses assumed premises to generate necessary conclusions. The following is a famous syllogism that illustrates deduction:

(Major) Premise: All men are mortal.

(Minor) Premise: Socrates is a man.

Conclusion: Socrates is mortal.

Induction or Baconian method, on the other hand, is a form of reasoning that begins not from premises but from observed particu-

38 For a recent champion of the Enlightenment, see the works of Steven Pinker, especially *Enlightenment Now: The Case for Reason, Science, Humanism, and Progress*, published in 2018.

lars; induction starts with the observation of data. For instance, let's say we wanted to find out what causes burnout in college students. Bacon's inductive method might work like this:

1. Make a list of cases in which burnout occurs.
2. Make a list of cases similar to these, but where burnout does not occur.
3. Use inductive method to discover the factors that are always present when burnout occurs.
4. Make a hypothesis about that causal factor.
5. Test (and test again) that hypothesis.

This method of inquiry later became known as the scientific method, thus explaining Bacon's honorific title as the method's father.

Bacon is also often credited with the saying, "Knowledge is power." He was not interested in speculative, abstract knowledge; he was no theoretical scientist. He wanted to acquire knowledge that could be put to use to better people's lives; you might say he pursued applied science. He writes, "[Knowledge] is not an opinion to be held [...] but a work to be done; and I am laboring to lay the foundation not of any sect or doctrine, but of utility and power."[39] Pursuing this utilitarian knowledge, Bacon breaks from the past: unlike so many of his intellectual predecessors, he does not believe that longstanding authorities and old books hold a monopoly on truth; rather, truth can be found by any individual who methodically, scientifically, inductively studies nature.

Bacon in fact distrusts older ways of pursuing knowledge. In the *Novum Organum*, Bacon maintains that the mind has, over time, acquired some bad habits. He refers to these bad habits as "idols of the mind." These idols include our natural propensity for gullibility; we are too eager to believe because we are superstitious,

39 Francis Bacon, *The Great Instauration* (New York: Simon & Schuster, 2012), 8.

or because we *want* to believe, or because we are prejudiced to see things one way. In short, in order to think more clearly, we need to think more impartially and objectively. This is of course the *modus operandi* of science. Allowing personal preferences or subjective opinions to influence one's work is anathema in the world of the sciences.

Carrying the banner for science (called "natural philosophy" at the time), Bacon proposed a total reconstruction of knowledge, thereby launching one of the first and most influential forays on behalf of the Scientific Revolution.

## John Milton, *Areopagitica* (1644) and "Of Education" (1644)

### *Areopagitica*

In 1643, British Parliament passed an ordinance for the licensing of the press. In order to be licensed, any book slated for publication had to be approved by the Stationers' Company, which was basically a censorship body. John Milton (1608-1674) was himself mentioned in the ordinance, for he had recently published his controversial book entitled *Doctrine and Discipline of Divorce* (1643), in which he argued that divorce should be granted on the grounds of irreconcilable differences; Milton even marshaled biblical evidence to support his positon. Although common today, this position was scandalous—even nearly unthinkable—at the time. In any case, *Areopagitica* argues against censorship and for the freedom of the press. His argument did not persuade Parliament.

Milton's title alludes to a written oration by Isocrates, delivered in the fifth century B.C.E. in his home city of Athens. Seeking to reform Athenian morals, Isocrates made a case for the use of censorship. This allusion obviously makes Milton's title ironic, since he argued against censorship. The title might also allude to the Apostle Paul's sermon on Mars Hill to the Areopagus four-hundred years later. After all, Milton's pamphlet and Paul's sermon converge upon the same idea: that even distorted and obscene ideas may contain surprising kernels of truth—in Milton's case, as found in a bad book; in Paul's case, as found in the religion of the pagans.

Milton launches multifarious arguments in *Areopagitica*. Here are just a few:

- Immoral books cannot corrupt spiritually sound Christians. Riffing off of Paul's dictum that "to the pure, all things are pure" (Titus 1:15), Milton writes, "Knowledge cannot defile, nor consequently the books, if the will and conscience be not defiled."[40]
- Censoring books will not make people more virtuous; it will simply make people sheltered, thereby doing their virtue a disservice. In order for virtue to strengthen and build its muscle, it must be tested. Censoring books will thus create morally flabby people. (Savvy readers will realize that Milton might be, in effect, challenging the student conduct codes enforced at Christian universities like PBA. Milton might say that the rules of accountability enforced by PBA's Office of Student Accountability are counterproductive: they do not create stronger Christians, just sheltered Christians.)
- Some of the books that are censored may later turn out to have contained some truth. Our apprehension of truth is ongoing; we never know where truth might turn up, even in a book that was once deemed dangerous.

This last point relates to what is perhaps Milton's most historically influential claim. The publication of many books contributes to what was later called the public sphere, a literal and figurative space of public debate and discussion. The public sphere could be a book, a pub, a coffee house, the floor of a political chamber,

40 John Milton, *Areopagitica and Of Education* (Wheeling, Illinois: Harlan Davidson, 1986), 16.

a periodical, or even a Parisian salon; the public sphere encompassed all of these. Milton recommends that we let all opinions and perspectives circulate in this public sphere, even if some of those opinions and perspectives are wrong or morally dubious. Why? Because eventually truth will rise to the top; truth will win: "And though all the winds of doctrine were let loose to play upon the earth, so Truth be in the field, we do injuriously by licensing and prohibiting to misdoubt her strength. Let her and Falsehood grapple; who ever knew Truth put to the worse, in a free and open encounter."[41]

### "Of Education"

"Of Education" prescribes an educational program for students aged twelve to twenty-one. The emphasis placed on learning the languages of the most literate western civilizations is part of Milton's legacy to centuries of education. Even into the twentieth century, serious students had no choice but to learn Greek and Latin; these were the languages of the learned. The focus on languages also tips Milton's hand as a humanist. Reading Greek and Latin gave students entrée into the very worlds of Plato and Epicurus, worlds that drew the fascination and admiration of humanists ever since literary explorers during the High Renaissance brought to Italy recovered classical texts and antiquities from across the Mediterranean.

Perhaps most importantly, the fundamental aim of Milton's pedagogy, the end goal of his educational program, points to Milton's identity as a distinctly *Christian* humanist: "The end then of learning is to repair the ruins of our first parents by regaining to know God aright and out of that knowledge to love him, to imitate him, to be like him, as we may the nearest by possessing our souls of true virtue, which being united to the heavenly grace of faith makes up the highest perfection."[42] Here Milton unites the

41 Ibid., 50.

42 Ibid., 50.

contemplative and active life. Learning cultivates a love of virtue and truth, which then motivates an obedience to God.

### John Bunyan, *Pilgrim's Progress* (1678)

Bunyan's *Pilgrim's Progress* is a bibliographical marvel. Only one other book has sold more copies: the Bible. It has been translated into more than thirty European and 130 non-European languages. By 1792, the book had already gone through 160 editions. In the over three hundred years since its publication, *Pilgrim's Progress* has never been out of print.

What makes these feats even more remarkable is the fact that the book was written by a relatively uneducated author. Bunyan (1628-1688) writes in his autobiography, *Grace Abounding to the Chief of Sinners* (1666), that, when he was a child, "it pleased God to put it into [my parents'] hearts to put me to school, to learn me both to read and write."[43] His formal education did not extend far beyond that. Consistent with this inauspicious genesis, *Pilgrim's Progress* gained popularity by first capturing the attention of the lower and middle classes. Only later, and in some cases grudgingly, did some of the *literati* acknowledge its merits—some, definitely not all. Edgar Allan Poe called it "a ludicrously overrated book."[44] On the other hand, Rudyard Kipling offered it high praise, identifying Bunyan as the "father of the novel."[45]

Its generic identity is a bit muddled. With Kipling, one is on relatively safe ground in identifying *Pilgrim's Progress* as a novel. After all, the text contains an extended narrative along with a few

---

43 John Bunyan, *Grace Abounding to the Chief of Sinners*, in *The Whole Works of John Bunyan*, ed. George Offor (London: Blackie and Son, 1862), 6.

44 Edgar Allan Poe, "Hawthorne's 'Tales,'" in *On Novels, Essays, and Travels—Marginalia*, eds. Edmund Stedman and George Woodbury (New York: Charles Scribner's Sons, 1914), 32.

45 Rudyard Kipling, "The Holy War," in *The Writings in Prose and Verse of Rudyard Kipling*, ed. Charles Balistier (New York: Charles Scribner's Sons, 1919), 35.

other standard characteristics of the novel, such as the use of prose and the representation of conflict and resolution.

Its status as an allegory, however, complicates its generic identity as a novel, which always includes the element of character development; this element is lacking in *Pilgrim's Progress*. After all, the protagonist's name—Christian—limits his development. Can Christian cease being Christian? Christian's situation is similar to that of the seven dwarfs in the Snow White story: Grumpy will always be grumpy; otherwise, we will have to change his name. So can his character ever really develop?

Nevertheless, *Pilgrim's Progress* is textbook allegory, which is defined as "a form of extended metaphor in which objects, persons, and actions in a narrative are equated with meanings that lie outside the narrative itself."[46] Thus the "Slough of Despond" is literally, within the narrative, a quagmire; it is also a metaphor, outside the text, for the despair caused by sin. Throughout the text, the allegory operates consistently and precisely, offering one-to-one correspondences between literal objects or characters within the text and concepts, people, and places that lie outside the text.

Many of Christian's conflicts concern confrontations with characters who allegorize ecclesiastical persecution. This is because Bunyan was a Puritan, a dissenter who worshipped outside the Anglican Church, which was (and is) the official church of England. In 1649, the Puritans and other dissenters put a temporary stop to that after defeating the royalists in the English Civil War, which began in 1642. Upon their victory, the Puritans executed Charles I, disestablished the Anglican Church, and ushered in an unprecedented era of English history: the Interregnum, when England had no monarch. However, the Interregnum failed, and in 1660, Charles's son, Charles II, established his place as king and restored the monarchy.

46 *A Handbook to Literature*, eds. C. Hugh Holman and William Harmon (New York: MacMillan, 1992), 11.

At that point, Charles II enacted various pieces of legislation to reinstate and increase the authority of the Anglican Church and therefore marginalize (punish) dissenters. These pieces of legislation were known as the Clarendon Code, named for the Earl of Clarendon, Charles II's chief minister. Thus the Corporation Act (1661) required all occupants of governmental offices to take communion in the Anglican Church. The Act of Uniformity (1662) required all clerics to use the Book of Common Prayer, the official devotional and liturgical text of the Anglican Church.

But it was the Conventicle Act (1664) that got Bunyan into trouble. This Act made it illegal for five or more people to engage in worship outside the auspices of the Anglican Church. As a dissenting minister, Bunyan repeatedly defied this law. He preached to the Puritan flock (numbering in the thousands) in the fields and in the marketplaces. In the end, Bunyan spent twelve years in prison for his defiance of the Conventicle Act. During this time, he supported his family by making shoelaces. He could have walked out of his prison cell anytime during those twelve years, on one condition: that he attend services like all faithful Englishmen and women in an Anglican Church and that he cease and desist from preaching to the Puritans. He refused, and in the end was freed only after Charles II passed the Declaration of Indulgence, which offered some amnesty to dissenters like Bunyan.

### Descartes, *Meditations on First Philosophy* (1641)

Descartes is often considered the founder of modern philosophy and the creator of what twentieth-century epistemologists called the Enlightenment project. *Meditations on First Philosophy* is one of Descartes's philosophical treatises that establish these formidable identities for the Frenchman.

In the opening pages, Descartes resolves to doubt everything that he had been taught and everything that he thought he knew; later commentators identified this endeavor as methodological/

Cartesian doubt. Descartes starts from philosophical scratch and purports to proceed with objectivity and impartiality, not assuming anything to be true.

Among the beliefs he does not assume to be true is the belief that the external world exists. After all, in order to believe that the external world exists, he has to trust his sense perceptions; and he recognizes that his "senses sometimes played [him] false."[47] Consequently, Descartes eschews the philosophical orientation that came to be known as empiricism, which maintains that true knowledge is derived from the senses. Instead, Descartes firmly plants his philosophical flag in what came to be called rationalism, the philosophical orientation that true knowledge comes from the mind alone, independently of the senses. From this commitment to rationalism proceeds Descartes's primary criterion for truth: whether or not an idea is "clear and distinct." If it is, we are likely in the territory of truth; if it is not, we have wandered into the muddled regions of uncertainty at best and befuddlement at worst.

Employing this methodology, Descartes arrives at three truths he holds to be indubitable. These three truths become the foundations of his first philosophy. (It is for this reason that the Enlightenment project became synonymous with foundationalism, the notion that all respectable epistemologies must be founded upon unassailable propositions or foundations.) The first truth (or foundation) is the proposition that the self exists. Here is how Descartes arrives at this truth: although he can doubt all things, Descartes cannot doubt that he is doubting. The locus of this doubting-activity is the self; therefore, the self must exist, for the doubting must be taking place *somewhere*. The fact that he can think necessarily implies that he exists. In his *Discourse on Method*, this is phrased in the immortal words, "I think; therefore I am."[48]

47 Rene Descartes, *Discourse on Method and the Meditations*, trans. F.E. Sutcliffe (London: Penguin, 1968), 66.

48 *Ibid.*, 53.

The second truth (or foundation) is the proposition that God exists. Descartes's argument for the existence of God bears striking similarities to the ontological argument as it descends from eleventh-century monk philosopher, St. Anselm. The argument goes something like this:

1. All of our ideas have a cause.
2. We have an idea of God.
3. The actual existence of God is the only adequate cause of our idea of God.
4. Therefore, God exists.

As with the first truth, this second truth—as expressed in the above syllogism—strikes Descartes as being clear and distinct. How else could we have an idea of an omnipotent, omniscient, and perfectly good being unless that being really existed?

Although the third and final truth is, like the first two truths, one of Descartes's foundations for first philosophy, it piggy-backs on the second; that is, without first establishing the second truth, the third truth would never make it. This third truth is the following: the external world exists. Previously, Descartes doubted that the external world exists because his senses occasionally played him false. But the certainty that God exists restores Descartes's trust in his senses. Why? Because God is no deceiver. God would not trick us into perceiving an illusory world. Being perfectly good, God endows us with the empirical equipment that faithfully represents in our minds images that accurately correspond to what exists outside of us.

These then are the three indubitable truths, the foundations, of Descartes's first philosophy.

## Alexander Pope, *Essay on Man* (1734)

Despite its misleading title, the *Essay on Man* is a poem, one that has been called the "Everest of eighteenth-century poetry, as *Paradise Lost* was the Everest of seventeenth-century poetry."[49] The poem bears the marks of its time: it is didactic and philosophical, grand and sweeping in its subject. The poem is written in heroic couplets: the lines rhyme and are crafted in iambic pentameters. An "iamb" is component part of a line in poetry that consists of an unaccented syllable and an accented syllable; one iamb is measured as one "foot" of a line. "Pentameter" means five feet. A poem written in iambic pentameters thus has five iambs per line, or ten syllables per line.

One major concern of the poem centers on the so-called "problem of evil": why does God allow bad things to happen? Riffing off of *Paradise Lost*, Pope ambitiously sets out to "vindicate the ways of God to man."[50] He does so by pointing to a metaphor that you have seen before, most notably in Pico's *Oration on the Dignity of Man*: the Great Chain of Being. Pope traces this Chain from the top of creation (God) to the bottom (inanimate matter). He shows how intricately connected the Chain is, how all the gradations within the Chain are necessary. If you fiddle with even the most minute link in the Chain, you wreak havoc upon the whole. The Chain is the beautiful and grand handiwork of God.

From our perspective on the Chain, however, things occasionally look amiss. Earthquakes and tsunamis sometimes wipe out a few thousand people; cancer will at times prevent children from reaching their fifth birthday. The problem here is that we have a limited perspective; we see everything from our angle on the Chain. From a cosmic perspective, from God's perspective, one would see

---

49 Geoffrey Tillotson, *et al.* Introduction to *Essay on Man*, in *Eighteenth-Century English Literature*, eds. Tillotson, *et al* (New Jersey: Prentice Hal, 1969), 635.

50 Pope, *Essay on Man. The Rape of the Lock and Other Poems*, ed. Martin Price (New York: Signet Classic, 2003), 96, l. 16.

that everything *as a whole* is working out exactly as God intended. The *partial evil* we see amounts to *total good* from God's perspective. All *apparent* chaos adds up to order. Intellectual historians have identified this outlook as an important part of the eighteenth-century worldview and have called it *Discordia Concors.* The apparent discord is harmonized into a cosmic good (concord).

After fleshing out this poetic theodicy, the poem assumes a tone of rebuke redolent of the way Yahweh tongue-lashed Job. How *dare* you question God? Do you know what God knows? Do you see what God sees? You have a limited perspective; you see only a fragment of the whole. If you *could* see the whole, you would see the Chain from top to bottom, perfectly good and perfectly just, as God designed it.

The poem bears the mark of its time and place in another way. Religious differences, leading to violence, stirred in the Augustans a desire for peace and unity. As a Catholic in a Protestant country, Pope acutely experienced this desire. He therefore registers in the poem the dangers of religious zeal. Religious zeal leads to self-righteousness, schism, and, too often, bloodshed. Pope therefore sounds a call for charity—what we might call "tolerance" today. In so doing, he downplays theological particularities, the specific doctrines that separate Bible-believing Christians from deists. His religious sensibilities are attuned to the most general and common religious beliefs, mainly the belief in a Supreme Deity. Despite being grounded on religious principles, the *Essay on Man* has not one reference to Jesus Christ. For this reason, some have seen in Pope—as they see in Isaac Newton—evidence of a burgeoning deism.

Though not exactly a fervent Catholic, Pope offered numerous statements—as seen in the following letter—that make it hard to conclude that he was anything but a Christian, though oftentimes a conflicted Christian: "I sincerely worship God, believe in his revelations, resign to his dispensations, love all his creatures, am in charity with all 500 denominations of Christians, however violently they treat each other, and detest none so much as that profligate race who would loosen the bands of morality, either under the pretence of religion or freethinking. I hate no man as a man, but I hate vice in any man; I hate no sect, but I hate uncharitableness in any sect."[51]

## Jonathan Swift, *Gulliver's Travels* (1726)

*Gulliver's Travels* is a work of prose satire, divided into four parts. In the first part, Gulliver is shipwrecked on the island of Lilliput, where the inhabitants are one inch tall. Gulliver learns that Lilliput is at war with a neighboring country called Blefuscu over rival interpretations of their holy text: on what side to crack open an egg. Blefuscu aligned itself with the big-end faction, Lilliput adhered to small-end dogma. This ridiculous war, along with its absurd cause, satirizes the religious wars of Europe. Within Lilliput, political dissension springs from shoe-heel heights, pitting the High-Heels against the Low-Heels. This asinine difference satirizes the skirmishes between rival political parties in England. Gulliver himself does not escape Swift's scathing humor—more specifically, Swift's scathing scatological humor. Gulliver details, for instance, his unpleasant experience of defecating in his Lilliputian-built house. Later, Gulliver urinates on the Lilliputian princess's chambers to douse a fire. Of these scatological episodes, Henry Miller comments, "The name Swift was like a clear, hard pissing against the tin-plate of the world."[52] George Orwell noted that Swift "thought about human dung incessantly, as is evident throughout his works."[53] We might draw a larger conclusion. In

51 Pope, Letter to Henry Brooke (Dec. 1, 1739), in *The Works of Alexander Pope* (London: John Murray, 1886), 223.

52 Quoted in Frances Wilson, *Literary Seductions: Compulsive Writers and Diverted Readers* (New York: St. Martin's, 1999), 63.

53 Quoted in Philip Bounds, *Orwell and Marxism: The Political and Cultural Thinking of George Orwell* (New York: Tauris, 2016), 18.

the Enlightenment (as in the Renaissance), humankind was placed upon a pinnacle, endowed with reason and dignity. Swift flicks humankind off of that pinnacle and drops it into the sewer, thereby challenging the high view of humanity gaining traction at the time. In this way, Swift is one of the few writers of the time who called into question Enlightenment principles.

In part two, Gulliver is left ashore in Brobdingnag, where the inhabitants are over fifty-feet tall. After Gulliver tells the king of Brobdingnag about England—its government, church, and judiciary—the king proclaims, "By what I have gathered from your own relation [...] I cannot but conclude the bulk of your natives to be the most pernicious race of little odious vermin that nature ever suffered to crawl upon the surface of the earth."[54] Here the satire is heavy-handed.

In part three, Gulliver visits the flying island of Laputa. Here Swift pokes fun at scientists, philosophers, and other men of learning. These pie-in-the-sky intellectuals lack common sense. They aim to reconstitute feces for consumption. They develop cures for constipation by blowing air through the anus. (See how much Swift likes to write about poop?)

In part four, Gulliver travels to the country of the Houyhnhnms, the talking horses. These creatures are preeminently reasonable. Pure rationality and logic lead them irresistibly to true beliefs about everything from statecraft to poetry. They afford females the same opportunities as males. They are, in a sense, Enlightenment heroes. However, they also have a latent dark side. They experience no love in courtship and marriage, no joy in birth, no grief at death. And while Gulliver affirms their excellence in poetry, that excellence is confined to technical proficiency. In short, they are like Spock from the *Star Trek* television and movie series: logical, but not emotional. Nevertheless, Gulliver admires and comes to love Houynhnhnm civilization, but the Houyhnhnms force him to leave because he is

54 Swift, *Gulliver's Travels* (New York: Penguin, 1967), 173.

not one of them and, in fact, more closely resembles the Yahoos, the filthy and violent creatures that plague the land.

The identification of Yahoos as human returns us to Swift's low view of humanity, what one might even call his misanthropy. This has been a vexed issue in Swift scholarship. Perhaps it is best to let Swift speak for himself in this excerpt from a letter to Alexander Pope: "I have ever hated all nations, professions, and communities, and all my love is towards individuals. But principally, I hate and detest that animal called man, although I heartily love John, Peter, Thomas, and so forth."[55]

### Samuel Johnson, *Rasselas* (1759)

*Rasselas* is a philosophical tale or apologue, defined as a didactic or moral fable. Unlike a novel, *Rasselas* has no individualized characters; instead, characters assume rhetorical positions. Think of *Rasselas* as a narrative essay; think of the very first sentence of the text as the narrative essay's thesis; think of the many episodes piled together in the text as anecdotal evidence for the thesis. According to Joshua Reynolds, Johnson wrote *Rasselas* in one week to earn some quick money to help pay for his mother's funeral.

Prince of Abyssinia (modern-day Ethiopia), Rasselas disconcertedly finds himself unhappy in the Happy Valley, where "every desire was immediately granted."[56] His tutor Imlac informs him that he is not alone in his dissatisfaction, despite the fact that no one who resides there has an ostensible reason for unhappiness. An experienced and wise sage, Imlac informs Rasselas that unhappiness reigns everywhere, even outside the Happy Valley. Rasselas resolves to find out for himself so, along with Imlac, his sister Nekayah, and Nekayah's maid Pekuah, he escapes the Happy Valley. They are determined to find a "choice of life" and thus happiness itself.

55 Quoted in *The Complete Works of William Thackeray* (London: Andesite Press, 2017), 244.

56 Johnson, *Rasselas* (Oxford: Oxford UP, 1991), 3.

Outside the Happy Valley, they explore all stations of life: the rich, the poor; the young, the old; stoics, hedonists; the married, the single. Alas, all stations of life are found wanting; happiness is nowhere to be found. As Imlac had informed Rasselas even before they escaped the Happy Valley, "Human life is everywhere a state in which much is to be endured, and little to be enjoyed."[57] In the final chapter, entitled "The conclusion, in which nothing is concluded," the travelers decide to return to the Happy Valley.[58]

Happiness is an important theme of much eighteenth-century literature. Bringing his sober-minded realism to bear on the theme, Johnson paints happiness as a quixotic goal, forever out of reach. In his *Life of Johnson*, Boswell records Johnson's thunderous answer to the question, Is man *ever* happy? "Never, except when he is drunk."[59] Johnson's pessimism is not eccentric; his voice joins a chorus of voices from the period that declare the impossibility of achieving happiness. As a Christian, Johnson defers happiness to life after death. (This is the theme of Johnson's famous poem, "The Vanity of Human Wishes," which might be read as a companion piece to *Rasselas*.) For this reason, the latter chapters of *Rasselas* are particularly important—specifically the chapters set among the catacombs where the characters discuss immortality and the nature of the soul.

### Voltaire, *Candide* (1759)

Like Johnson's *Rasselas*, *Candide* is a philosophical tale or apologue. Like *Rasselas*, *Candide* episodically chips away at optimistic views of the world. While *Rasselas* undermines the hope that happiness is possible, *Candide* squares off against the theistic article of faith that God is on his throne and all is right with the world. Unlike *Rasselas*, *Candide* employs dark humor to attack this optimistic article of

57 *Ibid.*, 31

58 *Ibid.*, 122.

59 James Boswell, *Life of Johnson* (Oxford: Oxford UP, 1980), 618.

faith. Reading *Candide* is like watching a Quentin Tarantino film: you should laugh and be horrified at the same time.

Voltaire specifically takes aim at the philosophy of Wilhelm Leibnitz (1646-1716), a German thinker who coined the term "theodicy," which means an attempt to justify the existence and benevolent nature of God given the fact of suffering in the world. To oversimplify, Leibnitz argued that God, being perfectly good, will necessarily always do what is best and thus created the "best of all possible worlds." Leibnitz obviously did not deny that suffering exists in this best of all possible worlds; but given the proposition that God always does what is best, then there must be sufficient reason for this suffering in the best of all possible worlds; we simply cannot always understand it. Leibnitz's theodicy bears strong resemblance to Pope's theodicy in his poem, *An Essay on Man*.

What finally made this theodicy (in either form) untenable and even laughable to Voltaire was the 1755 earthquake that struck Lisbon, Portugal. After the devastating quake crumbled the foundations of the city, those fortunate enough to survive gathered in the Lisbon harbor, thanking God for their survival…until a sixty-foot tall tidal wave, caused by the earthquake, engulfed them. In the end, nearly 100,000 died. Given such a tragedy, how, asked Voltaire, could this be the best of all possible worlds?

The eponymous name of the text's protagonist, Candide, means candor, truth, innocence. Episode after episode, these values are challenged as Candide desperately clings to the philosophy of the best-of-all-possible worlds. He is guided by his tutor, Pangloss, whose name means all tongue or all talk. From beginning to end, Pangloss, like a grinning idiot, airily upholds Leibnitz's optimistic philosophy, despite the horrific carnage that besets him and everyone he cares for, and despite the attestations of Martin, who calls optimism "'the mania of maintaining that everything is well when we are wretched.'"[60] "'You are very hard,'" Candide tells Martin. "'That is because I have lived,'" Martin replies.[61]

The famous conclusion of the apologue has launched a thousand interpretations. What is meant by the refrain, "We must cultivate our gardens"?[62] Does it register the limitations of what we can understand (like the problem of suffering) and thus enjoin us to work, to stay busy, in order to anesthetize our minds—to work without theorizing? Is the refrain meant to re-orient our focus from otherworldly concerns to human concerns? Is it thus a call for moral realism, a summons to find answers within ourselves rather than in non-falsifiable theological postulates? Cross reference this interpretation with Voltaire's rousing call for self-sufficiency in his Philosophical Dictionary: "When Nature created our species she gave us certain instincts: self-love to preserve ourselves, benevolence for the preservation of others, the love which is common to all species, and the inexplicable gift of being able to combine more ideas than all the other animals put together. Having thus given us our share, she said: 'Now do the best you can.'"[63]

Regardless, *Candide* posed a threat to Christianity. For many present-day atheists, the text is heralded as the Enlightenment's call-to-arms, which, by mid-eighteenth century, came to resemble Voltaire's own battle cry: to liberate humankind from religious superstition and ignorance and champion reason, tolerance, and equality. Enlightenment scholar Peter Gay eloquently sums up how *Candide* heeded this battle cry:

> Its central target, after all, is Leibniz, and Leibniz was the great compromiser of the age. He was the accommodating metaphysician who sought to reconcile religion and

60 Voltaire, *Candide*, in *The Portable Voltaire* (New York: Penguin, 1977), 282.

61 *Ibid.*, 306.

62 *Ibid.*, 326 and 328.

63 Quoted in Anthony Pagden, *The Enlightenment and Why It Still Matters* (Oxford: Oxford UP, 2013), 96.

> philosophy, the principles of Christianity to the principles of rationalism, the theologian who attempted to justify God to men with arguments which a philosopher steeped in Cicero could respect. *Candide* denies that any such accommodation is possible; the book is like a slap in the face of an adroit and benevolent envoy, a firm rejection of negotiations on any basis, and hence, in essence, a declaration of war on Christianity.[64]

**Goethe, *The Sorrows of the Young Werther* (1774)—spoiler alert: do *not* read this gloss before reading the novel.**

Goethe's novel is often identified with the *Sturm und Drang* (Storm and Stress) movement in Germany. According to *A Handbook to Literature*, the *Sturm und Drang* movement "was characterized by fervor, enthusiasm, restlessness, the portrayal of great passion, and a reliance on emotional experiences and spiritual struggles."[65] As such, *Sorrows* is often labeled a pre-Romantic or early Romantic work.

In a letter to a friend, Goethe provided a synopsis of the novel's plot: "I present a young person gifted with deep, pure feeling and true penetration, who loses himself in rapturous dreams, buries himself in speculation, until at last, ruined by unhappy passions that supervene, in particular an unfulfilled love, puts a bullet in his head."[66] The novel is thought to be roughly autobiographical. The character of Charlotte (or Lotte) is based on Charlotte Kestner, daughter of a bailiff in the German town of Wetzlar. The character of Albert is based on Charlotte's husband, Johann Kestner. Goethe,

64 Peter Gay, *The Enlightenment: The Rise of Modern Paganism* (NY: Norton, 1995), 203.

65 *A Handbook to* Literature, eds. C. Hugh Holman and William Harmon (NY: MacMillan, 1992), 460

66 Quoted in Clancy Martin, *Love and Lies: An Essay on Truthfulness, Deceit, and the Growth and Care of Erotic Love* (NY: Farrar, Straus and Giroux, 2015), 117.

of course, bears resemblance to Werther. Perhaps due to this autobiographical dimension, Goethe claimed that he wrote the novel in four weeks, in a trance of inspiration. (If you have a chance, watch *Young Goethe in Love* (2011), a film which plays on the doubled Goethe/Werther identity.)

The characters of Albert and Werther represent two competing worldviews. Albert espouses commonsense, practicality, and rationality. In his world, suicide is always wrong, for actions must be dictated by clear and logical motives; suicide is unreasonable. As such, Albert might be read as an embodiment of Enlightenment principles. Werther, on the other hand, resides in a *Sturm-und-Drang* world, where passion often overwhelms reason. Werther is impulsive and unconventional. In his world, suicide may be justified at times, for actions cannot always be judged by motives because our motives are often irrational or, at the least, beyond reason. As such, Werther might be read as the Enlightenment's antithesis, what will later be called Romanticism. Like Romanticism, Werther seeks liberation from conventions, which inhibit true genius; a true artist's only guide is nature. Like Romanticism, Werther is emotionally indulgent; he luxuriates in powerful emotion.

The Werther/Romanticism parallel is exemplified in Werther's interest in a poem by Ossian entitled *Fingal*. Ossian was supposedly a third-century Gaelic warrior and bard. The discovery of his poem created a literary sensation throughout Europe, gratifying the decidedly romantic interest in primitive genius.[67] Perhaps for this reason, Ossian occasions a climax in the novel's plot. While reading the poem aloud, Werther shares an erotically charged moment with Charlotte, one in which they weep together, "merg[ing] their tears."[68] This unique act of intimacy, at least according to Werther, makes Charlotte his forever. Not long thereafter, for the first time

67 It later turned out that the poem was a forgery, one that was incidentally detected by Samuel Johnson.

68 Goethe, *The Sorrows of Young Werther*, in *Goethe: The Collected Works, Volume 11*. Trans. Victor Lange and Judith Ryan (New Jersey: Princeton UP, 1995), 80.

in the novel, Werther addresses Charlotte with the familiar German *Du* rather than the formal *Sie*.

In the end, however, Charlotte chooses convention and safety: she remains with Albert. Tellingly, when Werther sends a note to Albert, requesting his pistols, Charlotte herself fetches them. Werther takes comfort in knowing that the instrument of his death passed through Charlotte's hands.

After its publication, the novel apparently created what has been called the "Werther effect." Young people began to imitate Werther: dress like him, talk like him, act like him. According to legend, a rash of suicides fell hard on the heels of the novel's release.

### Immanuel Kant, "Answering the Question: What Is Enlightenment?" (1784)

This short essay, originally published in a German periodical, is an important and unique textual artifact. It is important because it offers us clear definitions of the Enlightenment by a major Enlightenment figure. It is unique because, in terms of linguistic history, the Enlightenment had not really started yet, at least for English speakers. According to the Oxford English Dictionary (OED), the first recorded use of the term *Enlightenment* with a capital E was in 1825. Kant's essay was published in 1784. How is this possible? Did the OED make a mistake? No, if you remember that Kant wrote in German; he used the German word *Aufklärung*. Nevertheless, Kant provides us an on-the-ground, real-time definition of an historical phenomenon that has just gotten started. (A historical equivalent might be a music critic writing about rap in the late 1970s.)

A key image in the essay is the image of a child. Just as a child depends on others to do everything for him or her, so the unenlightened mind exists in a state of intellectual dependence; it believes what it is told. Just as maturity entails doing things for yourself, so the enlightened person thinks for himself or herself. What holds a person back from enlightenment, from becoming intellectually mature, is not a lack of intelligence. It is a lack of courage, the courage to think for yourself. Enlightenment means to free oneself from authorities—intellectual, religious, and political authorities—and find truth on your own.

A key distinction in the text is that between the civic use of reason and the public use of reason. Civic reason is employed when individuals are working within their civic capacity—within, say, their civic duty as military officers. Military officers cannot use their reason to question the orders that have been given to them by their superiors; their *civic* reason is limited. But a scholar, using *public* reason, should most definitely be free to question military plans and campaigns. A pastor, within his civic duty as pastor, cannot question Christian dogma. But outside of his official capacity as pastor (maybe he dabbles in deism in his spare time) he is free to use reason to question that same Christian dogma.[69] Indeed, he will necessarily do so if he possesses Kant's characteristics of enlightenment: the willingness to emerge from intellectual maturity and the daring to think for yourself.

### Edmund Burke, *Reflections on the Revolution in France* (1790)

Fashioned as a letter to a young Frenchman, *Reflections on the Revolution in France* is a polemic against the French Revolution. The writing of this lengthy "letter" was motivated by the 1789 sermon of Richard Price; entitled "On the Love of Our Country," Price's sermon praised the revolutionary activity in France, likening it to the British Glorious Revolution of 1688. Burke's *Reflections* was popular among traditionalists and conservatives; it is said that King

69 I will leave it to the reader to decide if this leads to a sort of intellectual schizophrenia. Do I believe one set of claims when I wear my civic-reason hat and another set of claims when I don my public-reason hat? Nevertheless, if Kant spells out in this essay a credo of the Enlightenment—think for yourself—then it would seem that some people, depending on their occupation, are free to abide by this credo only on their own time.

Louis XVI of France himself translated the work into French, three years before he was sent to the guillotine.

Burke believed that the French Revolution was an attack on political first principles. These first principles are embodied in the French royal family, which Burke found to possess symbolic value worth protecting. Specifically, the French royal family symbolized tradition, submission to authority, and honor. As a conservative Whig, Burke wanted to conserve these values. He defended the traditional view that a healthy society required social hierarchies that involve a necessary deference to those above from those below. That is, peasants should know and respect their place as well as the places of those above them on the hierarchy. Burke's version of equality amounts to an equality without confounding ranks, an equality within one's station in the social hierarchy. Burke repeatedly refers to these traditional ideas as "natural ideas"; they accord with human nature; they are a "natural" order.

Conversely, Burke maintained that the revolutionaries and their allies symbolized social chaos, atheism, and moral collapse. They represent a disastrous rupture from the past, one that will overturn a relatively stable political system that has existed for centuries. The revolutionaries are a mob of ignorant degenerates, a cabal of atheistic terrorists. Burke also sees the revolutionaries as a threat to the three necessary ingredients of a well-ordered city-state: religion, the nobility, and learning. Burke believed that an attack on one was an attack on all: if you take down the nobility, religion will fall along with them; if you allow the uneducated revolutionaries to destroy learning, religion will fall as well.

Often viewed as an embodiment of classic conservatism, Burke did not like political change. He proudly declared, "Four hundred years have gone over us [English]; but I believe we are not materially changed since that period. Thanks to our sullen resistance to innovation, thanks to the cold sluggishness of our national character, we still bear the stamp of our forefathers."[70] (If Burke were running for office today, his campaign slogan might be, "No changes in 400 years and proud of it!") And if changes *do* occur, they must take place slowly; such slow, organic change is the only way a country can survive the trauma that change often brings.

### Thomas Paine, *Rights of Man* (1791)

*Rights of Man* is a direct response to Burke's *Reflections*. While the latter is characterized by eloquence and sophistication, the former is written to the commoner in a direct and economical style. Published in a cheap pamphlet edition, one affordable to the lower and middle classes, the work was estimated to have sold 200,000 copies in its first year.

One principle argument of *Rights of Man* is the following: it is simply wrong for a country's citizens to be beholden to political policies of which they have no say. Citizens should have a voice in how they are governed. Traditional political policies were established by the privileged and thus tend to benefit the privileged—that is, the nobility; these policies moreover tend to oppress the poor, ensuring that they remain poor. While Paine concedes Burke's point that these policies are age-old, appealing to their duration is an arbitrary claim. Why should the poor be forced to adhere to policies for the mere reason that those policies are old?

What Burke finds sacrosanct, Paine identifies as tools of oppression. Paine, for instance, supports the separation of church and state. Religion lost its "native mildness" and became "morose and intolerant" once it established the "connexion which Mr Burke recommends": "By engendering the church with the state, a sort of mule-animal, capable only of destroying, and not of breeding up, is produced, called *The Church established by Law*."[71] While

70 Burke, *Reflections on the Revolution in France*. In *Eighteenth-Century English Literature*, Eds. Geoffrey Tillotson, *et al* (New York: Harcourt Brace, 1969), 1282.

71 Paine, *Rights of Man* (NY: Dover Thrift, 1990), 46.

Burke maintains that religion and learning cannot exist without the aristocracy, Paine would like to see the aristocracy come to an end. Paine calls for the abrogation of primogeniture, whereby all the wealth of a family passes to the firstborn son. "Establish family justice," writes Paine, "and aristocracy falls."[72] Paine's proposal for revised tax codes likewise undermines the aristocracy. He advocates luxury taxes and a progressive tax rate whereby the wealthy pay considerably more on taxes; Paine wishes to level the unevenness of wealth distribution.

Paine lampoons Burke's sympathy and compassion for the French king and for the nobility. How sorry is Burke, Paine scoffs, how "extremely sorry, that arbitrary power, the power of the Pope, and the Bastille, are pulled down." Meanwhile, continues Paine, "not one glance of compassion, not one commiserating reflection, that I can find throughout [Burke's] book, has he bestowed on those who lingered out the most wretched of lives, a life without hope, in the most miserable of prisons."[73]

Paine's attack on Burke and support for the French Revolution are animated by the spirit of the Enlightenment. Consider the source of Paine's authority for his arguments in *Rights of Man*. His authority is obviously not tradition or the church. His authority is reason. It is *reasonable*, though not necessarily in accordance with tradition and the church, to conclude that all people are born equal and thus have inalienable rights. It is *reasonable*, though not necessarily in accordance with tradition and the church, to conclude that the focus of a government should be on what Paine calls "public utility"[74]—that is, on the public, the common people, not the aristocracy or the clerical class.

Nevertheless, the battle between Paine and Burke created a pamphlet war—an eighteenth-century version of a culture war—

72 Ibid., 42

73 Ibid., 17

74 *Ibid.*, 71.

that embroiled nations. In good old twenty-first century American style, the rhetoric of this war was incendiary. Many of Paine's opponents were conservative Christians. Hannah More, who became a spokesperson for British evangelical Christians, declared, "From liberty, equality and the rights of man, Good Lord deliver us."[75]

### Mary Shelley, *Frankenstein* (1818)

In her preface, Shelley relates that she began *Frankenstein* in the summer of 1816 in Switzerland. She, her soon-to-be husband Percy Shelley, and Lord Byron agreed to write tales of the supernatural. Mary Shelley was the only one of the three to complete a tale, one that came to her in what she described as a "half-waking nightmare."[76]

*Frankenstein* is a novel, more specifically an epistolary novel. Most of the epistles (or letters) of the novel are written from the character of Robert Walton to his sister. As the novel progresses, the accretion of indirect narrators makes the novel particularly rich and dense. That is, when the novel begins, the narration comes to us second-hand: we receive the story from Robert Walton writing to his sister. Later, we receive the story from Victor Frankenstein talking to Robert Walton writing to his sister. Still later, the narration comes through the voice of the creature talking to Victor Frankenstein talking to Robert Walton writing to his sister. These layers of narration create a voyeuristic, spooky effect: we look from a distance at events described by unreliable narrators. Gazing helplessly at gruesome spectacles that may or may not be real is a foundational ingredient of the horror genre.

*Frankenstein* might also be described as a Gothic novel, a genre that came into existence in 1765 with the publication of Horace Walpole's *The Castle of Otranto.* The Gothic genre includes the

75 Quoted in Karen Swallow Prior, *Fierce Convictions: The Extraordinary Life of Hannah More* (NY: Thomas Nelson, 2014), 201.

76 Quoted in Dinah Birch, *The Oxford Companion to English Literature* (Oxford: Oxford UP, 2009), 390.

following elements, all of which appear in *Frankenstein*: wild landscapes; possibilities of incest (Victor marries his "sister"); the toxic effects of guilt and shame; omens; and voyeurism (the sensation of watching and being watched).

In addition to being an epistolary or Gothic novel, *Frankenstein* might also be considered a work of science fiction, or at least a forerunner of science fiction. This identification makes sense if you keep in mind that science fiction is defined as, among many other things, a narrative that imagines a radical technological or scientific advance. The advance in *Frankenstein* is, of course, the man-made creation of a man.

Some read the novel as a parable, a reading made especially plausible given the novel's subtitle, *the Modern Prometheus*. Just as Prometheus stole fire from the gods, foolhardily surpassing his limitations, so too has humankind stolen secrets from nature, overstepping the God-given boundaries of knowledge. In this sense, *Frankenstein* could be read as an admonition against the reckless use of science: a sort of pushback against the Scientific Revolution.

Another important interpretive issue of the novel: doublings of character. First consider the similarities between Robert Walton and Victor Frankenstein: both are self-educated and over-reaching, pushing the limits of knowledge. Next consider the parallels between Victor Frankenstein and the creature: both become wracked by guilt and rage. Indeed, consider how this particular doubling of character played out in popular culture through the centuries. Why in popular mythology is the creature called "Frankenstein"? Nowhere in the novel is he named as such.

This leads to another issue ripe for exploration: how much responsibility is the creature to bear for its murderous actions? How culpable is it? All the creature wanted was companionship and love. From the moment he was created, the creature received nothing but hatred, disgust, and violence; he never had a chance. Perhaps Victor Frankenstein—not the creature—is the monster in this novel.

## CHAPTER SIX

# THE WORLD OF DESPAIR AND HOPE

**Beate Rodewald and Michael Von Cannon**

*Continuity and Change*

After the emergence of Romanticism discussed at the end of the previous chapter, the late eighteenth and early nineteenth centuries saw Romantic priorities grow into dominant themes; belief in individuals' natural rights and confidence in the autonomous self shaped main characters in fiction as well as the public response to actual historical figures. The elevation of personalities was tied to the development of national senses of identity; that is, several countries in Europe saw a cultural, national identity tied to admired figures. (For example, Giuseppe Garibaldi in Italy is much credited with bringing about Italy's unification.)[1]

But it would be too simple to see Romanticism simply as a

1 Some information about the political and geographical situation in Europe, especially the steps towards unifying Italy, and equally important, the (first) unification of Germany, will help a lot in appreciating some topics, as, for example, questions concerning "identity"—individual as well as national. The inner-European maneuvers among states will shed light on the larger context of Imperialism and Colonialism.

reaction to the Enlightenment's emphasis on reason. As a new, what you might call "modern," sensibility emerged, Romanticism was as much influenced by the Enlightenment as it was reacting to aspects of it. Certainly, both foregrounded humanity's potential and ability as well as human endeavors to liberate people from confining structures, both literal and metaphorical. Concepts like "class," "race," and "gender"—even though they would not have been articulated using these terms—complicated (and challenged) the revolutionary ideals of "*liberté*, *égalité*, and *fraternité*." How exactly did the supposedly "universal" rights called for relate to actual conditions for real individuals? Through many of the texts read in this semester, we will see that the relationship between the universal and the individual, the general and the specific, provides a thread that runs through a multitude of texts.

The Enlightenment and, more importantly, responses to it still dominate twenty-first century discussions of Western intellectual history. Probably the most significant change the Enlightenment brought about was that "science" acquired a seat at the table, so to speak—even though "science" had not been established as a separate sphere of investigating life on earth; joining philosophy and religion/theology, science became accepted as an equally authoritative source of knowledge only in the nineteenth century. Discussing the origin of the word "scientist," J. A. V. Chapple explains,

> The word *science* once meant knowledge acquired by study. Not until the nineteenth century did its meaning tend to be restricted to the systematic study of the material and natural universe. Early scientists were usually called "natural philosophers" but in 1840 William Whewell wrote in his *Philosophy of the Inductive Sciences*, "We need very much a name to describe a cultivator of science in general.I should incline to call him a Scientist." Incredible as it may

now seem, that is the very first use of the word *scientist* cited in the Oxford English Dictionary.[2]

One of the guiding principles shaping theories in several disciplines in the nineteenth century was the attempt to articulate how change over time has occurred, and to articulate it without resorting to philosophical or metaphysical premises that depend on abstractions such as "universal reason" or "human nature"; instead, many of the influential writers of the time approached their subjects in hopes of deriving scientific laws based on observable, empirical realities of human existence. Probably the most explicit acknowledgement of Darwin's effect on non-biological investigations was provided by Friedrich Engels in his funeral speech for Karl Marx. And, while the quotation is rather long, it is worth quoting in its entirety because it combines many of the preoccupations of the time. It connects Darwinian ideas about biological evolution to Marxist ideas about changing economic relations among social classes to Hegelian notions concerning the role of religion, art, and philosophy in Western culture. The favorite questions of the time were the following: what is "Progress," how do our institutions reflect relations among classes, and how do our beliefs compare with other belief-systems? And for possible answers and explanations, most writers looked to history. Engels declared,

> Just as Darwin discovered the law of development of organic nature, so Marx discovered the law of development of human history: the simple fact, hitherto concealed by an overgrowth of ideology, that mankind must first of all eat, drink, have shelter and clothing, before it can pursue politics, science, art, religion, etc.; that therefore the production of the immediate material means of subsistence and consequently the degree of economic development

2 J. A. V. Chapple, *Science and Literature in the Nineteenth Century* (Houndmills, Basingstoke, Hampshire: Macmillan, 1986), 1.

> attained by a given people or during a given epoch form the foundation upon which the state institutions, the legal conceptions, art, and even the ideas on religion, of the people concerned have been evolved, and in the light of which they must, therefore, be explained, instead of *vice versa*, as had hitherto been the case.[3]

Engels's emphasis on the "material means of subsistence" reinforces the methodology of deriving scientific laws described earlier. The reorientation of research brought with it a reexamination of human beings as "knowing" subjects. Because material, empirically observable conditions were posited as the starting point for scientific approaches to any inquiry, the role of the researcher started to be reevaluated as well. After all, inquisitive investigators of the world are not located on a fixed platform above the earth, an Archimedean point from which an objective picture can be painted. As humans, we are interrelated in ways that are shaped by historical, cultural, and linguistic conventions of our particular context. How we talk about things oftentimes reveals as much about ourselves as about the things we talk about. Many prominent writers of the nineteenth century, such as Hegel and Nietzsche, were trained as philologists—that is, they studied the history and development of languages over time; this historical approach to language and culture predominated until the twentieth century; for instance, J.R.R. Tolkien, writing at the beginning of the new century, was trained as a philologist.

New theories in linguistic studies started to shift the focus from history to the *structure* of language; in other words, researchers investigated the relationships among various components of language at a given point in time. Swiss linguist Ferdinand de Saussure's *Course in General Linguistics* (1916) is generally considered the most influential contribution to this shift to a synchronic (non-his-

3 Karl Marx and Friedrich Engels, *The Marx-Engels Reader*, ed. Robert C. Tucker (New York: Norton, 1978), 681.

torical) approach; the shift in emphasis is usually referred to as the "linguistic turn." Philosophy and theory have been informed by this approach ever since.

*Language and Culture*

The philological approach of the nineteenth century was superseded by the emergence of linguistics and semiotics in the early twentieth century. Instead of researching chronologies and origins, linguistics (as a discipline) devoted more energies to studying synchronic contexts—in other words, it highlighted patterns, architectures, if you will, of language working in context. One of the most influential writers for cultural studies from the second half of the twentieth century onwards is Michel Foucault. In 1964, Foucault grouped Nietzsche, Freud, and Marx together due to a sort of family resemblance he saw in their respective approach to cultural analysis, or "themes concerning *the techniques of interpretation*."[4] The focus of Foucault's essay is, basically, the relationship between language, interpretation, and meaning. This sounds like a very broad and complex issue, and in a way it is, but looking over preoccupations in studies related to language, philosophy, and culture—especially in European academic and intellectual circles–Foucault's identification of unifying characteristics among these writers makes sense; the nineteenth century was, at least in Europe, dominated by the philological approach discussed above. Two statements from the opening of Foucault's essay are useful guideposts for understanding the shift to the synchronic or structural approach to language and its relation to the world of human understanding. Dealing with questions of interpretation, Foucault says, thinkers have always been aware that "first, [...] language does not say exactly what it

4 Gayle L. Ormiston and Alan D. Schrift, *Transforming the Hermeneutic Context: From Nietzsche to Nancy (SUNY Series, Intersections: Philosophy and Critical Theory)* (State University of New York Press, 1990), 59. [Emphasis in the original]

means," and second, "there are many other things in the world that speak, and that are not language."[5]

*History—How to Talk and Think about the Past*

The nineteenth century still saw efforts by philosophers to create all-encompassing explanatory systems. Hegel, for example, spent his life working on an elaborate theory of history, philosophy of history, and history of philosophy; and he did believe that change from one era to another proceeded rationally. He did not, however, claim to predict any future developments. The "absolute," the whole, he maintained, is in process of working itself out in emerging manifestations of consciousness. Moving from the particular to the universal, the absolute Spirit is the meaning of everything that comes to be known in the unfolding of history. And history unfolds dialectically, in a continuous process where every stage advances to a next, higher stage where remnants combine with reactions to become a synthesis, which, again, will lead to continued processes of such stages. Hegel had much confidence in the powers of human reason; he believed that this philosophical project of articulating the process of the principles (even "laws") of historical development would enable us to comprehend every aspect of reality.

This ridiculously simplified and abstract description of one of Hegel's main interests might serve to elucidate the tremendous influence his work exerted on other writers examined in the first half of The World of Despair and Hope. Examining "stages" provides the pattern for the work of Marx, Kierkegaard, Nietzsche, and Freud. Marx posits economic and work relations as the starting point for tracing historical development; Kierkegaard reverses Hegel in that, for him, the truth is not the emergence of the whole or absolute, but quite the opposite, truth is subjectivity and "faith begins precisely where thinking leaves off."[6]

---

5 Ibid.

6 Søren Kierkegaard, *Fear and Trembling: Dialectical Lyric by Johannes De Silen-*

Nietzsche's *Genealogy of Morality* endeavored to trace the history and origin of Western values and called for a thorough "revaluation" (or "transvaluation")[7] of those values. In calling for a radically "new" way of thinking about morality and values, though, Nietzsche might have inadvertently perpetuated some of the same principles he criticized. Some postmodernist writers (like Lyotard) will address this aspect of the call for new methods and theories.

Freud's *Civilization and Its Discontents* is a work in which Freud "psycho-analyzed" not individuals but societies at large; using his theories about the development (and repression) of sexual drives, he set out to diagnose contemporary society's "discontentment" as a kind of mental disorder. In the opening pages of the book, Freud says that he was provoked into further investigation into cultures by a response to his earlier book, *The Future of an Illusion* (1927), in which he criticized religious feelings as an illusion. The French writer Romain Rolland had responded to Freud, basically agreeing with him, but also arguing that all humans do share an innate religiosity, which he called an "oceanic feeling" of oneness. Freud replies that the sense of "oneness" is simply an initial stage of civilization, a stage he compares to infantile narcissism in the individual.[8] When the individual recognizes his or her separation from others—and eventual dependence on others for the fulfillment of desires—conflicting drives assert themselves. To oversimplify Freud's complex elaboration on the relationship between the individual and the world, one could say that in *Civilization and Its Discontents*, he applies his concepts of conflicting drives in individuals to civilization as a whole. Just as individuals navigate the road between

---

*tio*, trans. Alastair Hannay (London: Penguin Books, 2003), 82.

7 Friedrich Wilhelm Nietzsche, *On the Genealogy of Morality and Other Writings*, eds. Keith Ansell-Pearson and Carol Diethe (Cambridge, United Kingdom: Cambridge University Press, 2017), 152.

8 Sigmund Freud, *Civilization and Its Discontents*, eds. Todd Dufresne and Gregory C. Richter (Peterborough, Ontario: Broadview Press, 2016), 52.

maximizing pleasure and minimizing pain, so civilization struggles between conflicting impulses of bonding and fragmentation.

In the last few works by Freud, he seems more a philosopher than a psychoanalyst; but Freud was not the only one to wonder about the connections between the rapidly changing world and humans dealing with their new way of life. As Todd Dufresne explains, "Freud was part of a medical tradition that blamed advanced industrial society for contemporary mental illness, those ill-defined maladies (from fatigue to depression) classified under the almost meaningless rubric of 'neurasthenia'—blaming everything from the advent of railways to the widespread use of electricity in cities."[9]

### *The Future—Nineteenth-Century Innovations and the Notion of Progress*

Life seemed to speed up dramatically with the steam-powered printing press, electrical telegraphy, the dynamo, and gasoline-powered cars, to name only a few of the transformative inventions of the time. It is not surprising, then, that "progress" was on everyone's mind, and increasingly, the notion of progress became synonymous with scientific and technological innovation. The event that symbolized the progress already achieved, and more marvelous things to come, was the Great Exhibition of 1851 in London; it became a model for the World's Fairs for the rest of the century and onward. Prince Albert, Queen Victoria's husband, had organized the exposition, and in his speech on opening day, he tellingly articulated the vision that fuses the human ingenuity that the latest innovations displayed with the purpose of history itself: "Nobody who has paid any attention to the peculiar features of our present era […] will doubt for a moment that we are living at a period of most wonderful transition, which tends rapidly to accomplish that

9 Ibid, 117.

great end to which indeed all history points—the realization of the unity of mankind."[10]

Not only had science taken a seat at the table of authorities on knowledge and truth, but by the end of the century, it tended to crowd out knowledge that did not strictly follow its methods. Of course, this faith in science and progress was shattered soon after the beginning of the twentieth century. Dreams about more perfect futures faded when World War I showed that innovations in science and technology did not always automatically improve the lot of humankind; mustard gas and tanks (both used for the first time in the war) were specifically designed to be more efficient fighting and killing tools rather than beneficial contributions to society. But at the 1939 World Fair in New York, advertisements still echoed the triumphal optimism Prince Albert had expressed in London. A description of the General Motors exhibit read, "Since the beginning of civilization, transportation and communication have been keys to Man's progress, his prosperity, his happiness."[11]

The sobering insight of the war, though, continued to be reinforced by events of the next few decades. The varieties of totalitarianism, including Communism in the Soviet Union, Fascism in Italy, and Nazism in Germany, presented the extreme opposite of Enlightenment ideals of the autonomous, self-determined individual. More efficient ways of controlling and killing people were devised. And then came World War II.

The Holocaust and the atomic bomb are touchstones for rethinking the nineteenth-century claims about the ability of scientific research to eliminate human errors and biases. Whatever questions are pursued, whatever experiments are conducted, whatever perceived problems are addressed, scientific—or any

---

10 Qtd. in J. Richard. Middleton and Brian J. Walsh, *Truth Is Stranger than It Used to Be: Biblical Faith in a Postmodern Age* (Downers Grove, IL: InterVarsity, 1995), 18-19.

11 Qtd. in Alan P. Lightman, *Dance for Two: Selected Essays* (New York: Pantheon Books, 1996), 89.

other—research cannot extricate itself from the context of its existence; we pay attention to things we consider problems to be solved, we decide what problems deserve attention, and we allot resources to those problems we consider most urgent. And every individual is part of a larger community that articulates some shared objectives. In conversations involving any decisions that affect not only the individual, but also the communities of which the individual is a member, specific dilemmas become apparent. Science and technology are not morally neutral, and so it is important that not only experts in a given field talk to each other, but that different fields invite exchanges and solicit input from others.

The preponderance of science, asserting its voice in ascertaining the truths that can be known by human beings, led to a phrase coined by C. P. Snow in a lecture he gave in 1959; it is still used today: "the two cultures." (The full title of his lecture was "The Two Cultures and the Scientific Revolution.") Snow argued that the increasing separation of the sciences from the humanities was detrimental to both areas and that this division had moral implications. In 2009, on the occasion of the fiftieth anniversary of Snow's famous essay, Lawrence Krauss remarked that the "great cultural divide" separating the sciences and the arts still needs to be bridged in order to "further the progress of human knowledge and to benefit society."[12] For half a century, the questions raised in the "Two Cultures" debate have affected the curricula of colleges and universities in Europe as well as America. While technological developments in recent decades have complicated the picture somewhat, the digital age is still marked by a lack of communication between the arts and the sciences. At the same time, cultural criticism of the last half century has generated conversations from which might emerge more options than simple dualisms that are leftovers from the C. P. Snow "Two Cultures" debate of almost a century ago.

12 Lawrence M. Krauss, "C. P. Snow in New York," *Scientific American* 301, no. 3 (2009): 32.

While some theorists of the recent past continue the existential questioning that marked the nineteenth century's rejection of metaphysics, not all postmodern thinkers do. After all, the very term itself—postmodernism—simply tells us that we feel no longer "modern." Investigating strictly secular, scientific humanism provides opportunities to integrate more fully all "ways of knowing" that make us human.

*The Postmodern Condition*

Postmodernity arrived on the scene as a reaction to the worldviews of modernity and modernism. It advanced a modernist disenchantment with the Enlightenment celebration of "pure reason," substituting in its place epistemological uncertainty. At the same time, it rejected numerous tenets of modernism, including (but certainly not limited to) a belief in the individual and a faith in progress, an assumption that the breadth of human experience—conceptualized broadly in technological, economic, political, psychological, and artistic terms—could be fashioned anew. It was the theorist Jean-François Lyotard who, in "Defining the Postmodern," would connect the "the idea of modernity [...] with this principle that it is possible and necessary to break with tradition and to begin a new way of living and thinking."[13]

It turns out, a lot of new things were made in the modern period that spanned the late nineteenth and early twentieth centuries. Cinema, the airplane, the automobile, Penicillin, the radio, and nuclear fission were all invented or discovered during this period. New social norms started to appear too; for instance, with the advent of something as ordinary (by today's standards) as the car, the dating rituals of young people completely changed. Modernist writers and artists created modes of expression that had never been seen before, often informed by a liberal-humanist outlook

13 Jean-François Lyotard, "Defining the Postmodern" from *The Cultural Studies Reader*, Second Edition, ed. Simon During (New York: Routledge, 1999), 143.

that masterpieces could be original and could represent the universal human condition. New ways of understanding the depths of human psyche emerged with Freud's psychoanalytic understanding of sexual identity. Like Freud, Marx and Engels constructed a totalizing view of human nature undergirded—not by psycho-sexuality—but by economic relations. In *The Communist Manifesto*, they characterized all human history as a class struggle between the bourgeoisie and the proletariat, prophesying a revolution and eventual classless utopia on the horizon. New kinds of governments were also created. Fascist dictators like Benito Mussolini, Francisco Franco, and Adolf Hitler radically regimented their national communities (in Italy, Spain, and Germany, respectively) by stripping away everything oppositional, and even superfluous, to the empowerment of the State.

Having come of age under the shadow of Nazism, Stalinist communism, and Cold War capitalism, many postmodernists deeply mistrusted any totalizing practice as necessarily authoritarian. Some were not so sure that a "new" way of living was beneficial, nor was it even necessarily possible. Finishing his thought about how to define the modern, Lyotard declares, "Today we can presume that this 'breaking' [with tradition] is, rather, a manner of forgetting or repressing the past. That's to say of repeating it. Not overcoming it."[14] Phrased differently, the drive toward newness only forces oneself—and one's age—back to the past. In contrast to these moderns, postmodernists are keenly aware of their inheritance from the past. Whereas Lyotard seems to imply that knowing the past can lead to "overcoming it," no such causal relationship really exists in The World of Despair and Hope. For, as we'll see, the majority of postmodernists do not believe in the notion of an intrinsic, coherent self-identity, much less the concept of Enlightenment rationality, or the basic assumption that the past *must* give way through "newness" to the present and then future because

14 Ibid.

human history is a narrative of liberty, emancipation, ever-unfolding progress. Instead, self-identity is incoherent and performed, the world chaotic, and language about it always already insufficient.

If this all sounds nihilistic, it's not necessarily. Reason and the kinds of coherency it helps produce are not value-neutral for postmodernists; instead, the prioritization of reason is actually a quest for power with its own history of prejudices and violence. Thus, a turn toward incoherence—at least in the eyes of postmodern thinkers—involves the liberation of various individuals, identity groups, and ideas that, until this point in history, had been constrained. Likewise, numerous writers have perceived that postmodernity actually encourages strong ethical relationships with others in ways that might help us better understand our relationship to God.

*Language Trouble*

Let us start with something rather basic, something you've probably already experienced when encountering a postmodern text. It's hard to understand! Pick up a copy of Jacques Derrida's *Writing and Différance* or *Of Grammatology*, and a headache might soon follow; the writing is self-referential, illogical, at times contradictory, often playful. Not to be outdone by Derrida's inscrutability, Homi Bhabha even won the 1998 Bad Writing Contest (held by the Journal *Philosophy and Literature*) for a loquacious sentence from his book, *The Location of Culture*.

There is, however, a point to the style, a method to the madness, because Derrida, Bhabha, and other postmodernist theorists (such as Roland Barthes and Hayden White) sought to resist a traditional understanding of language as referential: the idea that words can and do refer to external things, to things outside of language itself. Derrida, for instance, advanced the work of structuralists (chief among them Ferdinand de Saussure), who claimed that language is only meaningful within a structure or system. Case in point: someone might argue that the color red inherently means, or symbolizes, anger; if you get angry, you might be referred to as a hot-head, after all. Yet, traffic lights use red to direct people to do the exact opposite: to slow down, not heat up. On Valentine's Day, red stands for affection; during the Christmas season, it signifies good cheer. On the U.S. flag, red stripes refer to sacrifice. In other words, red means something specific when it neighbors other colors like white and blue, or yellow and green, or when it occurs during a specific holiday. Similarly, the word "book" is meaningful in part because it's like but different from "cook" and "nook," just as the letter "b" mirrors "d," and "s" curvaceously re-interprets the angularity of "z."[15]

If words and even letters operate in contexts or in "structures" of language and, thus, cannot inherently refer to external reality, then post-structuralists followed that idea to its inevitable conclusion: there is no escape from language. In order to understand one word, we have to see it in the context of other words, and then in the context of still more words, *ad infinitum.* Self-referentiality leads to what Derrida refers to as "*différance*," which not only assumes that meaning depends on the differences between words but also that meaning remains forever deferred. In the absence of meaning, play abounds. Texts that writers and readers assume to have a single, unified meaning "deconstruct" themselves when their plural, sometimes contradictory meanings operate against each other. There are other ramifications, too. Writers could no longer assume elements of literature such as "character" and "plot" or even the process of "reading" itself. Instead, fiction becomes metafictional; stories talk about the process and limitations of story-telling and the experience of interpreting—as when your eyes fall on a

15 This paragraph references Saussure's *Course in General Linguistics*, which constructs a kind of roadmap for structuralism; as well, the difference between "s" and "z" echoes Roland Barthes's *post*-structuralist book *S/Z*, in which Barthes analyzes Honoré de Balzac's story "Sarrasine" by applying structuralism in a way that opens up the reading process to multiple interpretations, leaving the ultimate meaning of the story indeterminate and the need to find any ultimate meaning rather moot.

line from Italo Calvino's *If on a Winter's Night a Traveler* that reads, "The novel begins in a railway station, a locomotive huffs, steam from a piston covers the opening of the chapter, a cloud of smoke hides part of the first paragraph."[16] Additionally, postmodernist artists—writers, musicians, architects, and so on—could no longer believe in the originality of a work of art, or that art could reflect the artist's genius. Instead, art could only stitch together other, older styles and traditions into *bricolage* or *pastiche*.[17] These phenomena of deconstructed texts, metafictionalized narratives, and originality reconstituted as *bricolage* illustrate postmodern play.

Problems of unreliability do not just occur in literature, music, and architecture. In "The Historical Text as Literary Artifact," Hayden White famously asserts that even history—a kind of writing that one might imagine only traffics in objectivity—can be read as literature because the act of storytelling actually makes those facts meaningful in some way. Referring to such a process as "emplotment," White suggests that historians' abilities to narrativize the same historical event in different ways highlights how history and literature are not so different after all: "It does not matter whether the world is conceived to be real or only imagined; the manner of making sense of it is the same."[18] In order to assuage any fear that, in the absence of objectivity, historiography might encourage the spread of ideology and propaganda, White makes a thought-provoking claim. The assumption that history can be objective might actually encourage ideology-formation, he argues, whereas "by drawing historiography nearer to its origins in literary sensibility, we should be able to identify the ideological, because it

16 Italo Calvino, *If on a Winter's Night a Traveler*, trans. William Weaver (London: Vintage, 1998), 10.

17 Fredric Jameson, *Postmodernism, or, The Cultural Logic of Late Capitalism* (Durham: Duke UP, 2003), 17.

18 Hayden White, "The Historical Text as Literary Artifact," in *The Norton Anthology of Theory and Criticism*, ed. Vincent B. Leitch (New York: Norton, 2001), 1728.

is the fictive element in our discourse."[19] A seemingly objective and even scientific discipline like history is, at its foundation, based in narrative, which operates as discourse that can conceal and advance ideological agenda. This idea not only sums up White's point but also foreshadows the next two aspects of postmodernism.

*Against Grand Narratives*

In a powerful passage from his essay on "The Death of the Author," Roland Barthes states, "Literature [...] by refusing to assign a 'secret,' an ultimate meaning, to the text, (and to the world as text) liberates what may be called an anti-theological activity, an activity that is truly revolutionary since to refuse to fix meaning is in the end to refuse God and his hypostasis—reason, science, law."[20] If words do not reliably signify external things, and if the meaning of language (and not just *literary* but even ostensibly factual genres like history) is in considerable play, then such language problems necessarily challenge numerous grand narratives. These kinds of narratives totalize human experience into comprehensible form. They refer to the ways we give ourselves, our lives, and our relationships meaning by relying on pre-packaged "stories" that were written, revised, and reiterated long before we were ever born. These narratives are "grand" because they do not just make comprehensible our day, or our career aspirations, or even our love lives; they attempt to comprehend ourselves and our purpose here.

If there is one postmodernist who spent concerted effort addressing grand narratives and the need to dismantle them, it was Lyotard, specifically in *The Postmodern Condition*, which extends Barthes's vision while simultaneously advancing White's argument on narrative and knowability. In succinct fashion, Lyotard defines

19 Ibid.

20 Qtd. in Christopher Butler, *Postmodernism: A Very Short Introduction* (Oxford: Oxford UP, 2002), 24.

*postmodern* as "incredulity toward metanarratives."[21] Lyotard has two kinds of narratives in mind. In the first, or Hegelian, narrative, knowledge moves toward unity. In the second, or Marxist, one, humanity progresses onwards toward liberty and emancipation. Each narrative prioritizes science as the exemplary field of unified rational thought and as the vehicle for human liberation. For Lyotard, the natural sciences have traditionally delegitimized narratives and the kind of knowledge that can be acquired by reading them. Instead, traditional scientific discourse legitimates itself through empirical data, repeatable results, and denotative—or literal—language; however, in the postmodern world, science has lost its traditional Hegelian-Marxist goals of unity and liberation. Under the influence of a technological boom during the late twentieth century, it merely *performs* knowledge-seeking, thus turning knowledge into a commodity that can be sold and bought rather than as a truth that can help emancipate. Rather than being *the* legitimized field of knowledge production, science becomes one of many different "language games" (to use a phrase popularized by Ludwig Wittgenstein), each with its own vocabulary, set of genres, rules of conduct, and general style.

Although Lyotard spends most of his time critiquing grand narratives related to the natural sciences and the Enlightenment-era principles underpinning them, the fact of the matter is that "Lyotard later confessed [that] his knowledge [of science] was less than limited."[22] Understandably, he is remembered less for his perceptive insights on science—of which there are a slight few—and more for his call to challenge any field of knowledge, or grand narrative, that is seen as more legitimate than others. The list includes "Christian redemption, Enlightenment progress, Hegelian

21 Jean-François Lyotard, *The Postmodern Condition: A Report on Knowledge* (1979), trans. Geoff Bennington and Brian Massumi (Univ. of Minnesota Press, 1984), xxiv.

22 Perry Anderson, *The Origins of Postmodernity* (London: Verso, 2002), 26.

spirit, Romantic unity, Nazi racism, Keynesian equilibrium,"[23] in addition to Lyotard's perennial attacks on the utopian narrative of socialism, at least the totalitarian form it took under Stalin. Lyotard's goal is not to do away with all narratives but to envision a world of small rather than grand narratives, of local and regional kinds of interactions in which different kinds of stories all remain mutually harmonious in their plurality without issues regarding power or legitimation ever arising. To phrase it in a more negative light, Lyotard seems to give up on a modern metanarrative in which all knowledge can be organized into a hierarchy of unified reason (à la Hegel) and instead embraces a less vertical, more horizontal vision of free play where there might not be a power struggle, but neither is there a consensus on truth.

### *Power, Knowledge, Subject*

Gone are the days of Cartesian dualism, when an individual—suspicious of all bodily sensation as potentially fallible—can deny the existence of everything besides his or her own thoughts. Alone, disembodied so to speak, and free to follow reason's path, Descartes (in his *Meditations*) runs counter to the postmodern subject, which is always already embodied and positioned. Postmodernists often prefer to refer to the individual as a "subject" because it underscores the extent to which subjectivity—or one's sense of self—requires subjugation to power; to be a subject, one must first be subject-*ed*. When we think of power, we might quickly conceptualize some kind of authoritarian figure demanding that his subjects behave in certain ways while restricting them from or punishing them for behaving in others. Rather, for numerous postmodern thinkers, knowledge about one's self-identity actually depends on the enactment of power that could not be so directly wielded or exerted. It

23 Ibid, 31.

actually occurs innocuously through discourses, or socio-political practices like writing and even conversation.

Throughout his highly influential *The History of Sexuality*, Michel Foucault refers to the repression of sexuality in the nineteenth century. During this period of repression, something strange happened: "sex" became a unifying principle that drew together disparate things like one's behavior, feelings, appearance, and sexual organs. Prior to this point, heterosexual and homosexual acts were just that—acts; there was no heterosexual or homosexual sense of self-identity behind those acts. At the same time that "the free circulation in speech" on the subject of sex was repressed through prudishness and censorship, though discourse on the topic proliferated. Foucault refers to "the multiplication of discourses concerning sex in the field of exercise of power itself: an institutional incitement to speak about it, and to do so more and more," but only to speak about it in certain ways.[24] From this discourse, the artificial notion emerged that sex acts are not mere acts after all but manifestations of people's inherent identity. Hence, a causal reversal takes place: first, repression leads to the proliferation of writing and talking about sexuality and, from there, to the development of sex as intrinsic to individual identity; then, the artificial idea of sexual identity—the actual *effect* of such discourse—emerges as the *cause* of an individual's actions. In other words, it is precisely at the moment an individual declares his or her own self-identity that power asserts its...well, power.

Other thinkers, such as Adrienne Rich and Eve Kosofksy Sedgwick, would further develop the Foucauldian power-subject-knowledge relationship, specifically as it involves the marginalization of certain identity groups within the arena of human sexuality. For instance, in "Compulsory Heterosexuality and Lesbian Existence," Rich posits that lesbian relationships and

24 Michel Foucault, *The History of Sexuality, Volume 1: An Introduction*, trans. Robert Hurley (New York: Vintage, 1990), 18.

experiences have been erased by an "institution" of heterosexuality that prioritizes male power. It controls through the normalization of violent and criminal behavior (like sexual harassment and rape) as well as through restrictions on female autonomy and fulfillment. It occurs in the family unit, the school yard, the tax code, the courtroom, and the pornographic clip "as a means of assuring male right of physical, economic, and emotional access."[25] Radical for its time, Rich's argument lost its shock but not its resonance in the age of the #MeToo movement. For Sedgwick, in *The Epistemology of the Closet*, discourses on heterosexuality and homosexuality—or, better put, the dichotomy between those two as the only two options—actually restrict us from other epistemologies of sexuality. By delimiting sexual identity to two legitimate (but not equally accepted) manifestations, discourses on sex have powerfully denied access to other ways of knowing, to a freed-up epistemology that moves beyond the binary of being straight or being in, or out of, the closet, and toward more complex, and oftentimes less articulable, aspects of human sexuality.[26] Here, Sedgwick advocates for awareness about queer identities, which since the publication of her work has developed further into advocacy for other groups that now comprise LGBTQ+ communities.

Theorists have also applied the Foucauldian lens to the history of Western European imperialism and the conceptualization of racial and ethnic otherness. In *Orientalism*, Edward Said outlines the kinds of discursive practices that have led to the creation of "the Orient" and "Oriental" identity: "The Orient is an integral part of European *material* civilization and culture. Orientalism expresses and represents that part culturally and even ideologically as a mode of discourse with supporting institutions, vocabulary,

25 Adrienne Rich, "Compulsory Heterosexuality and Lesbian Experience," in *Feminism and Sexuality: A Reader*, eds. Stevi Jackson and Sue Scott (Columbia UP, 1999), 135.

26 Eve Kosofsky Sedgwick, *The Epistemology of the Closet* (Univ. of California Press, 1990), 35.

scholarship, imagery, doctrines, even colonial bureaucracies and colonial styles."[27] According to Said, Western individuals—ranging from archaeologists to writers—did not discover, or disinterestedly acquire, objective knowledge about the individuals they encountered in colonial spaces like French holdings in West Africa or British ones in India. Instead, they invented the idea of the Orient as well as the constellation of characteristics that would compose Oriental subjects "as a sign of European-Atlantic power over the Orient."[28] Developing the point further, theorists would ponder how imperialistic discourses inhabit the university, an institution historically referred to as the *ivory* tower. While some, like Gayatri Chakravorty Spivak, wonder if intellectuals' well-intentioned desires to give a voice to seemingly voiceless "subaltern" populations could be interpreted as a power play,[29] others such as Ngugi wa Thiong'o ask why African literature and culture have been marginalized while English literature and culture—and by extension U.S. and Western European literatures and cultures—have been legitimized as necessary subjects of inquiry for an undergraduate education.[30]

If power does not just marginalize individuals but also produces subjects (in order to control them), then another compelling site of power's potential is the "simulacrum," a term Jean Baudrillard popularized to refer to a topsy-turvy world in which the truly real has been replaced by the hyperreal. Fredric Jameson situates it squarely within the consumerist culture of late capitalism: "Appropriately enough, the culture of the simulacrum comes to life in a

27 Edward W. Said, *Orientalism* (London: Vintage, 1979), 2.

28 Ibid, 6.

29 Gayatri Chakravorty Spivak, "Can the Subaltern Speak?" in *A Critique of Postcolonial Reason: Toward a History of the Vanishing Present* (Cambridge, MA: Harvard, 1999).

30 Ngugi wa Thiong'o, Taban Lo Liyong, and Henry Owuor-Anyumba, "On the Abolition of the English Department" in *The Norton Anthology of Theory and Criticism*, ed. Vincent B. Leitch (New York: Norton, 2001).

society where exchange value has been generalized to the point at which the very memory of use value is effaced"[31] and this is due to the widespread "transformation of reality into images."[32] Commodities—things bought and sold at market—are eventually valued through the assigning of a monetary price, which does not necessarily reflect their actual (or "use") value based on the real needs they satisfy. So, for instance, a media-saturated simulacrum bombards us with advertisements that do not just reflect our desires and needs but actually create those things. If desire can be created, then there are more potential consumers of a given good or service, which means increased profits for companies producing those commodities. Yet, it's not only through overtly commercial endeavors, like ads, that the simulacrum alters our desires and needs. Images from movies and television, or from Netflix and Instagram feeds, force us to compare ourselves to, and pattern our lives on, mere representations. They alter, oftentimes imperceptibly, our goals, our sense of accomplishment, our idea of what's possible and what's not, even our self-worth. Sometimes, they alter those things to such an extent that we only feel like we're genuinely living when we're copying someone else's plot, scene for scene. Here's a question: when you received your acceptance letter from PBA, did you compare that moment in your life to a scene from a movie or show in which someone also receives the results of their university application? They always seem to say with dismay but a hint of hope, "It's a small envelope. I probably didn't get in." Did you say the same thing because that's what you're supposed to say, because that's what people—well, not *actual* people but actors playing characters—always say? If so, you've trespassed into the simulacrum; if you didn't, you might still be living in the simulacrum, whether you like it or not.

31 Jameson, *Postmodernism*, 18.

32 Jameson, "Postmodernism and Consumer Society," in *The Norton Anthology of Theory and Criticism*, ed. Vincent B. Leitch (New York: Norton, 2001), 1974.

All of this discussion of power could make you feel paranoid. Yet, if postmodernism teaches us anything, it's that there might not be a coherent "you" any longer, only a matrix of identity politics—including gender, sexuality, race, ethnicity, class, (dis) ability, education level, and so on and so forth—by which power exerts control. As Seyla Benhabib astutely observes, "The subject is replaced by a system of structures, oppositions and differances [sic] which, to be intelligible, need not be viewed as products of a living subjectivity at all. You and I are the mere 'sites' of such conflicting language of power, and 'the self' is merely another position in language."[33]

*Hope for the Postmodern Age*

If there is hope for the postmodern age, it is not the kind of hope to be found in the other "worlds" encountered through the honors curriculum. It might sound strange, though, to talk about something like hope, especially when there seem to be so many problems to despair over: the inability to escape language, the loss of the real, the advent of the simulacrum, the frailty of human beings under the pressure of powerful forces, and the contestation of all grand narratives, which leads to a Lyotardian social space in which any "truth" is as legitimate as any other.[34] These all distill into the commonly held and often repeated idea that postmodernists think everything is relative and, therefore, nothing is true—thus, why should they be arguing anything at all?

Oddly enough, there is a lot of hope. One virtue of postmodernism is that, by refuting the myth of individuality, light shines on

33 Qtd. in Butler, *Postmodernism*, 51.

34 Jürgen Habermas and others have decried such radical relativism, arguing that it would completely kill any possibility of developing and sustaining a "public sphere," where people could come together to discuss and debate ideas and, through civil engagement, influence political action. See, for instance, Habermas's *The Structural Transformation of the Public Sphere: An Inquiry into a Category of Bourgeois Society* (1962).

the oppressive work of power. To that effect, postmodern thinkers reveal how certain groups of people have historically been marginalized or made subordinate to other groups of people that have historically been perceived as better in some way. It challenges the assumed superiority of the West over the non-West, heterosexuality over other (seemingly "deviant") expressions of sexuality, masculinity over femininity, upper class over lower class, high culture over mass culture, Christianity over other religions or approaches to spirituality. It shows how power does not just operate in open conflicts between people but, discursively, in our very institutions, even colleges and universities. Ideally, it urges us all to create spaces of acceptance and inclusion.

In other words, postmodernism can help us forge more ethical relationships with others and, in so doing, might help us develop more just political systems and better ways of understanding and practicing Christianity. It should be remembered that Lyotard and other postmodernists were not calling for the delegitimizing of *all* narratives, but the grand narratives (like those propelling fascist and socialist totalitarian regimes) because they force human beings—sometimes violently, always powerfully—into the mold of a single, ideological schema. In *The Human Condition*, Hannah Arendt builds on this point by arguing that totalizing narratives, and the political systems they inaugurate, fail to appreciate and, in fact, work to suppress our "plurality": "Plurality is the condition of human action because we are all the same, that is, human, in such a way that nobody is ever the same as anyone else who ever lived, lives, or will live."[35] The prioritization of plurality—of uniqueness and singularity—has been with postmodern theories from the very start of this chapter. When Derrida, for instance, discusses the way literature deconstructs itself, one thing he means to express is that no reader can offer *the* interpretation of a work of literature; no

35 Hannah Arendt, *The Human Condition*, Second Edition (Chicago: Univ. of Chicago Press, 1998), 8.

reader can sufficiently say what a work means by describing it in a different way because literature, and the process of reading it, are part of a singular act.[36] If that goes for literature, then shouldn't it also for humanity? Here, though, you're probably nagged by a question, a really good one: How can postmodernists believe that each human is singular, that humanity is a plurality, if postmodernism itself marks the death of individualism?

The vast majority of postmodernists did not reject "the individual" outright but, rather, the two-fold notion that one's personhood is determined by the possession of an inherent or essential self-identity that, at its very core, is rational. Despite their rejection of Enlightenment reason, none of these thinkers—at least to our knowledge—ever denied their own individuality. Not merely replicas of what had come before or would come after, they believed in their own personhood, in a uniqueness that does not require essence. In other words, nobody needs to know exactly who they are—or that they are *essentially* anything at all—in order to demand they be treated as unique.

Numerous postmodern philosophers—among them Jean-Luc Nancy, Richard Rorty, and Emmanuel Levinas—have illuminated the way in which a resistance to Enlightenment notions about the rational self actually becomes a bedrock for the ethics of community. Without master narratives about historical progress, without faith in Enlightenment reason, without authoritarian forms of social order holding groups of people together, how could there exist the possibility of solidarity between distinct and ultimately irreducible individuals? Jean-Luc Nancy faces these kinds of questions head-on in *The Inoperative Community*. Writing in the wake of totalitarianism, he rejects any assertion that communities—national or otherwise—should be organized around some shared trait or focused on accomplishing some goal. Rather than promote

36 Derrida discusses this idea in a lot of different works. One of the most accessible is "An Interview with Jacques Derrida," in *Acts of Literature*, ed. Derek Attridge (New York: Routledge, 1992).

an operative, or workable, community, he draws upon Heidegger's existential idea of "being-with"[37] in order to argue that singularity always already requires co-existence, which is another way of saying that you can only be yourself by being with others. Such singularity ends when communities work toward a shared goal; it is sustained by "interrupti[ng]" the work of community, by inhibiting any attempt to totalize or otherwise restrict plurality.[38] Like Nancy, Rorty also identifies problems with "operative" forms of community. He observes that the rejection of Enlightenment reason as the core of individuality and as the guiding principle of a community can lead to greater solidarity between more diverse groups of people, including those historically denied the full benefits of personhood (for instance, women and people of color) during and after the Enlightenment: "[M]y position is not incompatible with urging that we try to extend our sense of 'we' to people whom we have previously thought of as 'they.'"[39]

It might be argued that Levinas would advance the most radical approach to the postmodern community. His terminology can be a little idiosyncratic; so, as a preface, when Levinas talks about encounters between people and the sense of responsibility that emerges, he does so by fixating on the "face," which is, but is not just, the actual face; it's that which one encounters in another human being that demands ethical treatment. It is also that which, in the end, cannot truly be comprehended: "The face is signification, and signification without context. I mean that the Other, in the rectitude of his face, is not a character within a context. Ordinarily one is a 'character': a professor at the Sorbonne,

---

37 Martin Heidegger, *Being and Time*, trans. Joan Stambaugh (Albany: State Univ. of New York Press, 2010), 117.

38 Jean-Luc Nancy, *The Inoperative Community*, ed. Peter Connor, trans. Peter Connor, Lisa Garbus, Michael Holland, and Simona Sawhney (Minneapolis: Univ. of Minnesota Press, 1991), 31. [Emphasis in the original]

39 Richard Rorty, *Contingency, Irony, and Solidarity* (New York: Cambridge UP, 1989), 192

a Supreme Court justice, son of so-and-so [... The face] is what cannot become a content, which your thought would embrace; it is uncontainable."[40] By providing a list of numerous contexts in which people might be identified, or might self-identify—through their occupation and family relations as well as their biological traits (for instance, hair color and height) and, of course, their race, gender, class, and so forth—Levinas does not want to imply that these things are unimportant, but that people cannot be fully understood in these contexts. Instead, they should be treated as irreducible. Responsibility for other people (and, thus, for their own responsibility for others), a concept as old as the Old Testament itself, changes our understanding of ourselves too. It tempers our "self-centered impulse for control over nature and others" in ways that should overhaul every single aspect of our social beings, from the way people conduct themselves in personal relationships and engage with the natural world, to the way they run universities and govern our cities, states, and nations.[41]

Reflection on postmodern community also extends to spirituality, to a re-envisioning of church community and communion with God. It's important to note that few postmodernists overtly theorized about God. Religion doesn't really show up in Baudrillard or Jameson; Arendt talks about the modern disavowal of God; Derrida has a quasi-religious appreciation for literature; spiritual implications of postmodern theories abound—and certain thinkers oriented toward the religious and the spiritual have brought them front-and-center. Many Christian thinkers have shown how postmodernism can actually help deepen one's faith. Some, like Stanley J. Grenz, see its usefulness while, simultaneously, rejecting some of its basic tenets: "Postmodern thinkers rightly alert us to the naiveté

---

40 Emmanuel Levinas, *Ethics and Infinity: Conversations with Philippe Nemo*, trans. Richard A. Cohen (Pittsburgh: Duquesne UP, 1985), 86-7.

41 Norman Klassen and Jens Zimmerman, *The Passionate Intellect: Incarnational Humanism and the Future of University Education* (Grand Rapids, MI: Baker Academic, 2006), 129.

of the Enlightenment attempt to discover universal truth by appeal to reason alone. Ultimately the metanarrative we [as Christians] proclaim lies beyond the pale of reason either to discover or to evaluate."[42] As the diction suggests, Grenz takes issue with Lyotard's dismissal of all grand narratives, proclaiming instead the truth of one narrative: the story of Jesus as the incarnation of God.[43]

According to James K. A. Smith, though, the suspicion of master narratives productively challenges us to see faith as more than a set of static creedal statements. Just as Lyotard does not reject narrative as a whole but sees how everything we undertake—including scientific endeavors that ostensibly marginalize narrative—actually require story-telling, Smith characterizes the Judeo-Christian tradition as a faith founded on stories, on myths and parables, and therefore on the deconstructive possibilities of interpretation. For Smith, as well as many other Christian postmodernists, the Derridean notion that we cannot escape or transcend language opens up the Bible to a space where multiple interpretations can co-exist, if for no other reason than that, even in the Gospel, certain events are described (that is, interpreted) in different ways.[44] The question, then, is not whether the Bible gives us unfettered access to objective truth, to a truth that "can be universally known by all people, at all times, in all places."[45] That ship has sailed. Instead, Smith is concerned with good versus bad interpretations, with diverse communities that establish different guidelines for

42 Stanley J Grenz, *A Primer on Postmodernism* (Grand Rapids, MI: William B. Eerdmans Publishing Company, 1996), 164-5.

43 Ibid, 164.

44 James K. A. Smith, *Who's Afraid of Postmodernism? Taking Derrida, Lyotard, and Foucault to Church* (Grand Rapids, MI: Baker Academic, 2006), 44. There are numerous other works that explore the relationship between Derrida and religion. Any list on the subject would have to include John D. Caputo's stellar work *The Prayers and Tears of Derrida: Religion Without Religion*. For further reading about the broader approach to Christian faith as narrative, see Hans W. Frei's *Theology & Narrative: Selected Essays*.

45 Ibid, 48.

Biblical interpretation, and with a deconstructive church focused on revelation rather than on the more logic-oriented "apologetics of demonstration."[46] Informed not just by Lyotard and Derrida but also by Foucault, Smith's version of the postmodern church would also uncover how power structures (he specifically discusses late capitalism and consumer culture) coercively shape people's identities.[47] Although Smith declines to fully apply a Foucauldian lens by observing how powerful and undesirable discourses operate *within* the church,[48] he does urge it to "recogniz[e] the structural goodness of disciplinary formation" as worshippers seek "to reflect the image of Christ."[49]

Ultimately, Barthes's declaration that the death of the author heralds the death of God (which, of course, echoes Nietzsche) might not be true after all. Postmodernism and Christianity do not have to be mutually exclusive. In fact, postmodernism can strengthen faith and church community. Through the rejection of Enlightenment ideals like objective rationality, it validates religious experiences and interpretations of the Bible that do not stand to reason; it encourages diversity rather than conformity; it challenges followers to embrace the social justice mission of Christianity. God in the postmodern age does not resemble the versions of God that have come before. That fact might not necessarily bring us easy comfort, but it should give us hope by empowering us to commit ourselves to justice and empathy, to plurality in the here and now.

46 Ibid, 53-8.

47 Ibid, 106-7.

48 For feminist theologians like Mary Daly, for example, discourse surrounding Christianity conceals misogyny, as evidenced in her pithy assertion: "if God is male then the male is God." See Daly's *Beyond God the Father: Toward a Philosophy of Women's Liberation* (Boston: Beacon Press, 1985), 19.

49 Ibid, 107. Smith identifies numerous spiritual disciplines, such as fasting, communion, meditation, and economic redistribution.

# The World of Despair and Hope Textual Glosses

## Johann Wolfgang von Goethe, *Faust* (1808)

In The World of Reason and Revolt, Goethe's somewhat autobiographical *Sorrows of Young Werther* epitomized the romantic emphasis on intense emotionality in contrast to the Enlightenment's focus on rationality and common sense. Goethe's *Faust* is much more difficult to characterize, especially if one takes into consideration that after the 1808 publication of Part I, Goethe spent several decades composing the much more allegorical Part II, in which he interweaves themes ranging from mythology and art to statesmanship, economics, science, and religion. Part II was not published until after Goethe's death.

It is tempting to read Faust, the character, in Part I as a personification of the by-then established romantic hero and to identify many of his reflections on the quest for true knowledge with Goethe, the author. However, this over-simplification would miss the impact the work had on subsequent treatments of the Faust-theme (as, for instance, in Thomas Mann's 1947 novel *Dr. Faustus*), especially in the context of nineteenth- and twentieth-century European culture. Kierkegaard's *Fear and Trembling* devotes about five pages to the discussion of the character of Faust; *Either / Or* also includes a discussion of him, and Bertrand Russell's essay "A Free Man's Worship" begins with a description of the opening scene of Faust in his study. The work has been adapted in all media numerous times and is frequently referred to as one of the greatest works of German literature.

The richness of Part I derives from Goethe's drawing on several traditional motifs that had been treated in legends, literature, and theatre for centuries; in the Christian tradition, the "Devil's Pact" (or temptation) goes back to Genesis 3:5, Matthew 4:1-11, and

Luke 4:1-13. Goethe's *Faust*, like Marlowe's 1604 *Dr. Faustus*, also drew from the *Faustbuch*, published in 1587 in Frankfurt, and other folklore sources. But Marlowe's medieval Faust differs dramatically from the character Goethe depicts in a post-Enlightenment world. David Lyle Jeffrey explains that in Marlowe's *Doctor Faustus*, the main character "signs a blood pact with Lucifer, exchanging his soul for the services of Mephistopheles [...]. The overreacher's subsequent magical exploits are more madcap and ribald than constructive and enlightening; Faustus dies a terrible death [...]. There is in Marlowe none of the romantic self-actualization of Goethe's *Faust*."[50]

While the characters and basic plot could be summarized as a repetition of the formula "devil tempts man, man accepts, transgresses," Goethe's treatment in Part I places the work firmly in questions grounded in the nineteenth century; several of the longer monologues by Faust illustrate the quintessential passion-driven, questing romantic protagonist who strives to transcend human limitations. Early critics pointed to the seeming lack of organization and the mixing of genres—what to make of the mixing of dramatic scenes with dream-like sequences and the interpolation of poetry (some written in blank verse) in *Faust*? What does the "Dedication" have to do with the "Prelude in the Theatre" and the "Prologue in Heaven"? The "Prologue in Heaven" presents a picture of the world as described by the character of the Lord and Mephistopheles, respectively; how does the exchange reflect emerging nineteenth-century ideas about the modern world? But Goethe's work was also shaped by the century's obsession over the relationship between the universal and the individual, the objective/external and the subjective/internal. In a conversation with his secretary Eckermann, Goethe made the following remarks about the two parts:

50 David L. Jeffrey, *A Dictionary of Biblical Tradition in English Literature* (Grand Rapids, MI: Eerdmans, 1992), 203.

"A far richer world is displayed," said I [Eckermann], "in this second part than in the first."

"I should think so," said Goethe. "The first part is almost entirely subjective; it proceeded entirely from a perplexed, impassioned individual, and his semi-darkness is probably highly pleasing to mankind. But, in the second part, there is scarcely anything of the subjective; here is seen a higher, broader, clearer, more passionless world, and he who has not looked about him and had some experience, will not know what to make of it."[51]

Due to the allegorical complexity of the piece, Part II is almost inaccessible to readers today, and editions (if they include any parts from Part II at all) limit themselves to excerpts and summary or paraphrases of the context.

### Søren Kierkegaard, *Fear and Trembling* (1843)

Written under the pseudonym Johannes *de Silentio*, Kierkegaard's treatise on Christian faith offers a powerful counterpoint to the organized religion of the Danish State Church and to the system of scientific thought imbued in G. W. F. Hegel's philosophy. Out of all the mysteries in the Christian faith, the one Kierkegaard chooses to meditate on is the story of God commanding Abraham to kill his own son, Isaac. Kierkegaard mulls over the Abraham-Isaac story by exploring three different stages or modes of life: aesthetic, ethical, and religious. Appropriating Hegel's dialectic approach to philosophy, he shows how the fusion of the aesthetic and the ethical leads to the religious stage, which is founded on faith in the absurd.

Before delving into the book, let us first provide a cursory overview of these three stages. The aesthetic stage does not just deal with art, or art appreciation, but with the way anything—even our own daily lives—can be appreciated as art objects. The main feature distinguishing the aesthetic from other stages is its imme-

51 Johann Wolfgang Von Goethe and Cyrus Hamlin, *Faust: A Tragedy: Interpretive Notes, Contexts, Modern Criticism* (New York: W.W. Norton, 2001), 544.

diacy. When, for instance, we immediately respond emotionally to our surrounding world and then construct idealized versions of our lives, first by cataloging pleasurable or beautiful things to be sought and ugly or painful things to be avoided, and second by imagining life as the pursuit—and eventual attainment—of a happy ending, we might be said to inhabit a purely aesthetic existence. For Kierkegaard, this stage is also "relative" because it remains inwardly focused on oneself, on one's personal ideals rather than on the actual world.

When an individual makes the outward turn from the ideal to the actual, from the self to the community, life becomes much less relative. It enters the second, or ethical, stage. Importantly, though, the aesthetic is not completely cancelled out in the ethical stage. Rather, following Hegel's idea of "sublation," the aesthetic is simultaneously left behind and retained. For instance, the aesthetic individual sees life in terms of personal preference, whereas the ethical individual moves from that relative position to the more absolute—what Kierkegaard also refers to as "universal"—position of the community by observing life in terms of good things that accord with customary or social norms and bad things that don't.

By adopting Hegelian sublation, Kierkegaard perceives the move from the aesthetic to the ethical as part of a dialectic. Within Hegel's system of thought, one idea moves to its dialectical opposite through the act of sublation. The second idea (in this case, the ethical) retains part of the aesthetic while also adding in new qualities, some of which challenge those found in the aesthetic stage. In other words, the system of thought moves dialectically from one idea to the next, and then the next, leading onward to ideas that become more and more sophisticated and comprehensive through a necessary application of logic that strives for universal understanding. Thus, at the start of Problema III in *Fear and Trembling*, Kierkegaard observes that "the ethical is as such the universal."[52] The ethical operates within a comprehensive system of right and wrong that accords with social norms applied not just to one individual but to all.

One kind of behavior that runs afoul of most social norms would be murder. Hence, an ethical reading of the Abraham-Isaac story would go like this: God tells Abraham to sacrifice Isaac; Abraham determines to keep his faith by following God's command; God, in response to the strength of Abraham's faith, saves Isaac. The ethical reading would highlight the fact that God does not order Abraham to murder but tests him by calling on him to sacrifice his son, nor does Abraham seek to kill but to obey God. It would also underscore the happy ending: God rewards Abraham's trust. Sacrifice, obedience, trust, salvation: all of these words could, and often do, show up in stated and unstated codes of social behavior that form the bedrock of civilized societies.

Kierkegaard does *not* read the story that way. Instead of an ethical hero, Abraham represents one of the few true "knights of faith." He does not believe in a logical system of ethics that accords with social norms. Instead he believes in the absurdity of faith; that is, faith actually begins where rational thought leaves off. "Where Hegel goes wrong," Kierkegaard observes, "is in talking about faith, in not protesting loudly and clearly against the honour and glory enjoyed by Abraham as the father of faith when he should really be remitted to some lower court for trial and exposed as a murderer."[53] Although he does not end up killing Isaac, Abraham thinks he will because he thinks God has ordered him. Resigned to losing his son, Abraham discovers that, in order to follow God, he must suspend the ethical.

In another dialectical maneuver, then, Abraham inhabits a thoroughly religious stage of life that retains *and* rejects certain

---

52 Søren Kierkegaard, *Fear and Trembling: Dialectical Lyric by Johannes De Silentio*, trans. Alastair Hannay (New York: Penguin, 1986), 109.

53 *Fear and Trembling*, 84.

aspects of the aesthetic and ethical. Like the aesthetic individual, Abraham promotes the particular rather than the universal. Illustrating a return to the individual himself, the book focuses on the inner turmoil of Abraham; of course, it refers to Isaac, Sarah, and other individuals, but the real story offers a potentially dangerous proposition: Abraham's faith in God forces him to live outside the law of his community. Consequently, the book refutes the kind of Hegelian dialecticism that transforms faith into a logical system revealed through customs and norms. Kierkegaard felt that such a perversion of faith had taken hold of the Danish State Church. At the same time that the religious stage rejects the ethical, it also retains the commitment to living with and for others, which is critical for the ethical stage. The problem for Hegel—and, of course, for Abraham—is that God just happens to be a radical Other who cannot be made comprehensible in any human system of understanding.

### Karl Marx and Friedrich Engels, *Communist Manifesto* (1848)

A "manifesto" is a public declaration or announcement issued by a person or group of people outlining goals and policies as part of developing a (often political) platform. The 1840s were a tumultuous time in many parts of the world, but especially in Western and Central Europe where, in 1848, uprisings occurred in many countries. Industrialization had significantly affected the lives of the working classes, both urban and rural, and calls for reforms were issued from many sides; but just as there were many causes for unrest in different places, there were different articulations of what particular change was needed, though many reformers embraced a wide range of liberal and socialist ideas. Throughout Europe, struggles between representational, constitutional forms of government and monarchical forms continued.

The most important works shaping socialist thought from the

mid-nineteenth century onwards were written by Karl Marx, who was commissioned by the "Communist League," an organization headquartered in London, to write the "Manifesto."[54] At the time, Marx was living in Brussels; it was Marx's friendship and collaboration with Engels that brought about the alliance between Marx and the "Communist League." Engels, whose father co-owned a textile factory in Manchester, England, had been affiliated with the organization; he had firsthand knowledge of working conditions in factories. Even though the British Parliament had passed several legislative acts to address working conditions, especially for children, the lives of most factory workers were pretty grim.[55]

Adapting Hegel's stage theory of history, Marx posited that the history of societies had been shaped by class struggles between the dominant class of any epoch and the oppressed classes of the time. Just as the bourgeoisie had been oppressed by the aristocracy in the eighteenth century, only to become the dominant class of the nineteenth century, so Marx argued, the proletariat or working class, oppressed by the bourgeoisie in the nineteenth century, would rise up and overthrow the oppressing bourgeoisie.

Central to his description of the struggle between the bourgeoisie and the proletariat is the analysis of capitalism as, according to Marx, a fundamentally exploitative economic system. In somewhat simplified terms, Marx says that before the Industrial Revolution, workers produced material objects that reflected the craft and skill of the worker; the product of labor was connected to the worker who produced it. The *commodity*, or the thing produced that could be sold for a price, was not completely separated from the worker.

After the arrival of steam-operated machines, workers were no longer paid for their skills, but rather for the hours they worked

54 Karl Marx, Friedrich Engels, *The Communist Manifesto: With Related Documents* ed. John Edward Toews (Boston: Bedford/St. Martins, Macmillan Learning, 2018), 6-7.

55 The Factory Act of 1833, for example, established that children between the ages of nine and thirteen were to work no more than nine hours a day.

in the factory and, thus, they became *alienated* from the materials they produced; workers had to turn themselves into hourly "units." In Marx's words, this change resulted in "resolving personal worth into exchange value."[56] Articulating the point more concretely, he writes that "these laborers who must sell themselves piecemeal, are a commodity"; instead of having worth as a human being, the worker "becomes an appendage of the machine."[57]

Marxist analyses of economic conditions were tremendously influential throughout the twentieth century and remain so in the twenty-first; perhaps the most well-known "Neo-Marxist" analysis of capitalism is the three-volume set by Michael Hardt and Antonio Negri (*Empire*, *Multitude*, and *Commonwealth*–published in 2000, 2004, and 2009, respectively). Together with Nietzsche and Freud, both of whom were a few decades younger, Marx significantly influenced theories of history and political thought to this day.

### Fyodor Dostoevsky, *Notes From the Underground* (1864)

This short novel is divided into two distinctly different parts. The first part seems to consist of random meditations on the part of the first-person narrator, whose name we never learn. The second part, chronologically set about twenty years before the reflections offered in Part I, recalls several encounters the narrator had with his classmates and some other people when he was twenty-four years old.

The "Notes" of Part I, consisting of eleven sections, offer observations about life in the middle of the nineteenth century; they include thoughts about society and commentary on the narrator's own life and sense of self. The seemingly unsystematic ruminations touch on many of the theories advanced by thinkers of the time, especially those who offered new approaches to tracing the development of civilizations over different epochs, and those talking about the relationship between human nature and different forms of soci-

56 Marx and Engels, 67.

57 Ibid., 70.

ety. Allusions, as well as direct references, evoke theories developed by Jean-Jacques Rousseau, Henry Thomas Buckle, Friedrich Schiller, and other writers well-known among the Russian intelligentsia. Some of the topics explored include the conflict between reason/science and human will, enlightened self-interest and desire, as well as the struggle to ground decisions on firm principles and the uncertainty of foundations.

A pervasive thread running through these "notes" is a deep questioning of all rationalist and materialist explanations of human nature; additionally, notions of what would constitute "progress" in any society are explored, among them varieties of socialism that became popular during the century. Like other nineteenth-century theories that attempted to apply scientific methods to the social sciences and humanities, socialist ideas (especially the ideas of Nikolai Chernyshevsky) are held up to examination—and found to be wanting.

The most intriguing aspect of the work is, undoubtedly, the character of the narrator; he, like the more well-known main characters of Dostoevsky's later works *Crime and Punishment* (1866) and *Brothers Karamazov* (1880), is a complex study in psychology. He is a personification of the complete opposition to all rationalist theories, but ironically ends up chained to a rigid logic, albeit an absurd one of acting out of nothing but spite. The very first paragraph of the novel, which opens the narrator's diatribe, sets "spite" up as his primary motive for anything he does: "I am a sick man [...]. I am a spiteful man"[58]; the rest of the chapter continues to refer to his "spite" (at least five more times) in contradictory and paradoxical ways. Here, clearly, is a main character who is not a traditional "hero."

Admittedly, the very notion of what exactly constitutes a literary "hero" has become more complicated, but for a long time,

58 Fyodor Dostoyevsky, *Notes from the Underground*, trans. Kirsten Lodge (Ontario: Broadview Press, 2014), 17.

scholarship discussing "heroes" or "protagonists" foregrounded admirable characteristics, nobility of character, or other qualities considered worthy of emulation. Since the appearance of the "Underground Man," more main characters of doubtful "merit" (of the traditional kind) have appeared in fiction, and "common" rather than "outstanding" characters people the landscape of fiction. It seems that readers have come to look more acceptingly on main characters who display lots of weaknesses as well as the occasional strength.

The second part, the remembered encounters between the narrator, his classmates, and others, includes episodes revolving around experiencing insult and humiliation in human interactions. The underground man devises several plans to evoke responses from other people in a deep desire to be acknowledged. One of the scenes involves an officer whose treatment of the narrator brings about the following comment:

> I was standing by the pool table without realizing that I was blocking the way, and he needed to get through. He grabbed me by the shoulders, and without a word–with no warning or explanation–picked me up from where I was standing and moved me, and then walked on by as though he hadn't even noticed me. I would have forgiven even a beating, but there was no way I could forgive him for moving me out of the way like that and then ignoring me so completely.[59]

Other encounters follow; among former classmates, the narrator feels unwelcome at a party. His description of their conversations with him are fragmented and seem more a continuation of him projecting his own hyper-self-conscious preoccupations on them rather than a report of the event. The evening ends with a visit to a brothel, where the narrator meets Liza. The narrator engages in

59 Ibid, 55.

meandering speculations about people saving other people; Liza, while telling him that he sounds like a book, seems capable of seeing beyond outward appearances. The narrator's "spite" asserts itself again when he tries to humiliate her; when he leaves, he casually tells Liza to stop by sometime. When Liza does, their exchange suggests that her character might provide an alternative to the rigid rational self-interest of the world the narrator rejects as well as to the other side of the coin, equally rigidly determined by the narrator's "spite." After all the contemporary theories engaged in discovering laws that could predict the next step an individual (or a community) might take, Dostoevsky seems to suggest that we might not want to look at our fellow human beings as if they were quantifiable by theories.

### Charles Darwin, *Autobiographies* (1876)

While Charles Darwin's name is synonymous with the theory of evolution articulated in his *On the Origin of Species* (1859), his short *Autobiographies* or autobiographical fragments and excerpts from his voluminous personal correspondence present fascinating insights into Darwin the person and how he saw himself and his work. Given that Darwinism fundamentally reoriented not only biological studies, but a wide range of approaches in disciplines like anthropology, philosophy, and sociology, it might be surprising to see that the portrait the texts paint is in many ways one of a typical inhabitant of nineteenth-century England.

Darwin's father and grandfather were physicians, and Darwin too began his studies with an eye on a medical career; this goal, however, was soon abandoned. His father suggested that he become a clergyman instead. Darwin records his reaction as follows: "I asked for some time to consider [...]. I had scruples about declaring my belief in all the dogmas of the Church of England; though otherwise I liked the thought of being a country clergyman."[60] This (maybe unexpected) moment in his memories is elaborated in a later selection of the *Autobiographies* ("Religious Belief"), which invites more nuanced engagement with his work as a naturalist and its relation to questions of personal faith and convictions.

Darwin did not intend for these writings to become available to the general public; rather, the longer pieces were written for his children and grandchildren. Instead of listening to Darwin the giant who dramatically shaped the scientific world from that day on, we hear about his health concerns, his obsession with collecting beetles, his tastes in reading material, and reflections on religion. The texts describe his private world, but they enable readers to trace how Darwin's worldview and attitude towards scientific endeavors emerged. Not surprisingly, we learn that he considered his voyage on the *Beagle* to be the crucial event that determined his career and the rest of his life. Darwin's encounters with some illustrious contemporaries are also recorded, the most well-known personalities being T.H. Huxley, Sir J. Herschel, Alexander von Humboldt, and Herbert Spencer, all prominent figures of the nineteenth-century scientific world.

Other observations in the *Autobiographies* echo themes pursued in some other prominent contemporary works, such as John Stuart Mill's *Utilitarianism* (1863). One example pertains to the differentiation between "higher" and "lower" pleasures.[61] Recalling his voyage on the *Beagle*, Darwin reports that he "discovered, though unconsciously and insensibly, that the pleasure of observing and reasoning was a much higher one than that of skill and sport. The primeval instincts of the barbarian slowly yielded to the acquired

60 Charles Darwin, *Charles Darwin: Autobiographies,* eds. Michael Neve and Sharon Messenger (London: Penguin, 2002), 29.

61 In Chapter 2 of *Utilitarianism*, Mill famously expanded on Bentham's theories concerning the "greatest happiness" by differentiating between quantity and quality of "pleasure."

tastes of the civilized man."[62] The topic of discussing the relative merit of various "pleasures" was not invented in the nineteenth century, though, and one could easily find related texts going as far back as Plato and Aristotle, as well as Stoic, Epicurean, and Christian sources. However, the way in which Darwin connects the hierarchy of pleasures with notions of individual improvement or development carries all the marks of modern thought since the Enlightenment. In her discussion of the *Human Condition* in the middle of the twentieth century, Hannah Arendt offers a concise description of the common features of "modern" ways of thinking:

> The coincidence of Marx's labor philosophy with the evolution and development theories of the nineteenth century–the natural evolution of a single life process from the lowest forms of organic life to the emergence of the human animal and the historical development of a life process of mankind as a whole–is striking and was early observed by Engels, who called Marx "the Darwin of history." What all these theories in the various sciences–economics, history, biology, geology–have in common is the concept of process, which was virtually unknown prior to the modern age.[63]

The notion of "evolution" displaced questions of higher purposes and ultimate ends that had been asked by philosophy and theology; now change over time supplied the data to be recorded so as to lead to scientific laws thought to be immune to human error.

## Friedrich Nietzsche, *Genealogy of Morality* (1887)

That Nietzsche is a key figure of nineteenth-century thought and a major influence on the following century is widely acknowledged. However, Nietzsche, like every other human being, did

62 Darwin, 44.

63 Hannah Arendt, *The Human Condition* (Chicago: Univ. of Chicago Press, 1998), 116.

change his mind occasionally, and at different times during his career, he focused on different topics. So, depending on whether one reads an early text (for instance, *The Birth of Tragedy*, published in 1872) or a late one (like the *Genealogy of Morality*), one picks up any one of many strands of Nietzschean thought that informed twentieth- and twenty-first century thought in a variety of disciplines, including anthropology, psychology, sociology, and political or cultural theory. Like some of the other writers studied in The World of Despair and Hope, Nietzsche offered a diagnosis of the state of nineteenth-century Europe, which he called "this mouldy, self-doubting present day."[64] *The Genealogy of Morality* best complements other texts read this semester in that it, too, uses the (Darwinian) motif of "change over time" that characterizes the century. *The Genealogy* traces the history and origin of Western values just as, several decades later, Freud will investigate the "discontents" or "discomforts" perceivable in and with culture in an attempt to identify the origin of those discomforts.

Nietzsche was highly skeptical of the trends that had been set in motion by the Enlightenment: he looked critically at the full-blown culmination of scientific methodology being applied to research in any field, even in investigating phenomena distinctly *not* subject to laws detectable in the natural world (as in, for instance, physics). In the third essay of *The Genealogy*, he issued the following direct warning: "let us be wary of the tentacles of such contradictory concepts as 'pure reason', 'absolute spirituality', 'knowledge as such [...].'"[65] His choice of phrases highlights his particular criticism of the philosophy of Immanuel Kant.

Particularly challenging for Christians is the fact that Nietzsche, whose father was a Lutheran minister, places much blame on Christianity and its dominance in shaping the culture and moral code

64 Friedrich Wilhelm Nietzsche, *On the Genealogy of Morality and Other Writings*, eds. Keith Ansell-Pearson and Carol Diethe (Cambridge, United Kingdom: Cambridge University Press, 2017), 66.

65 Ibid., 87.

of the Western world. But Nietzsche sees any other attempt at providing a single, universal, and comprehensive explanatory system as equally problematic; philosophical, religious, as well as scientific "systems" create, according to Nietzsche, a parallel (meta-physical) world that deprives a human being of life as it is lived in the here and now. Nietzsche's rejection of any dualism that attaches the true meaning of things to any such system is one of the reasons he is considered a precursor to the existentialist movement of the twentieth century.

In place of an explanatory system, Nietzsche offers a radical perspectivism, which means that we all explain or interpret from a vantage point; in other words, we are part of the picture we describe; there is no Archimedean point which would allow us an objective view. However, this perspectivism does not imply that assessing the "meaning" of anything is a complete free-for-all or that any interpretation is as valid as any other interpretation. Chapter 12 of the third essay of the *Genealogy* provides the most concise passage articulating Nietzsche's view:

> From now on, my philosophical colleagues, let us be more wary of the dangerous old conceptual fairy-tale which has set up a 'pure, will-less, painless, timeless, subject of knowledge', let us be wary of the tentacles of such contradictory concepts as 'pure reason', 'absolute spirituality', 'knowledge as such': – here we are asked to think an eye which cannot be thought at all, an eye turned in no direction at all, an eye where the active and interpretative powers are to be suppressed, absent, but through which seeing still becomes a seeing-something, so it is an absurdity and non-concept of eye that is demanded. There is only a perspectival seeing, only a perspectival 'knowing'; the more affects we are able to put into words about a thing, the more eyes, various eyes

> we are able to use for the same thing, the more complete will be our 'concept' of the thing, our 'objectivity'. [66]

It is somewhat ironic that Nietzsche's imagining an "overman" of the future consolidates Enlightenment ideas about self-determining human agents with Romantic notions of heroic, passionate efforts exerted because efforts need to be exerted–even if they aim at *nothing*. In the third essay of the *Genealogy*, Nietzsche writes: "That the ascetic ideal has meant so much to man reveals a basic fact of human will, its horror *vacui*; it needs an aim –, and it prefers to will nothingness rather than not will."[67] Statements like this may explain why his name is widely associated with nihilism; however, Nietzsche himself would probably be surprised that this aspect of his work drew so much attention.

### Sigmund Freud, *Civilization and Its Discontents* (1930)

Freud is generally considered to be the founder of psychoanalysis and, while his methods and conclusions have been largely superseded by later research, Freud's path-breaking work still provides points of reference for investigations into the workings of the human mind, especially the roles of conscious as well as subconscious elements and how they affect human behavior. The concept of the unconscious was not invented by Freud; however, his investigation of the unconscious dimensions of the human psyche for the purpose of developing therapies that might address and potentially remedy seemingly inexplicable behaviors was ground-breaking. As Ted Honderich explains, Freud's reports concerning his clients specifically aimed to demonstrate that "when the subject's loss of authority with respect to his own mental states is due to a process he called 'repression,' these states are subject to transformations

66 Ibid, 87.

67 Ibid, 68.

which render them unrecognizable by the subject and may have pathological consequences."[68]

So current practices of advising people to seek psychological or psychoanalytical help owe a debt to Freud—even if Freud's own analyses of individuals in early twentieth-century Vienna are generally considered of little use to psychoanalysts of our time. Freud's earlier works focused on exploring individual human beings' pathologies; *Civilization and Its Discontents* is a later text in a series of works in which Freud "psychoanalyzed" not individuals but societies and culture at large. The German word "*Kultur*" in the original title has broader connotations than the English "civilization"; it can mean "culture" as well as "civilization" and "society." Freud himself acknowledged his turn towards broader investigations into cultural changes in his later works. Given that the nineteenth century had been increasingly enthusiastic about the infinite possibilities of human progress, it should not surprise anyone that the horrors of the First World War gave people pause; are humans collectively really committed to making life better for everyone? Or does an old saying—"*Homo homini lupus*" [Man is a wolf to man]—more adequately describe how humans have treated each other? After quoting the Latin phrase, Freud asks, "Who, after all the experiences of life and history, will have the courage to dispute this claim?"[69]

When the book was published in 1930, Freud had already been living with cancer of the jaw for about seven years; he was preoccupied with death (even more so than before his diagnosis); while one ought to be careful with biographical explanations for writers' theories about the world and other human beings, some consider Freud's physical suffering as influential for his later, and often rather dark, view of culture.

68 Ted Honderich, *The Oxford Companion to Philosophy* (Oxford: Oxford University Press, 2005), 323.

69 Sigmund Freud, *Civilization and Its Discontents,* Eds. Todd Dufresne and Gregory C. Richter (Peterborough, (Ontario: Broadview Press, 2016), 85.

The big question Freud pursues in this work is the following: why have the structures humans have developed over time to improve both individual and collective conditions—*at the same time*—created the source of much misery? Freud wonders why it is that "however one defines the concept of civilization, it is patently clear that everything with which we attempt to protect ourselves against the threat from the sources of suffering belongs to that same civilization."[70] In eight chapters of *Civilization*, Freud discusses what aspects of culture create "discomfort," "discontent," or "unhappiness."In Freud's view, the biggest sources of discomfort are cultural demands that force individuals to renounce their "instincts"; what exactly Freud means by this term ("instinct") and an inextricably related term ("drives") will take some time to unpack in class discussion.

### Aldous Huxley, *Brave New World* (1931)

"Brave New World" has become a favorite phrase for people expressing either hope and confidence or fear and apprehension in view of changes, often related to technological or scientific developments in society. Huxley's 1931 novel (the title of which he borrowed from a line in Shakespeare's *The Tempest*) is one of the most well-known literary dystopias; paired with Orwell's *1984*, written in 1948, it presents one of several models writers envisioned as potential outcomes of social and cultural developments of the first half of the twentieth century. Advances in biological sciences, chemistry, and psychology might be used to remove all physical and emotional pain from people's lives and keep them in perpetual, stable comfort (though few readers would consider the state the inhabitants of Brave New World experience as "happiness").

Orwell's novel, by contrast, projects the political complexities of two world wars into the future and envisions the triumph of

70 Ibid, 64.

totalitarianism and the complete control of the population by propaganda and brain-washing techniques. For the last half century, writers have been pondering which of these nightmarish visions would be more pernicious—a world of blissfully delirious quasi-humans or the claustrophobic oppressiveness of a totalitarian regime. Huxley's own answer is recorded in a letter he wrote to Orwell in 1949: "Within the next generation I believe that the world's rulers will discover that infant conditioning and narco-hypnosis are more efficient, as instruments of government, than clubs and prisons, and that the lust for power can be just as completely satisfied by suggesting people into loving their servitude as by flogging and kicking them into obedience."[71]

Huxley came from a famous family that included several prominent scientists, and Huxley, too, had plans to become a doctor; however, a disease caused significant loss of sight when he was sixteen. Given that *Brave New World* presents themes and ideas debated in intellectual circles of the time, it is not surprising that most of the characters in the novel seem personifications of attitudes rather than psychologically complex individuals, a feature that is reflected in Huxley's choice of names for key figures like Bernard Marx, Lenina Crowne, Helmholtz Watson, and Mustapha Mond. Collectively, the names evoke primarily the following historical figures: Karl Marx, Vladimir Lenin, Benito Mussolini, Herbert Hoover, Mustafa Kemal Ataturk (founder of the Republic of Turkey), Leon Trotsky, and Hermann von Helmholtz (physicist and philosopher of science). Presenting the reader with a jumbled cast of characters mixing politicians, scientists, philosophers, and dictators, Huxley draws attention to the combined influence of social, scientific, and technological engineering in the world of the novel.

The work is sometimes referred to as a "novel of ideas" or even

---

71 Aldous Huxley, *Letters of Aldous Huxley*, Ed. Grover Cleveland Smith (New York: Harper Row, 1969), 605.

a "fable."[72] Readers in the last half century frequently assumed that the industrialized mass production of human beings in the novel is Huxley's unequivocal critique of the contemporary eugenics movement; however, comments in his nonfiction writings about eugenics and the uses of science for purposes of social reform present a more complicated picture of his views.[73] In the first few decades of the twentieth century, eugenics were widely discussed in England; Huxley participated in discussions on contemporary politics, scientific advancements, and moral issues. He wrote essays with titles such as "Are We Growing Stupider?" and "What Is Happening to Our Population?" in which he voiced concern about the "higher" classes' lower birthrates. Scholars have argued that Huxley's "ongoing support for so-called race betterment was typical of left-leaning British intellectuals in the inter-war period."[74] The novel *Brave New World*, though, includes enough undeniably satirical material to surmise that, while Huxley may have seriously considered theories concerning the potential merits of eugenics programs, he was also aware of the possibility that eugenics could bring about a nightmare, rather than contribute to improving societies.

About thirty years after the publication of the novel, Huxley wrote a collection of essays, *Brave New World Revisited* (1958), in which he examined the progress of his prophecies, addressing issues such as overpopulation, propaganda, the art of selling and brainwashing, drugs and political control, and education. Many points in his analysis can illuminate discussions of our own media-driven world.

72 Margaret Drabble and Jenny Stringer, *The Concise Oxford Companion to English Literature* (Oxford: Oxford University Press, 1993), 68.

73 This lesser known side of Aldous Huxley is discussed in detail in David Bradshaw's T*he Hidden Huxley: Contempt and Compassion for the Masses*, 1920-36 (London: Faber and Faber, 1994).

74 J. Woiak, "Designing a Brave New World: Eugenics, Politics, and Fiction," *The Public Historian* 29, no. 3 (2007): 106.

## Hannah Arendt, *The Human Condition* (1958)

While reference works generally identify her as "theorist" or "political philosopher," Arendt herself resisted such categorizations; one of the many German-Jewish people who left Germany in 1933, she went to France and worked for refugee organizations until her emigration to the United States in 1941. Her most well-known works informed discussions inside and outside academic circles and greatly influenced subsequent cultural criticism.[75]

Arendt did not separate her personal beliefs from her academic work. She was skeptical of the grand philosophical explanations the Western tradition offered for why humans act the way they do and what kinds of actions humans are capable of. The events of World War II led her to revisit Western intellectual history in order to delineate what the truly free political life could mean. Her works frequently turn to topics related to totalitarianism, the nature of freedom, and the capacities of thought and judgment. Her *The Origins of Totalitarianism* (1951) is a standard reference for studies of totalitarian movements; it also informs our understanding of the concept of "ideology."

In *The Human Condition*, Arendt traces the word "politics" to its origin in the *polis* of the Greek city-state, where the "active life" referred to participation in a "freely chosen form of political organization and by no means just any form of action necessary to keep men together in an orderly fashion."[76] After the disappearance of the ancient city-state, Arendt contends, "the term *vita activa* lost its specifically political meaning [...]."[77] The *polis* was followed

75 Scholarship highlighting Arendt's influence on subsequent cultural criticism include Steve Buckler's *Hannah Arendt and Political Theory: Challenging the Tradition* (Edinburgh: Edinburgh University Press, 2012). Also, for newly collected and edited articles by Arendt, see Hannah Arendt, *Reflections on Literature and Culture*, ed. Susannah Young-ah (Stanford, CA: Stanford University Press, 2007).

76 Hannah Arendt, *The Human Condition* (Chicago: University of Chicago Press, 2012), 13.

77 Ibid., 14.

by the "rise of the social," by which she means "the institutional differentiation of modern societies into the narrowly political realm on the one hand—the state and its apparatus—and the realms of the economy and the family on the other."[78] This modern social world brought about a decline of the "public sphere" where equals deliberate about shared interests.[79] Since Arendt, there have been numerous critiques of this notion of the public sphere—with feminist and postmodernist critics highlighting the limitations of ideas concerning the "common good" when it comes to actual lived experience in multicultural societies (especially in the face of globalization); the "common good," unfortunately, often neglected to consider every human being in favor of privileged groups.

Historically, the lack of differentiation among words that denote "activity" has, according to Arendt, led to misleading political and economic theories (as, for example, in Marx and Locke). Structurally, the book charts the transformations over time of the kinds of activities that occupy people's lives: labor, work, and action. Arendt insists on clear differentiation of the terms in order to illuminate historical changes in the structure of societies. Her definitions are as follows:

> Labor is the activity which corresponds to the biological process of the human body [...].The human condition of labor is life itself. Work is the activity which corresponds to the unnaturalness of human existence [...]. Work provides an 'artificial' world of things, distinctly different from all natural surroundings [...]. Action, the only activity that goes on directly between men without the intermediary of things or matter, corresponds to the human condition of plurality, to the fact that men, not Man, live on the earth

78 Seyla Benhabib, "The Embattled Public Sphere: Hannah Arendt, Juergen Habermas and Beyond," *Theoria* 44, no. 90 (1997), 3.

79 This Arendtian public sphere was elaborated upon in Habermas's 1962 *The Structural Transformation of the Public Sphere.*

> and inhabit the world. While all aspects of the human condition are somehow related to politics, this plurality is specifically *the* condition [...] of all political life.[80]

Plurality, then, is essential for the possibility of agency, of initiating something new. The possibility for change (or the space of hope) appears when Arendt's plurality is complemented by her notion of *natality*; in Arendt's words,

> The fact that man is capable of action means that the unexpected can be expected from him, that he is able to perform what is infinitely improbable. And this again is possible only because each man is unique, so that with each birth something uniquely new comes into the world [...]. If action as beginning corresponds to the fact of birth, if it is the actualization of the human condition of *natality*, then speech corresponds to the fact of distinctness and is the actualization of the human condition of *plurality*, that is, of living as a distinct and unique being among equals.[81]

Speech and action for Arendt are "the modes in which human beings appear to each other"[82]; being seen and heard by others makes human life more than mere existence. In dialogue about shared interests, we are engaged in a process of judging, a process that constitutes freedom and action. Linda Zerilli summarizes Arendt's account of political judgment as follows: "We don't have to hold these truths to be self-evident any more than we have to hold men and women equal or the rose beautiful; *nothing compels us*. There is nothing necessary in what we hold. That we *do* so hold is an expression of our freedom. In the judgment, we affirm our freedom and discover the nature and limits of what we hold

80 Ibid., 7.

81 Hannah Arendt, *The Human Condition*, 178.

82 Ibid., 176.

in common."[83] What we hold in common is *contingent*—rather than fixed—once and for all. Many postmodernist thinkers would agree with Arendt.

## Aleksandr Solzhenitsyn, *One Day in the Life of Ivan Denisovich* (1962)

As the title indicates, this short novel chronicles the events of an ordinary day in the life of the fictional Ivan Denisovich Shukhov, who is a prisoner in a Soviet prison camp in Siberia in the 1950s. Solzhenitsyn himself spent eight years in a "gulag" and would have been intimately familiar with the routines of such a camp. It would be tempting to see the "diary entry" of Ivan Denisovich as a slightly edited account of Solzhenitsyn's personal experience, but it is a work of fiction, rather than an autobiography. Unlike other works of prison literature you may have encountered (for instance, Boethius's *Consolation of Philosophy* and Bunyan's *Pilgrim's Progress*), the work was not written while the author was in prison. It was, in fact, first published in a Soviet literary journal; why, one might ask, would a Soviet magazine publish something so indicting of the Soviet regime?

Given the political and cultural context of 1962 (the height of the cold war), it is important to trace at least a rough outline of the tumultuous times in both worlds on either side of the "iron curtain" during the second half of the twentieth century. After World War II, the only two countries in the Western world that were not completely devastated were the United States and the Soviet Union–the former a democratic society, the latter a communist one. For several decades after the end of the war in 1945, the two competed over which parts of Europe would develop as allies to either side, with Germany being split in two. In the Soviet

83 Linda Zerilli, ""We Feel Our Freedom": Imagination and Judgment in the Thought of Hannah Arendt," *Political Theory* 33, no. 2 (2005), 183. Emphasis added.

Union, different factions advanced models on how to more effectively compete economically with the capitalist economies of the West. In such a climate, some Russian leaders found it advisable to allow well-known public figures, like Solzhenitsyn, to speak about the extreme conditions under the harsh Stalinist regime, which ended with Stalin's death in 1953.

Solzhenitsyn was awarded the Nobel Prize for Literature in 1970. Political climates changed again in the Soviet Union, however, and in 1974 Solzhenitsyn was exiled. He moved to (West) Germany, then Switzerland, and finally to the United States in 1976. He lived in Vermont until 1994 when he returned to Russia, after the Soviet Union had been dissolved in 1991.

In the second year (1978) of his eighteen-year exile in the United States, Solzhenitsyn delivered a commencement address at Harvard that created such public debate that the "Ethics and Public Policy Center"[84] published a book in 1980 entitled *Solzhenitsyn at Harvard: The Address, Twelve Early Responses, and Six Later Reflections.* Given Solzhenitsyn's role in the relations between the Soviet Union and the United States, influencing public announcements and perceptions of the two countries' respective views, *One Day in the Life of Ivan Denisovich* remains a text that speaks powerfully to this complicated period in history.

The story itself is rather sparse; while the description of the treatment the prisoners receive illustrates the inhumanity of totalitarian oppression, the focus of the narrative is the inner world of the protagonist rather than his external circumstances. Seemingly minor details, like managing to get an extra bowl of soup or hiding a piece of bread, affect the state of Ivan Denisovich Shukhov's mind as much as any action the prison guard takes. Relationships among the prisoners, also known as *zeks*, and interactions between them and their guards shape how they individually and collectively *live.* It is significant that Shukhov is not a hero figure in the traditional

84 https://eppc.org/about/

sense; he is an ordinary peasant, subject to the whims of a regime that imprisons people randomly and that does not adhere to any sense of justice. The work and senseless routines the prisoners are subjected to seem designed to strip them of their very humanity. The camp team includes more than twenty people, but only a few of them are developed in some detail; they include Alyosha, a Baptist; Tsezar, a film director; and Tyurin, who is the leader of the work team. The question that pervades the work is how one can maintain human dignity in such a world. The various degrees to which the individuals exhibit their humanity in the most minute acts and gestures affect the reader more strongly than would graphic descriptions of cruelty and abuse.

### Richard Rorty, *Contingency, Irony and Solidarity* (1989)[85]

Prominent literary scholar Harold Bloom called Richard Rorty "the most interesting philosopher in the world."[86] When he died in 2007, Rorty was eulogized as the "most famous philosopher in the world." [87] Like the other postmodern figures discussed in this chapter, Rorty can be identified as a post- or anti-foundationalist thinker. Like Derrida, for instance, he believed that we cannot rise above language. In *Contingency, Irony and Solidarity*, he rejects the commonsensical notion that language is used to represent the way the world *really* is and is thus a medium for conveying truth, which already exists "out there" somewhere. Rorty does not believe that truth is "out there"—only the world is. Rorty likewise rejects the commonsensical notion that language is used to express the way we *really* are inside; again like the other postmodernists described in this chapter, Rorty does not believe that we have an intrinsic self.

85 This gloss was written by Samuel Joeckel.

86 See back cover of the Cambridge UP edition of *Contingency, Irony and Solidarity*.

87 Mark Edmundson and Richard Posner. Qtd. in Stephen Metcalf, "Richard Rorty: What Made Him a Crucial Philosopher?" *Slate Magazine*, June 18, 2007.

Rorty thinks that language is a tool—not a medium—that we used to create truth: truth about the world and truth about ourselves.

Consistent with the postmodern notion of the inescapability of language, Rorty uses the word "vocabularies" to describe the system or network of words we use to create truth. (He is also content to use Wittgenstein's word for this same phenomenon: "language games." Other similar terms are "conceptual framework" and "*Weltanschauung*.") Over the centuries, people have used different vocabularies. For instance, in the eighteenth century, Thomas Paine made use of a liberal-Enlightenment vocabulary; in the twentieth century, Marx helped create the vocabulary of communism. Sometimes, people living at the same time use different vocabularies. The musical vocabulary of a country-music fan is vastly different from that of someone who listens to hip-hop. Rorty argues that rival vocabularies like these are incommensurate. You cannot appeal to independent criteria to adjudicate their differences because no such criteria exist. You cannot rise above language, which means you cannot rise above perspective (Nietzsche again!).

Vocabularies can be divided into types of language: literal and metaphorical language. Literal language is the language we are used to, the language that most everyone speaks. For instance, in the days of Copernicus most everyone spoke the language of Aristotelian cosmology: the earth was the center of the cosmos, and planets stuck to their spheres. Metaphorical language is a new language, something we are not used to. To return to the previous example, Copernicus began using a new language—he deployed a metaphor—that no one quite understood at first; it sounded weird. Eventually his metaphor caught on, and people came to believe that the sun is the center of the universe.

Just as Rorty rejects the traditional scientific account of things (science as the steady march toward scientific truth), so Rorty rejects the traditional philosophical account of things. Traditional philosophers like to ask questions like, "How do you know?" Rorty thinks this is, at best, an unproductive question or, at worst, a meaningless question. Rorty believes there is no non-circular way to defend beliefs. Rorty dismisses the notion that beliefs can be grounded on foundations or on anything essential; he replaces phrases like "philosophical judgments" with words like "descriptions" and "re-descriptions." All of our beliefs are contingent, explained by the time and place we happen to live. However, this does not mean you must be resigned to the way things are during your time and place. If you are unhappy with the status quo, deploy a metaphor (as did Copernicus...or Mary Wollstonecraft or Martin Luther King, Jr.).

And here we arrive at one difference between Rorty and other postmodernists. Rorty seeks political solidarity around the classical aim of liberalism. Other postmodern thinkers are leery of power structures—even a liberal power structure—as agents of oppression. Foucault, for instance, was wary of liberal solidarity for two reasons. First, as Rorty himself explains, Foucault "is not prepared to admit that the selves shaped by modern liberal societies are better than the selves earlier societies created."[88] Foucault worries that liberal societies might perpetrate the very oppression they seek to minimize. Second, Foucault seems suspicious of the very notion of solidarity to begin with. As he explains, "I do not appeal to any 'we'—to any of those 'we's whose consensus, whose values, whose traditions constitute the framework for a thought and define the conditions in which it can be validated."[89]

Rorty has no such qualms. He defines a liberal as someone who thinks that "cruelty is the worst thing we do."[90] A liberal thus seeks to eliminate as much cruelty from society as possible; sensitivity to other people's suffering and humiliation creates the conditions for solidarity. For this reason, Rorty insists upon a separation between

---

88 Richard Rorty, *Contingency, Irony and Solidarity* (Cambridge: Cambridge UP, 1989), 63.

89 Foucault, Conversation with Paul Rabinow. In *The Foucault Reader*, ed. Paul Rabinow (New York: Pantheon, 1984), 385.

90 Rorty, xv.

the private and public self. The danger of self-creation is that the language of the private self can easily be imposed on other people; during acts of self-creation, one is tempted to ask another, "Do you believe what I believe?" This sort of question leads to a dangerous "us-versus-them" mentality. Acts of self-creation can generate violence of various kinds against others. Rorty thus recommends keeping the public and private selves separate; do not try to reconcile the two. The goal of the private self is autonomous self-creation, to be able to pronounce in one's own terms, "Thus I willed it."[91] The goal of the public self is to stop cruelty, a project that begins by asking the question, "Are you suffering?"[92] You need not use the same vocabulary as someone else in order to relieve his or her suffering.

91 Ibid. 101.

92 Ibid. 198

# CONTRIBUTORS

**Jenifer Elmore** is Professor of English and Chair of the English Department at Palm Beach Atlantic University. She received a B.A. in English at the University of the South, where she benefitted from an intense liberal arts experience similar to the Supper Honors Program. She went on to earn an M.A. and Ph.D. in English at Florida State University before joining the PBA faculty in 2005. In addition to her courses in English, she teaches Writing About Literature and The World of Christendom and Islam and has also taught The World of Reason and Revolt and The World of Despair and Hope.

**David Horkott** is Associate Professor of Philosophy at Palm Beach Atlantic University where he has taught philosophy, humanities, and honors courses since 2002. He earned a master's degree in systematic theology from Wheaton College. His doctorate was completed in a Great Books program at the University of Dallas. He is chair of the philosophy department and faculty sponsor of the philosophy club. For the past three years, he has served as the university's Faculty Fellow for Service-Learning. His research interest is Nietzsche studies. He has presented papers at Nietzsche conferences hosted by Cambridge, Warwick University, University of Glasgow, and Baylor. He is currently working on a monograph with this working title, *How Reading Nietzsche Can Make You a Better Christian*. Dr. Horkott regularly teaches three Supper Honors courses: The World of Polis and Covenant, The World of Humanism and Reform, and The World of Reason and Revolt.

**Samuel Joeckel** is Professor of English at Palm Beach Atlantic University. He regularly teaches The World of Humanism and Reform, The World of Reason and Revolt, and The World of Despair and Hope; he has also taught honors-elective courses on comedy and humor. He is the author of *The C.S. Lewis Phenomenon* and a novel, *Golden Notes*. He is co-editor of *The Christian College Phenomenon.*

**Nathan Maxwell** came to PBA in January 2009 as an adjunct instructor in the School of Ministry. Prior to coming to PBA, Dr. Maxwell served for three years as instructor of biblical studies and director of technology at the South Texas School of Christian Studies, a collaborative extension campus for Howard-Payne University, and Logsdon Seminary. At the School of Christian Studies Dr. Maxwell taught biblical Hebrew and courses in Old Testament studies for undergraduate and seminary students. Dr. Maxwell's primary interests are Old Testament poetics and hermeneutics. His dissertation focused on analyzing poetic voice in the book of Psalms, and he subsequently has presented papers at the regional and national Society of Biblical Literature on the function of poetic voice within the Psalter.

**Jordyn Patrick** (BA, MLitt) attended Palm Beach Atlantic University from 2012-2016 where she completed her Bachelor of Arts in History. She was a student in the Frederick M. Supper Honors Program and attended the University of Oxford for the 2015 Hilary term where she specialized in Anglo-Saxon Archaeology of the Early Christian Era. Following her graduation from PBAU, Jordyn attended the University of Glasgow and obtained her master's degree in Celtic and Viking Archaeology. She currently works for Archaeology Scotland, an organization that shares her passion and commitment to inspire communities and people to discover, explore, and care for Scotland's archaeological heritage.

**Francisco Plaza** is Professor of Politics at Palm Beach Atlantic University. He received his Ph.D. in Politics at The Catholic University of America. He served as Alternate Representative of Venezuela to the Organization of American States. He founded the first liberal arts bachelors program in Venezuela. His published works include *El Silencio de la Democracia* and "Beyond Tyranny: The Totalitarian Spirit of the Venezuelan Regime." In the Frederick M. Supper Honors Program, he teaches The World of Polis and Covenant, and The World of Caesar and Christ. Professor Plaza is married to Yocoima Plaza, and they have seven children.

**Gary R. Poe** is Professor of History and Chair of the History Department at Palm Beach Atlantic University. Dr. Poe has been teaching at PBA since 1995 and working in the Honors program since 2002. He received his Ph. D. in Christian History from The Southern Baptist Theological Seminary focusing on the Early Church. He teaches The World of Polis and Covenant, The World of Caesar and Christ, and The World of Christendom and Islam, as well as honors elective courses in the Suppers Honors Program. In addition to these courses, Dr. Poe has led many of the Honors travel study trips to such places as England, Germany, Turkey, Greece, and Israel.

**Beate Rodewald** has been teaching in the PBA Honors Program since 1989; she taught the original interdisciplinary team-taught version of the program and served as director from 1996 to 2001. She was a member of the team that redesigned the program in its current form. On a regular basis, she teaches four of the six worldview classes: The World of Christendom and Islam, The World of Humanism and Reform, The World of Reason and Revolt, and The World of Despair and Hope. She has also taught The World of Caesar and Christ. Rodewald's special topics courses include "Utopia," "Autobiography/Confession," "Time and Memory" as well as a Study/Travel trip to Germany.

**Tom St. Antoine** is Professor of Communication and Director of the Frederick M Supper Honors Program at Palm Beach Atlantic University. He has directed the honors program since 2000. Dr. St. Antoine has a Ph.D. from Louisiana State University, an M.A. from Florida Atlantic University, and a B.A. from PBA where he was a member of the first class to complete the honors program. In 2009 he received the Corts Award for teaching excellence. He has published his research on rhetoric, higher education, and honors education in a variety of books and journals. In the honors program, he teaches the first-year experience class, rhetorical eloquence, and the honors capstone.

**Elizabeth Stice** is Associate Professor of History at PBA. In the honors program, she teaches Polis and Covenant, Caesar and Christ, and Humanism and Reform. She did her PhD in history at Emory University, an MA in history at the University of Hawai`i, and her BA at Messiah College.

**Michael Von Cannon** is a faculty member in the Department of Language and Literature at Florida Gulf Coast University. Prior to FGCU, he was a postdoctoral fellow in English at Louisiana State University. Well before that, he was a student in the Frederick Supper Honors Program at Palm Beach Atlantic University. Von Cannon has published on Ernest Hemingway, F. Scott Fitzgerald, H.D. (Hilda Doolittle), and Edgar Allan Poe. Since 2013, he has written the annual chapter on Hemingway and Fitzgerald for *American Literary Scholarship*. Currently, he is co-editing the final volume of Hemingway letters, which will be published through Cambridge University Press.

Made in the USA
Columbia, SC
11 January 2024

30318506R00226